CHARLES SIMPSON

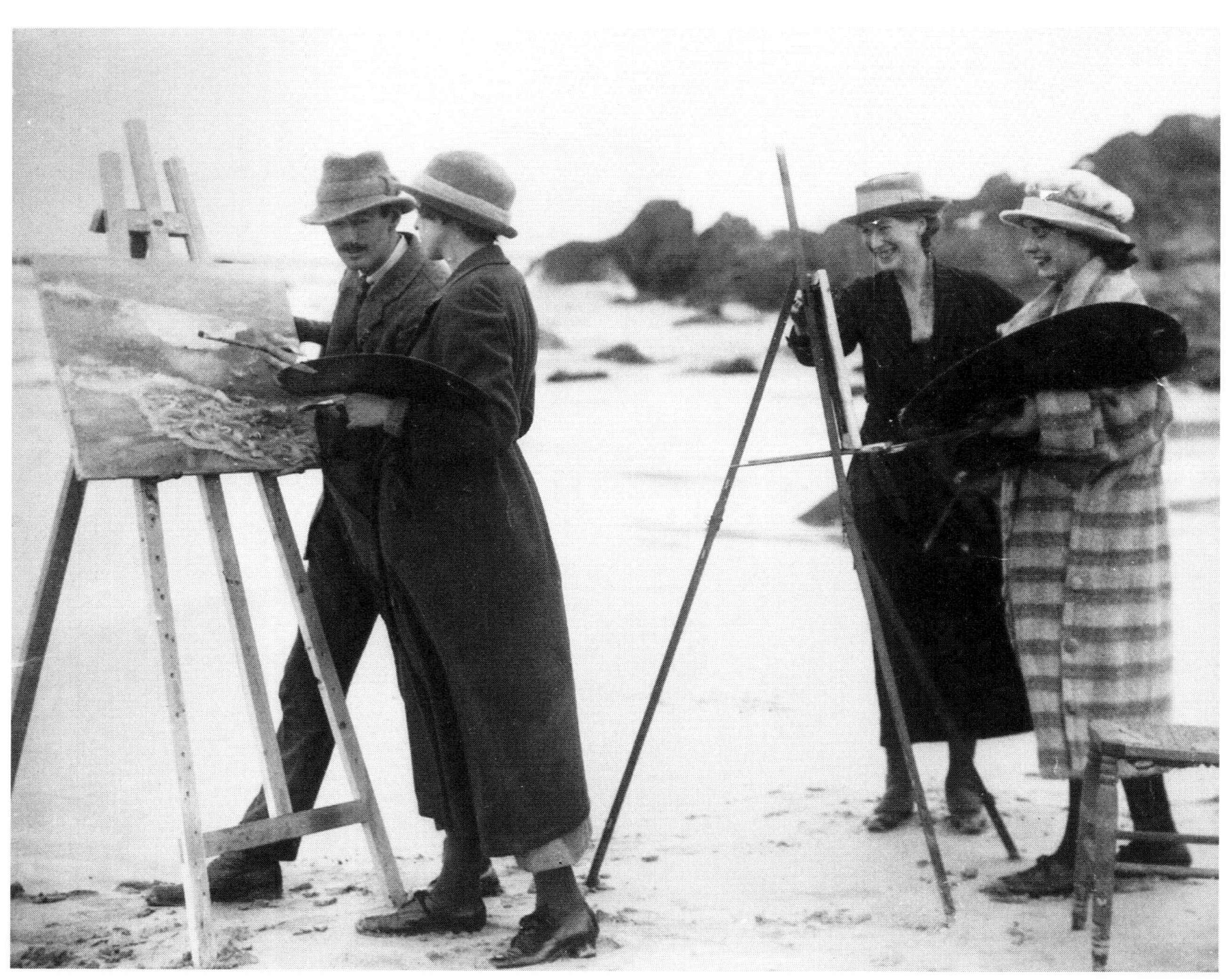

Charles Simpson: Painter of Animals & Birds, Coastline & Moorland

JOHN BRANFIELD

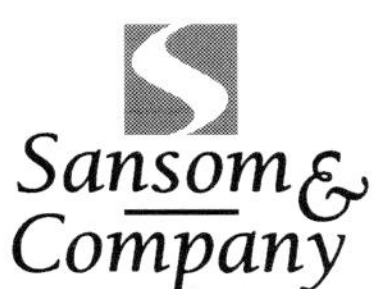

in association with

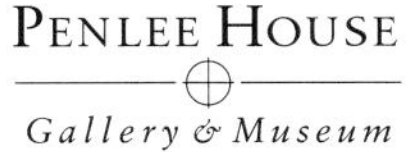

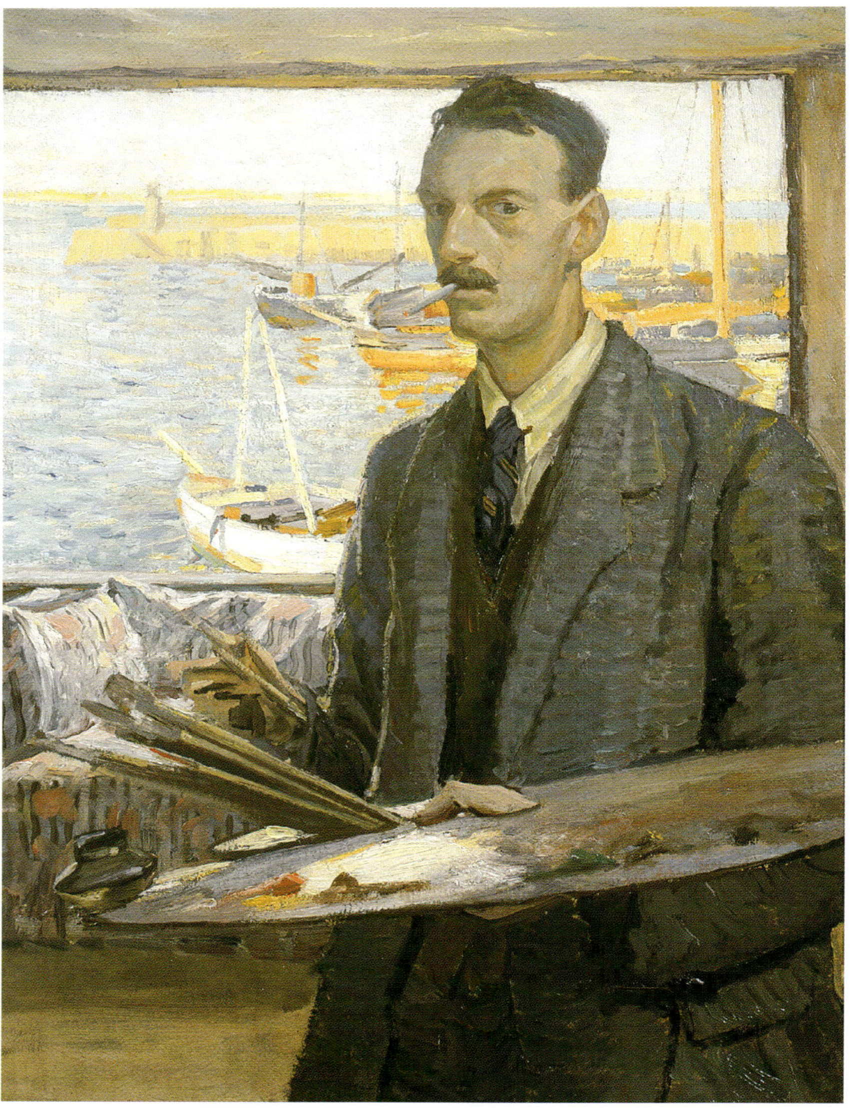

First published in 2005 by Sansom & Company Ltd., 81g Pembroke Road, Bristol BS8 3EA, in association with Penlee House Gallery and Museum, Penzance.

© *John Branfield*

All paintings and family photographs © The Simpson Estate

ISBN 1 904537 43 X

British Library cataloguing in Publication Data:
A catalogue record for this book is available from the British Library

Designed and typeset by Gendall Design, Falmouth, Cornwall
and printed and bound in Malta by Gutenberg Press Ltd.

Text set in Monotype Sabon 10/16pt

Sponsored by Porthminster Gallery, St Ives

ABOVE
Self-portrait
c1918, Charles Simpson
Oil on canvas, 40 x 30 in
Reproduced by kind permission
of David Messum

FRONT COVER
Crossing the stream
Oil on canvas, 11 x 15 in

FRONTISPIECE
Charles and Ruth Simpson teaching
on Porthmeor Beach, St Ives
c1920, photograph, WCAA

Contents

Acknowledgements

I was fortunate to have known Leonora, the daughter of Charles and Ruth Simpson. She revered her father and after his death in 1971 the house and studio in Penzance remained unchanged until her own death in 2003. Her family papers, including Ruth's wonderfully vivid letters home when she was a student at the Forbes School of Painting in 1911 and 1912, went to the Penlee House Gallery and Museum, Penzance, and they are now in the West Cornwall Art Archive (WCAA) at Trevelyan House. Together with Charles Simpson's own writings, they have been the main source of my material. I am grateful to Dr Melissa Hardie and the staff at Trevelyan House for all their help.

I am greatly indebted to David Tovey, who very generously gave me the benefit of his wide knowledge of St Ives art and his own research into Simpson's paintings. I should also like to thank John Anderson, Jane and Hugh Bedford, Colin Bradbury of Venture, Truro; Pem Bridger, Douglas Connor, Betty Chellew, Richard and Alison Davidson, Michael Day of Burlington Paintings, London; David Evans, the late Tim Evans, Jonathan Grimble of the Porthminster Gallery, St Ives; Hilary and Thornley Gwennap, Victor James, Kevin Hearn of New Street Books, Penzance; Simon Hendra and Viv Hendra of the Lander Gallery, Truro; Edna Hocking, Vivienne and Garnet Hocking, Chris Insoll, Jean and Tim Jones, Richard Kay of Lawrence Fine Art Auctioneers, Crewkerne; Tom Kilner, Barbara and David Kirk, David Lay of the Penzance Auction House, Colin Manning, Richard Mather, David Messum of Messum's Fine Art, London and Marlow; Ed Nadarin, Tara Physick of Jordan and Chard Fine Art, Maryella Pigott, Jane Powell, Tony Pratt of the Canterbury Auction Galleries, Jane Skinner, Penny Smith, Leon Suddaby, Chris Trant of the Mill Gallery, Ermington; Archie Trevillion, Michael Truscott, John and Angela Wheeler, Marion Whybrow, David Wilkinson of The Book Gallery,

St Ives; Douglas Chomé Wilson of Chomé Fine Art, Bath; Jean Wilson, Trevor Woodman and Austin Wormleighton.

Institutions that have been helpful are Christchurch Art Gallery, New Zealand; The Cornwall Centre, Redruth; The Cornwall Family History Society, Truro; Derby Museum and Art Gallery; Doncaster Museum and Art Gallery; Dunedin Public Art Gallery, New Zealand; The Grundy Art Gallery, Blackpool; Laing Art Gallery, Newcastle upon Tyne; Nuneaton Museum and Art Gallery; Penzance Library; Plymouth Museum and Art Gallery; Royal Cornwall Museum, Truro; Russell-Cotes Art Gallery, Bournemouth; St Ives Library; St Ives Trust Archive Study Centre and The Walker, Liverpool.

A book like this could not be produced without the support of the family and I am extremely grateful to Deirdre Stone and Annie Coultas for permission to reproduce Charles Simpson's paintings and to quote from his writings; John and Elaine Haddock have been very helpful. Finally I should like to thank John Sansom of Sansom & Company, Hanna Oakes of Gendall Design and all the staff of Penlee House Gallery and Museum.

Author's Note
Charles Walter Simpson was always known to family and friends as Walter, at first to distinguish him from his father, also named Charles. In a family or social context I refer to him as Walter; if the reference to him is primarily as a painter I use his surname. He signed his work C.W. Simpson, Charles W. Simpson or Charles Simpson. Unless otherwise indicated, all paintings are from private collections.

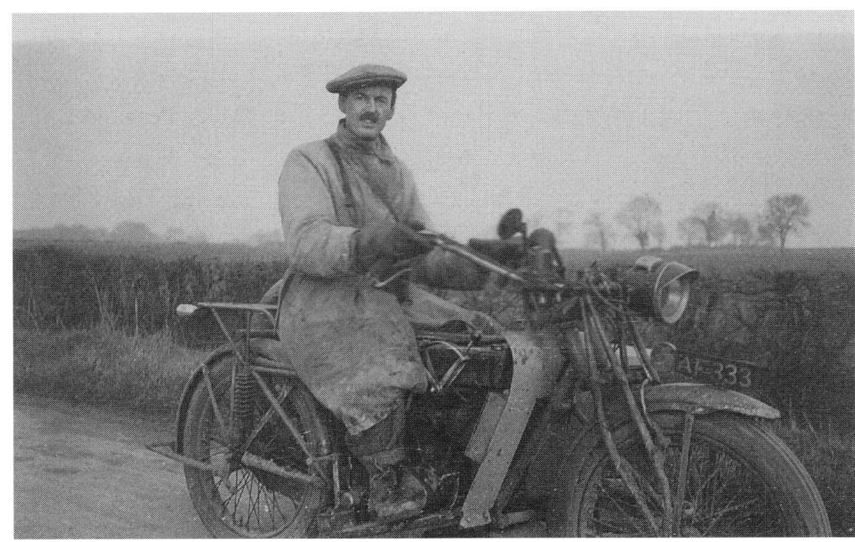

Simpson on his motorcycle
c1925, photograph, WCAA

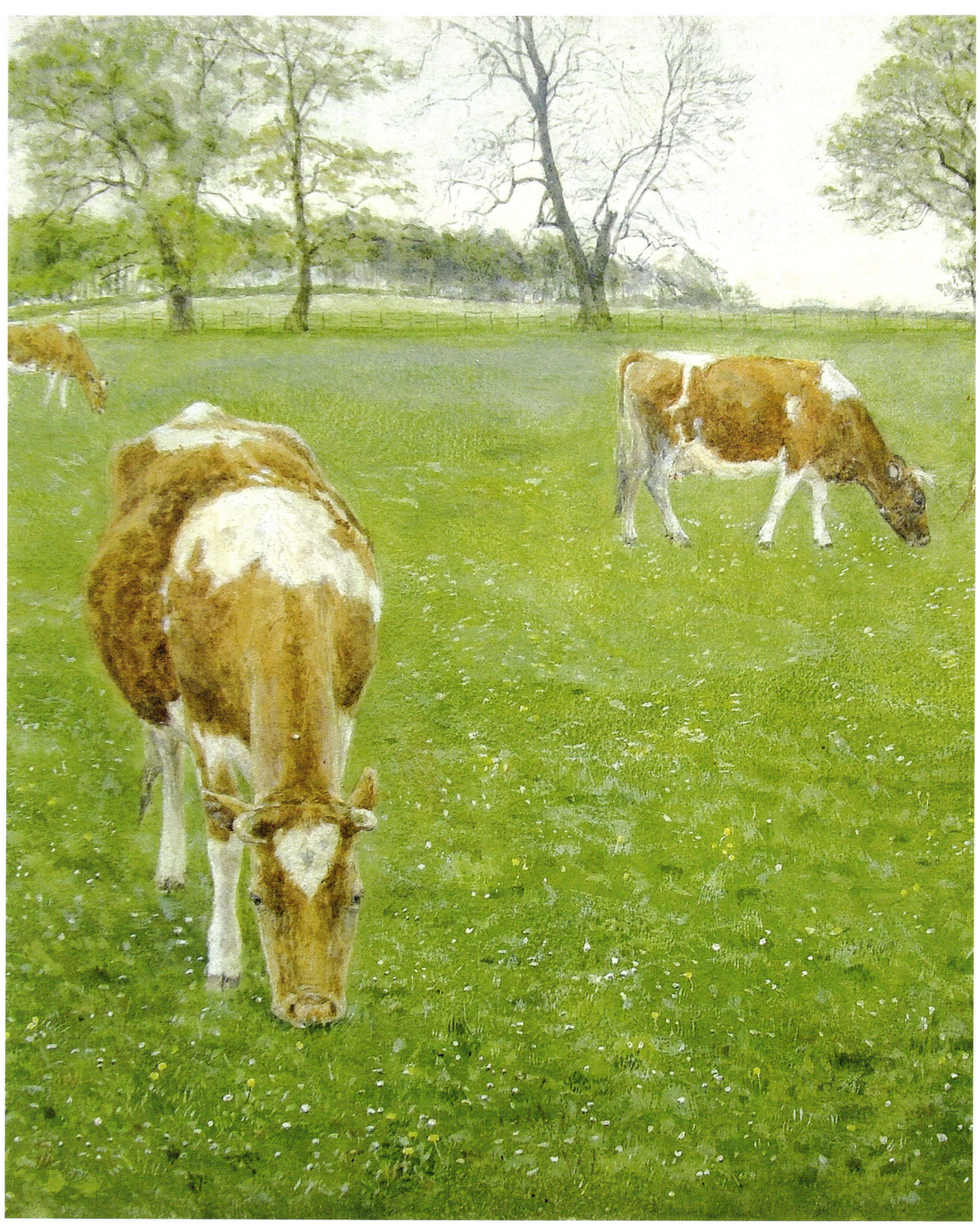

Pickhurst Manor: Boyhood

CHAPTER ONE

'The train steamed out of the station of Elmers End, the change on the journey
from London to the branch line for Hayes in Kent. The carriages were old
and the seats dusty and faded, the glass of the windows was dull and the
view further obscured by clouds of white smoke that blew past them, casting
shadows on the grass bank of a cutting or twirling away among the branches
of small trees that bordered the line. In one compartment were four children,
a little boy, Charles Simpson, called by his second name, Walter, and his three
sisters, Gaynor, Dolly and Mary; with their mother and a nurse. The children
had counted many stations since leaving London… And now, after the change,
there were only three. Eden Park and West Wickham were passed. The
children crowded to one side of the compartment, hands pressed against the
windows, rubbing the glass panes.'

So begins Charles Simpson's memoir *The Fields of Home*. The children
with their mother and nurse had left their home in Bournemouth, where they
lived when their father was abroad with his regiment, and were on their way
for a long summer holiday with their grandparents. Pickhurst Manor was
where their mother had grown up. It was close to London but in the 1890s
was deep in the Kent countryside, on a hill looking across a valley to the
common beyond. The house was built of golden-red brick, partly covered
with Virginia creeper, and had rows of white-framed windows. There was a
large conservatory at one end and a terrace ran the full length of the building.
Below a grassy slope were walled fruit and kitchen gardens, a vinery and
peach-house. Behind the manor were stables and farm buildings.

The family station omnibus, drawn by a pair of horses and driven by
the coachman with a footman in attendance, was waiting for them. They
were soon at the gate, opened by the lodge-keeper, and swept along the
gravel drive, past lawns and a rose garden, to the front door. Their relatives
gathered in the hall while the butler and footman carried away the luggage.

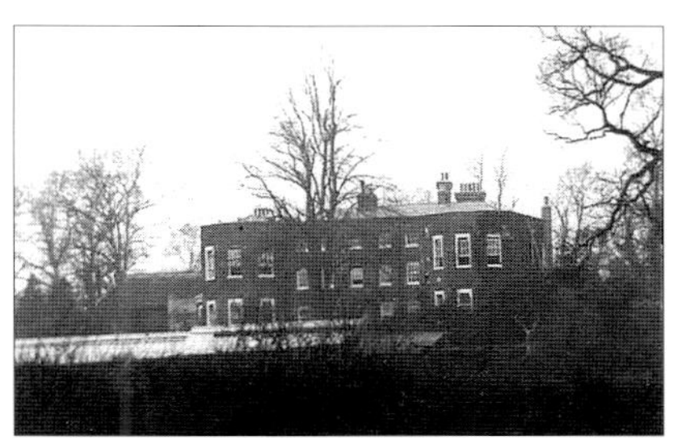

ABOVE
Pickhurst Manor, Kent
c1885, postcard

PAGE 8
Detail from ***The Cow Field***
(the Farm at Pickhurst Manor)
1903, watercolour, 9.75 x 13.5 in
Painted when Simpson was eighteen

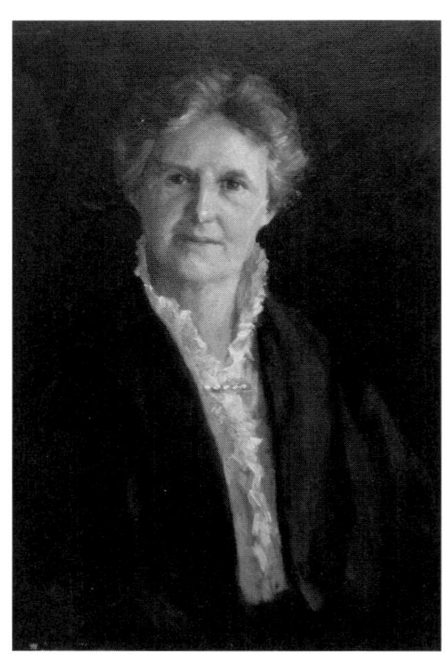

Nora Simpson, Charles Simpson's mother
Painting by Ruth Simpson
c1914, oil on canvas, 23 x 19 in

Walter's grandfather, Charles Frederick Devas, was of French Huguenot descent. Originally the family had lived near Bromley, until the house had been engulfed by Greater London. 'Pickhurst Granny', as Walter called her, was from an Anglo-Irish family, the Alexanders. She waited to greet her daughter Nora and her four grandchildren in her sitting room off the large drawing room. She wore black, with a white lace cap on her head; an old fox terrier lay at her feet. Around the walls of the drawing room hung her watercolours of Italian landscapes.

The children had tea in the nursery. The day and night nurseries were in a far part of the rambling house, on either side of a long corridor where they could run and make as much noise as they liked. They ate rich dripping cake and butter from the farm, beneath the hunting prints on the walls. After his sisters had gone to bed Walter went to his mother's room to say goodnight before she went down to dinner. The candle-light was reflected in the mirror of the dressing table and shone on her silver trays and brushes.

On his own Walter sat eating a last slice of cake. Silently a mouse came up the table leg and advanced across the cloth. It was hardly visible amongst the shadows cast by the lamp. He watched as it took a crumb and vanished. In the morning he always freed the mice that had been caught in traps set in a cupboard on the nursery corridor, then couldn't wait to go to the farm. John, the hired man, was his hero. He helped him tend the hens and turkeys, the ducks on the pond. He went ferreting with him, the tally of rats kept by a row of tails nailed to a board in the cowshed. He followed him across the fields to take up the mole traps. John promised to let him use his shotgun when he was older. Later, when he had his own room high up in the house, he would pack the bodies of rats and moles in lime and stacked the boxes in the wardrobe. They were discovered before the bodies were reduced to skeletons and John was blamed for 'putting ideas into his head'. At lunch, the only meal he had in the dining room, he would recount what John had done and what John had said. When he started to copy John's accent, this was considered too much.

The pasture was full of buttercups and the cows lay among them, their brown and white sides half-hidden by the yellow flowers. His sisters in white sun-bonnets crossed the meadows and raced to claim their favourite trees, to which they had given names, the Staircase Tree and the Omnibus Tree. At four o'clock John called in the cattle for milking and they entered the dimly lit cowshed, its rafters hung with cobwebs. The names of the dozen Guernseys were written in white letters on black above their stalls,

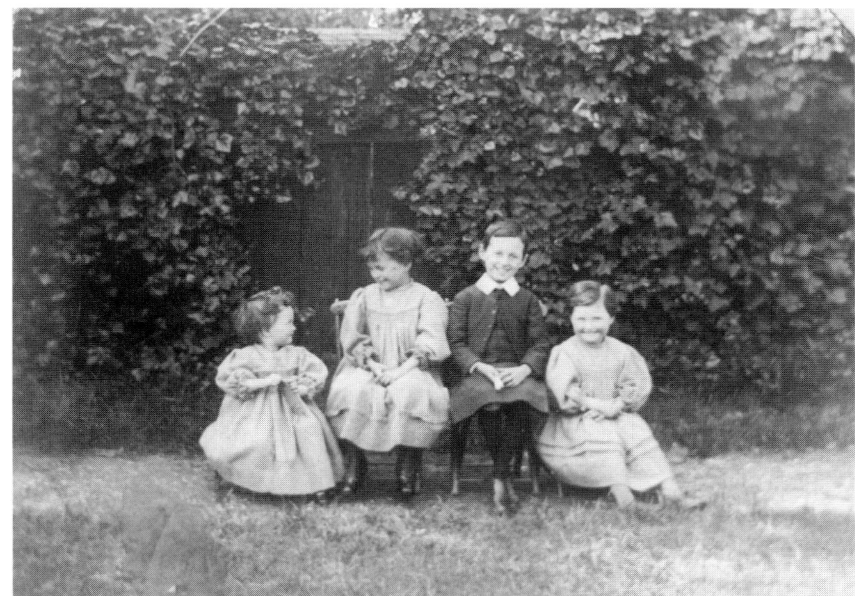

Charles, always known to the family as
Walter, and his sisters in the early 1890s
WCAA album

all beginning with L: Lindon, Lady, Lass, Lilac, Lavender. The children
would rub Lass's ears as she waited her turn. Lindon and Lass were the
subjects of Walter's early watercolour sketches, exact portraits of each
animal, Lindon quite dark for a Guernsey and Lass much paler, the gold
and white of her colouring catching a green reflected from the grass.

As milking finished they would hear the sound of the carriage returning
to the stable yard after taking Mrs Devas for her afternoon drive. The
coach house and stables were away from the farm and seemed a less
friendly place to the children. The coachman was elderly and dignified and
the grooms adopted his aloofness. The carriage horses in their stalls were
well-groomed, as polished as the landau, brougham, wagonette and station
omnibus in the coach house, and had as little individuality. Everything was
ordered and spotless. Walter preferred the informality of the farmyard and
John's friendship. But John was not thought well of in the house, he was
too individual and not obsequious enough. He always dressed in a cloth
suit rather than corduroy trousers tied below the knee or breeches and
leggings like the gardeners. He was gentle, hating the taking of life. As
his job required it he did it as efficiently as possible. Walter was drawn to
watch him when he killed poultry for the table, feeling a scientific interest
and a sense of awe. He noticed the red blood on the creamy white neck of
an Aylesbury duck. He pored over the books on big game hunting in the
billiard-room library and stalked rabbits through the grass. He had an
airgun and longed to shoot a sparrow but never succeeded. His catapult
was more deadly but when he occasionally managed to kill a bird its limp

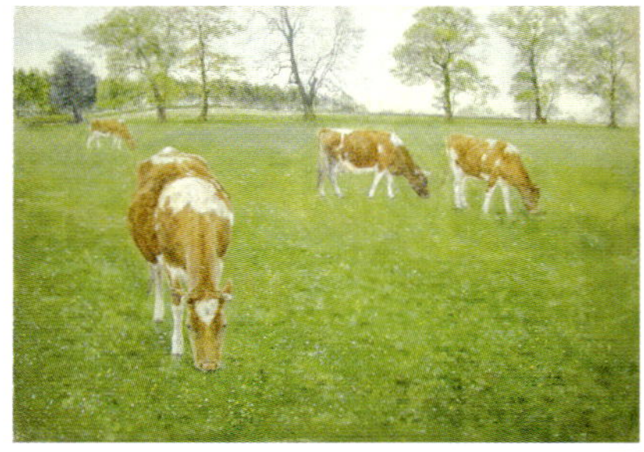

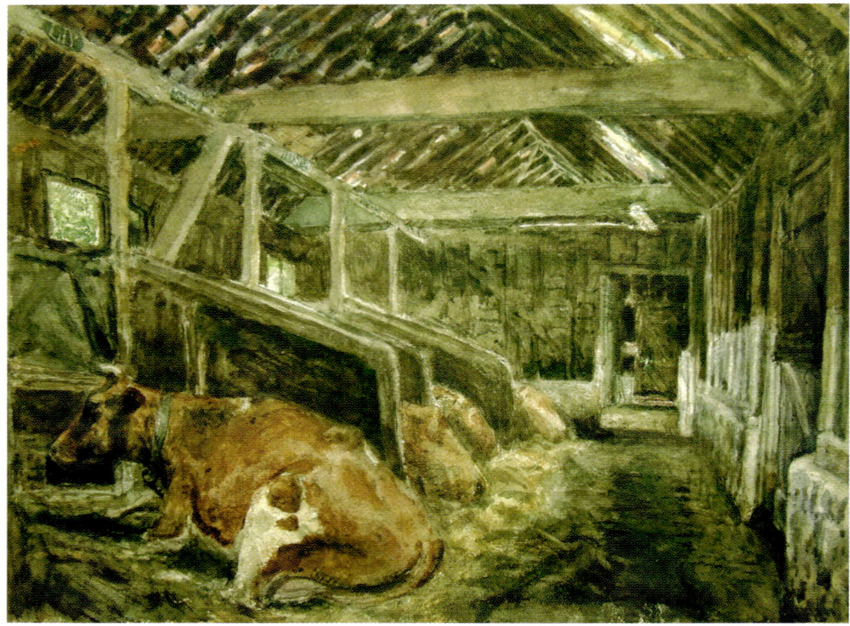

body filled him with remorse. The combination of unsentimentality and tenderness was characteristic of his later animal and bird paintings.

Charles Walter Simpson was born on 8 May 1885 at Camberley in Surrey, where his father was at the Army Staff College. Charles Rudyerd Simpson had a reputation as a horseman amongst the hard-riding junior officers. He was usually in the lead at the meets of the College Drag Hounds, clearing almost impossible fences and having many a fall. He was found one day unconscious in a ditch with an unconscious horse lying on top of him. One of Walter's earliest recollections was of being held in his mother's arms and watching his father breaking in a young horse. Like the families of all servicemen, they moved house frequently, though only Pickhurst was 'home'. Another early memory was of being pushed in his pram along a road outside Dublin as the red-coated soldiers of his father's regiment marched by to the accompaniment of *The Lincolnshire Poacher* played by a fife and drum band. When his father was at the War Office they lived in Argyll Road near Holland Park, when he was abroad they stayed in Bournemouth, which was the home of his father's sister Gaynor. Auntie Gay was a musician, though poor health prevented her from following a professional career. After walks on the beach with their mother, they would call on her for tea and afterwards she would play and sing. She introduced Walter to the music of Beethoven, a love of which remained throughout his life. It was Auntie Gay who treasured Walter's childhood drawings, keeping them in a scrapbook. It is a thick, bulging volume with a broken spine, labelled *Charles Walter Simpson. This book was begun at 3 years and finished at 10 years old. Gaynor A. Simpson – her book.*[1] He was best at drawing animals; sometimes his mother put in the figures. Beneath a drawing of a lion attacking a giraffe, Gaynor added *aged four years.* The family went back to Dublin again and Walter spent hours at the zoo sketching the lions. When he flicked a paintbrush at a sleeping lioness she reached through the bars and tore his jacket from shoulder to cuff.

Whenever they moved house the children took their pets with them, cats, rabbits and guinea pigs. In London they always visited the pets department of the Army and Navy Stores, usually going home with a tortoise in a paper bag though they longed for something more exotic, a meerkat or a monkey. Their father returned to the Staff College as a lecturer and here at Camberley Walter had a donkey to ride, though it was not suitable for following the drag hunt. He went to the meets and made pencil sketches, usually of riders thrown from their saddles as they crashed over a big fence. The drawings amused the officers and one was reproduced in a book before he was ten years old.

Although he grew up in a family of girls – a fourth sister Judy was born several years after the others – he followed his boyish occupations and the girls shared his interests. He formed a butterfly collection, revelling in the thrill of the chase. The brief pang of regret for a life snuffed out was soon forgotten in setting and pinning the insects with the beautiful colours and patterns of their wings. He collected birds' eggs, observing the rule of never taking more than one egg from a nest. Of all his sisters, Mary was the

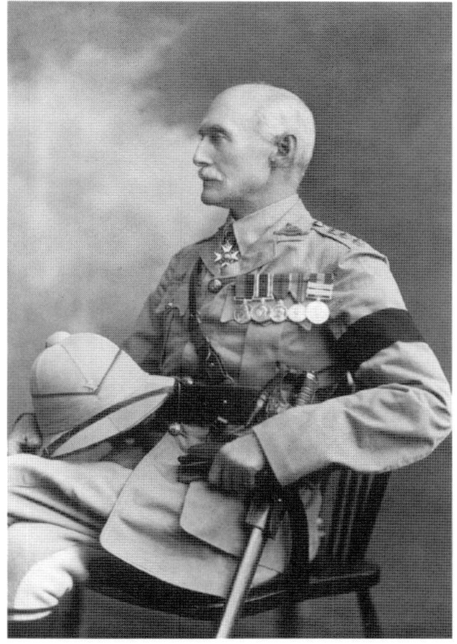

ABOVE
Major General Charles Rudyerd Simpson, Colonel of the Lincolnshire Regiment

BELOW LEFT
Charles Walter Simpson aged nineteen in 1904 with his four sisters, Gaynor, Mary, Judy and Dolly

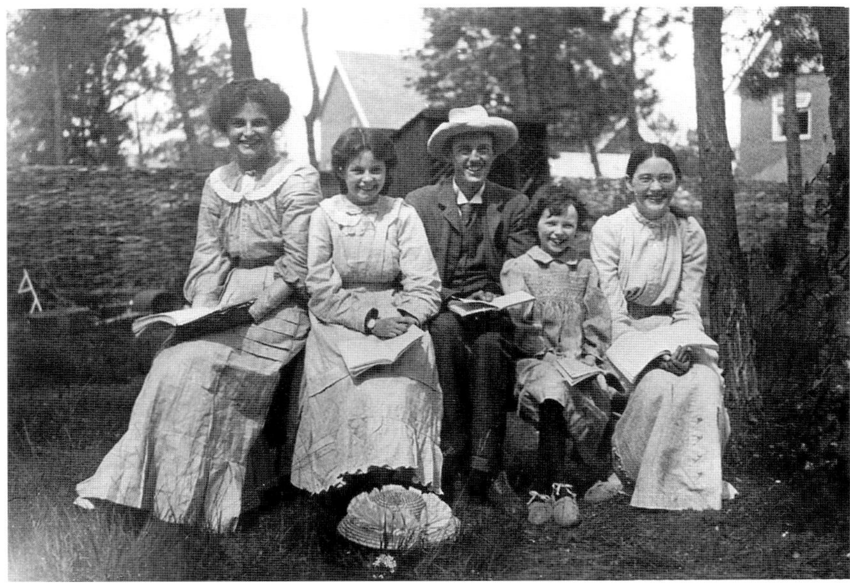

closest, loving the farm as much as he did. Together they bought and studied books on agriculture. He made a model farm for her, painting the animals and cutting them out of stiff paper. He made farm buildings with detachable roofs to give access to the stalls, each with the name of its occupant. There were horses and carts, everything down to the smallest detail of milk-pails and milking stools. Away from the farm, it enabled them to relive their lives there.

They were always sad at the end of the summer to leave Pickhurst for a visit to their father's parents at Millmead House, Guildford in Surrey. It was a sombre place, full of dark furniture. The garden too was dark and shaded, enclosed on three sides by the town. Grandfather Simpson was an austere character, a retired barrister who rode into town, upright and dignified on his tricycle. Millmead Granny was his second wife, their father's mother having died when he was five. She was a Williams, of Welsh descent, and had a love of music. She knew many famous people, Felix Mendelssohn, Charles Dodgson and George Frederick Watts, who painted her portrait. The children felt uncomfortable with her and one day when summoned from the playroom at the top of the house refused to go down: they missed meeting Lewis Carroll. It was through Millmead Granny that Walter visited Watts at the age of twelve, showing him the drawing of a lion. 'You can hear the roar coming out of his mouth,' said Watts kindly. Walter's grandmother admonished him for painting cattle, saying that he should paint beautiful women instead.

His father returned from India to raise the 4th Battalion of the Middlesex Regiment, based at Woolwich. The family moved again, to a large house with a garden that ran down to a reservoir next to the Arsenal. Walter grew up with little formal education. He was never sent away to school, often having periods of illness. He was expected to follow his father into the army and in 1900 at the age of fifteen he went to a tutor to prepare for the exams. He had a volatile grey pony of 13 hands called Will o' the Wisp, which he rode every afternoon after lessons. The pony was a good jumper and he practised over hurdles in preparation for a course arranged by his father at the cavalry riding school. Sometimes he rode to Plumstead Common to watch the training of cavalry recruits, returning home to sketch what he had seen.

Will o' the Wisp was stabled with his father's charger Abu Hamed, the horse that he had ridden at battles in the Sudan. There was a soldier groom but Walter looked after the pony himself. After lessons one day he saddled him, mounted and rode out of the yard. It was windy, there was washing on the line and the prop blew down as he was passing. The pony shied and swung around. The bridle snapped and Walter was thrown to the ground against a wall, the pony stepping on his head. It left the mark of the iron shoe imprinted around his left ear. 'It's all right,' he told the groom. It was how a good sportsman like his father would behave, showing no reaction to a tumble. He remounted and joined his father for an afternoon's practice over the hurdles. He was thrown again and once more ignored it.

He felt no ill effects and two weeks later decided to spend a few days at Pickhurst. He rode out of Woolwich on Will o' the Wisp, through the built-up area and around the outskirts of London until he reached the familiar lanes of Kent. He rode up the drive from the lodge to the stables and left his pony in the care of a new coachman. He slept in his old white-panelled bedroom at the top of the house and heard the rain falling softly on the creeper-covered walls outside. When he awoke he was as eager as ever to see the farm and the fields, but as he went downstairs the pain began.

For weeks he was desperately ill, the blow from the pony's hoof having damaged the mechanism of his ear. It affected both hearing and sight, and other complications threatened. The pain was intense and it seemed as though he would be permanently deaf. When he had recovered a little he was taken to Bournemouth to convalesce. He spent many months there, his only solace the music that drowned the discordant noises in his head. He had always loved the music of Beethoven but now it became a passion. He identified with the composer, knowing that Beethoven too became deaf. To compound his problems, he had occupied a room in hospital where the previous patient had been a boy with TB and he had caught the infection. The doctor advised plenty of fresh air and a second year's complete rest by the sea.[2] His father's regiment had left Woolwich and it was not convenient for the family to join him, so Nora Simpson took a house at Deal in East Kent and moved there with her invalid son and four daughters.

He wandered through the quiet countryside between Deal and Sandwich, exploring byways and hamlets hidden between the hills inland from the sea. He searched for subjects to paint, the ewes with their lambs in a field, a bull in a pen, a team of horses passing through a village. He felt the timelessness of the landscape, where it seemed that the Romans had landed only yesterday, and he reflected on the fate that had led him to do the one thing that he really wanted to do, to spend his days painting. Was it an unlucky accident when he fell from his pony at Woolwich? Or was it lucky? There was no question now of joining the army. Could he make a career as an artist?

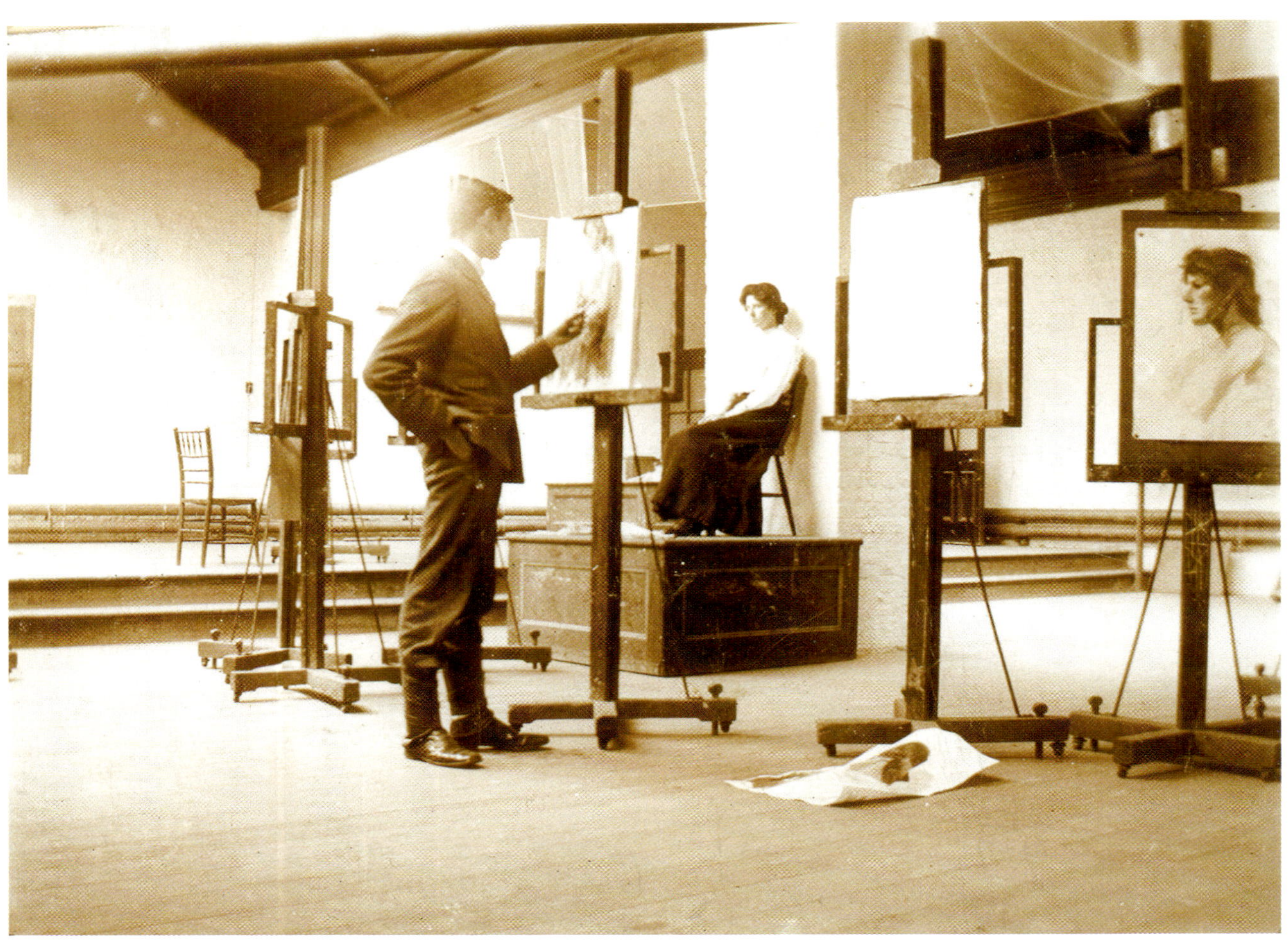

Sketching from a model at the
Herkomer School of Art, Bushey
1904, photograph, WCAA album

Bushey, Newlyn and
Norfolk: Apprenticeship

CHAPTER TWO

What had seemed merely a daydream became a possibility. He went back to
discuss it with George Frederick Watts R.A., who had been so encouraging
when Walter showed him his drawing of a lion some years earlier. Watts
lived at Limnerslease, a beautiful house among trees on the Hog's Back
near Guildford in Surrey. He painted allegories with titles like *Progress*
and *Hope*, the famous image of a blindfolded female figure crouching on
a globe and holding a broken lyre. His contemporaries regarded him as
'England's Michelangelo' for his monumental works that dealt with large
social and philosophical themes. His literary subjects drawn from Bocaccio
and his historical scenes were far removed from Walter's interests, but the
young man felt that he could talk to the old master as one artist to another
and it helped confirm him in his decision. What inspired him most of all
was the size of Watts's canvases and he was filled with a desire to work on
a large scale, resulting in the huge landscapes of cattle coming across the
moors or seascapes of wheeling gulls.

Walter had been entirely self-taught and if he was to be a professional
artist he needed some training. The Royal Academy Schools and The Slade
were out of the question; his health was still too uncertain to undertake a
demanding five-year course. He submitted a drawing to the Bushey School
of Painting and was accepted. The school had been founded by Hubert von
Herkomer, a Bavarian who had lived in England since the age of eight. An
immensely successful artist, he was made Slade Professor of Art in 1885.
One of his best- known paintings is *Hard Times* of the same year, in which
an out-of-work labourer, with his wife and children sitting exhausted on
the grass verge at his feet, stares at the road ahead winding into a flat,
bleak landscape. Herkomer settled in the village of Bushey in Hertfordshire
as it was convenient for London and he had no intention of running an
art school until a neighbour who wanted lessons for his niece offered to

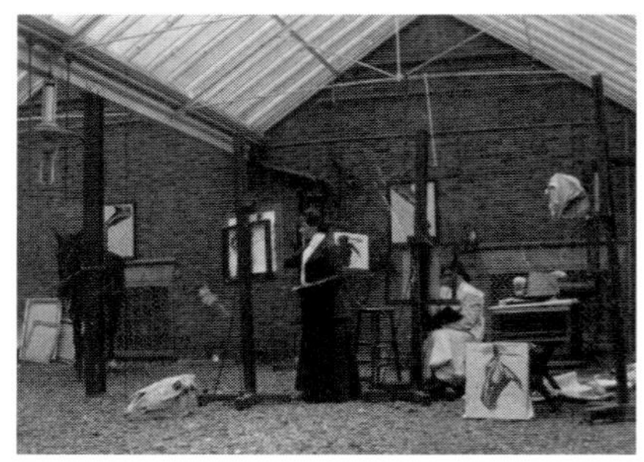

One of the studios at Bushey was designed so that horses could be brought in as models
Photograph, WCAA album

finance it. He designed an Arts and Crafts building and it opened in 1883 with thirty-two students.

Herkomer had hated his own repressive art training at Southampton, South Kensington and Munich, and wanted to create a school where students were able to express their own individuality. Unusually for the times, he had mixed classes, men and women painting together except in the life room. They were encouraged to broaden their interests, producing a magazine, performing plays for which they designed and made the sets and costumes and giving concerts; they even made films. Under his autocratic leadership, by the 1890s Bushey had become a thriving art colony with former students staying on in studios in the neighbourhood. One of these was Lucy Kemp-Welch, whose teaching in the school made its name synonymous with animal painting and was the reason for Walter's choice.

In the classroom she had been a shy and rather overlooked student but, back in the tiny sitting room of her lodgings, she painted an eight-foot canvas of gypsies she had seen driving horses through the village. Fellow students carried it to one of Herkomer's regular sessions of criticism: he was astounded by it. The picture was exhibited at the Royal Academy in 1895 and was followed each year by another large painting. The Chantrey Bequest bought *Colt Hunting in the New Forest* in 1897, establishing her reputation. When Charles Walter Simpson enrolled at Bushey in 1904 she had taken over the running of the school as Herkomer was a sick man. Later she bought it outright.

For a student of nineteen, Simpson already had a clear idea of what he wanted to paint and how to approach it. From boyhood he had drawn and painted directly from his subject, the countryside and its animals. In Kemp-Welch he had an example of someone doing this very successfully. She was a committed plein-air painter and she too liked large canvases. She had wooden packing cases built around them; they were delivered to the site and secured. With the barn-like doors open, she could work on the painting and fasten it at the end of the day. It might stay outside for up to three months. If the subject made it impossible to set up a canvas in front of it, as with the sudden excitement of gypsies riding through the village, she made sketches, trying to capture fleeting moments and training herself to memorise scenes that passed too rapidly to record. She then used these notes to build up a picture in the studio. These were practices that Simpson was to use all his life.

Lucy Kemp-Welch painted the countryside and its animals, though her interest was almost exclusively in horses, with which she felt a strong identification. She made the famous illustrations for *Black Beauty*. She personalised her animal subjects: her colts are free spirits, her stallions stand with their magnificent manes lifted by the wind against a threatening sky, her shire horses are wonderfully strong but exploited as they haul a tree trunk out of the forest. Simpson never projected his own feelings on to the animals he painted. To do that, he felt, was to be like a conductor who imposes too personal an interpretation upon a piece of music.

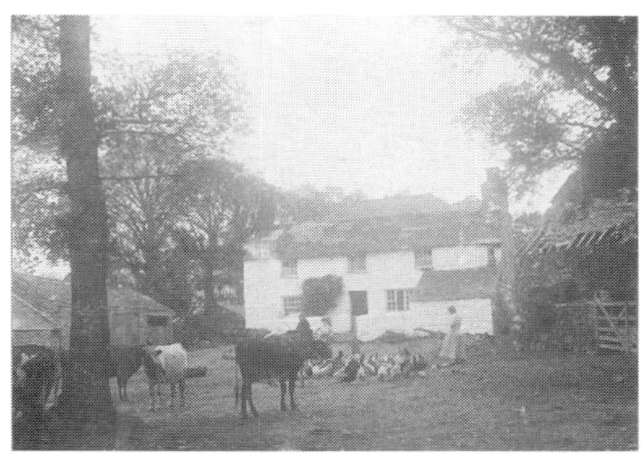

Tregethas Farm, St Erth
c1900, photograph

The animal painter he admired most was J.A. Arnesby Brown, who had been a student at the Herkomer School some fifteen years earlier. Arnesby Brown's favourite subject was cattle; he painted them with truth and simplicity under large skies which as well as being an important part of the composition fix the moment, the time of day and season. Simpson thought he was one of the few great painters of cattle in three centuries of European art. Arnesby Brown lived in East Anglia but usually spent the winters at St Ives in Cornwall. He painted on a farm near St Erth, a village on the narrowest part of the county before it widens to the Penwith peninsula. This area between north and south coasts, only six miles apart, is less 'Cornish' in character than the moors and cliffs further west. It's a gently rolling landscape, unspectacular and secretive, with an old manor house and a few farms, narrow lanes and high hedges.

In an act of homage after leaving Bushey, Simpson went to Cornwall in 1905 to stay at Tregethas Farm, where Arnesby Brown had painted. The farm was a mixed holding of about ninety acres, approached by a long winding track leading to the house, built in the seventeenth century and surrounded by tall elms. There was a cobbled yard and a range of two-storey granite farm buildings with slate roofs, the date 1817 above one of the doors. The tenant farmer John Hocking and his wife Laura had three daughters, Ada, Elsie and Winnie. They welcomed Walter into the family and gave him a studio on the top floor of a barn. It had a pattern of pigeon-holes in the wall and John Hocking put two skylights into the slates.

'A barn for a studio, and miles of open country round; a team of horses working near at hand; bullocks in the straw-yard; the dairy herd waiting the hour of milking by the field gate; to stay on a farm, canvases stacked on the dusty barn floor,' he wrote, 'that is the ideal of the pastoral animal painter.' With weeks ahead in which to make sketches, he took out a new canvas every day and looked for a subject. Once he had begun, nothing distracted him. 'The palette is loaded with paint, scraped, and loaded again. The flies settle on it, pollen dust or stray leaves drift over it; the rain may fall (it gives quality to the paint); but the picture grows hour by hour.

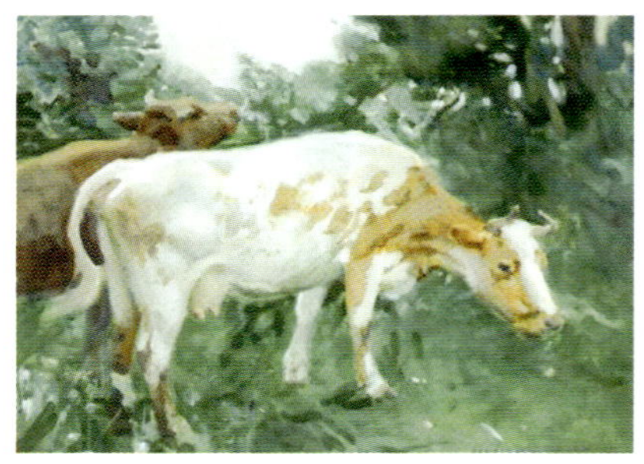

The colour box lies in the grass; empty tubes are tossed into it; two or three brushes have fallen under foot; they lie unheeded, the day is changing and work must be fast.' The farm kept shorthorns, the most paintable of cows with their rich reds and splashes of white. Simpson followed them in the fields, noticing all their attitudes. He loved the slow movement as they grazed, turning the head and neck to cover as large an area as possible before taking a graceful step, the last snatch at some grass as the stride began. He observed the way they disposed their weight during feeding, the arch of their backs and the stretch of their necks.

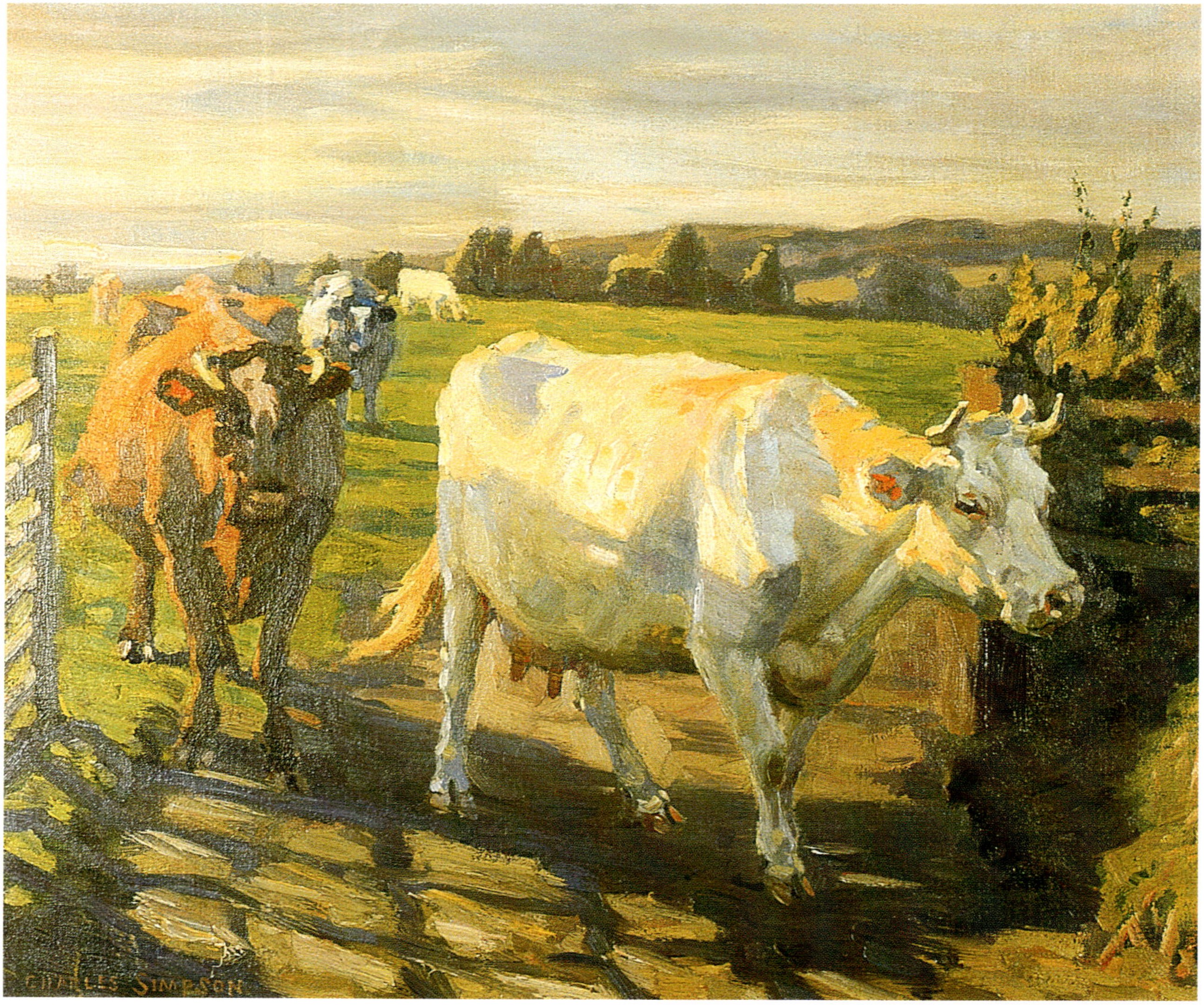

Beyond the farmhouse an avenue of trees led to a pond and the beginning of marshy ground, a scene he recognised from Arnesby Brown's pictures. Here he too painted cattle standing at the water's edge and a farm horse drinking from the pool. Other pictures were less influenced by the older painter: the dim cowshed at milking time, the light falling on Ada's white apron and the spotted white flanks of a cow and shining through the open door at the far end on to chickens scratching in the straw; Elsie standing with the cows in the yard at dusk, as the lamplight shines behind the window of the farmhouse; a tranquil scene of the yard in the sun with the barn and hayricks and a few hens. The horse drinking at the pond was the first picture he ever exhibited. His first success at the Royal Academy was in 1907 when he showed *Autumn Ploughing*; the following year *The Hayfield* was accepted and in the next year he sold his first picture at the Passmore Edwards Gallery in Newlyn. In 1910 he was back again at the Academy with *Milking Time*.

Tregethas was within easy reach of the art colonies of Newlyn and St Ives. It was a short walk through the lanes to St Erth station, on the main Paddington to Penzance railway. A branch line from St Erth ran past the saltings at Lelant and along the side of the Hayle estuary and St Ives Bay, past wide sandy beaches and through cuttings to arrive at the station above Porthminster Beach. The St Ives painters, dominated by the seascape artist Julius Olsson and including Arnesby Brown, Noble Barlow and Algernon Talmage, were interested primarily in sea and landscape, in capturing the different moods of the weather and the effects of light. Simpson, believing a picture should be a whole, the fields and sky painted with the same intensity as the animal, took lessons from J. Noble Barlow in St Ives.

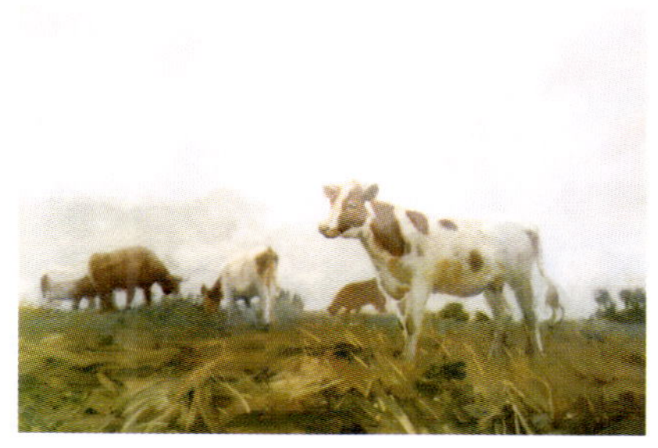

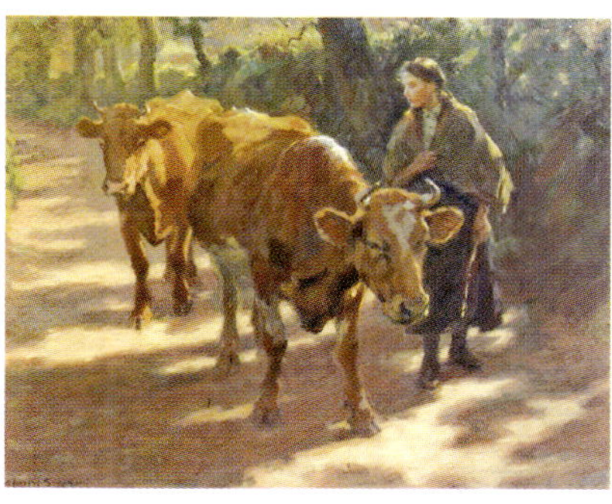

TOP
Cows in a Pasture
1913, gouache, 24 x 30 in
Courtesy of Porthminster Gallery, St Ives

ABOVE
Cows in a Lane
Oil on canvas, 45 x 55 in

BELOW LEFT
The Stackyard (Chywoone Farm)
Oil on canvas, 28 x 34 in
Photograph by Venture, Truro

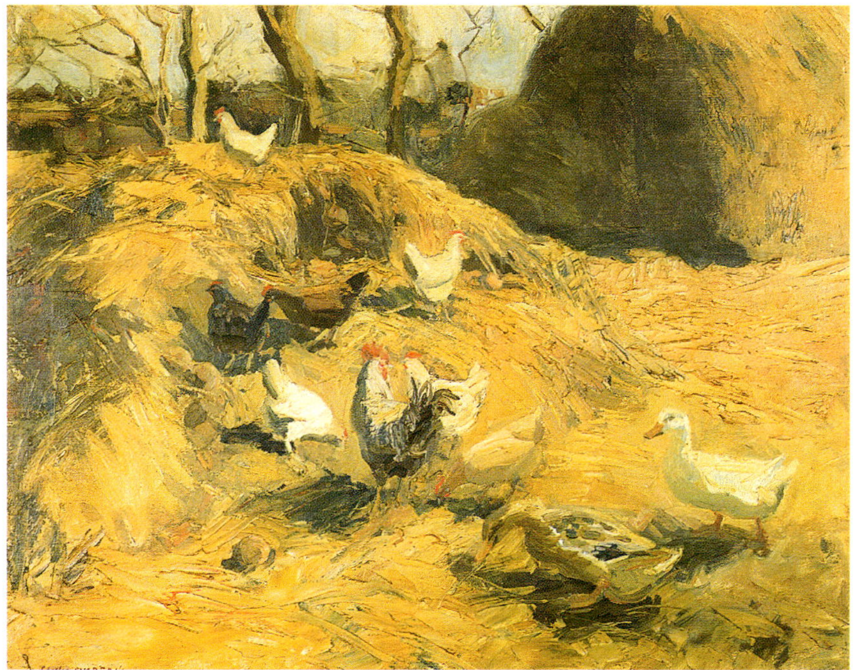

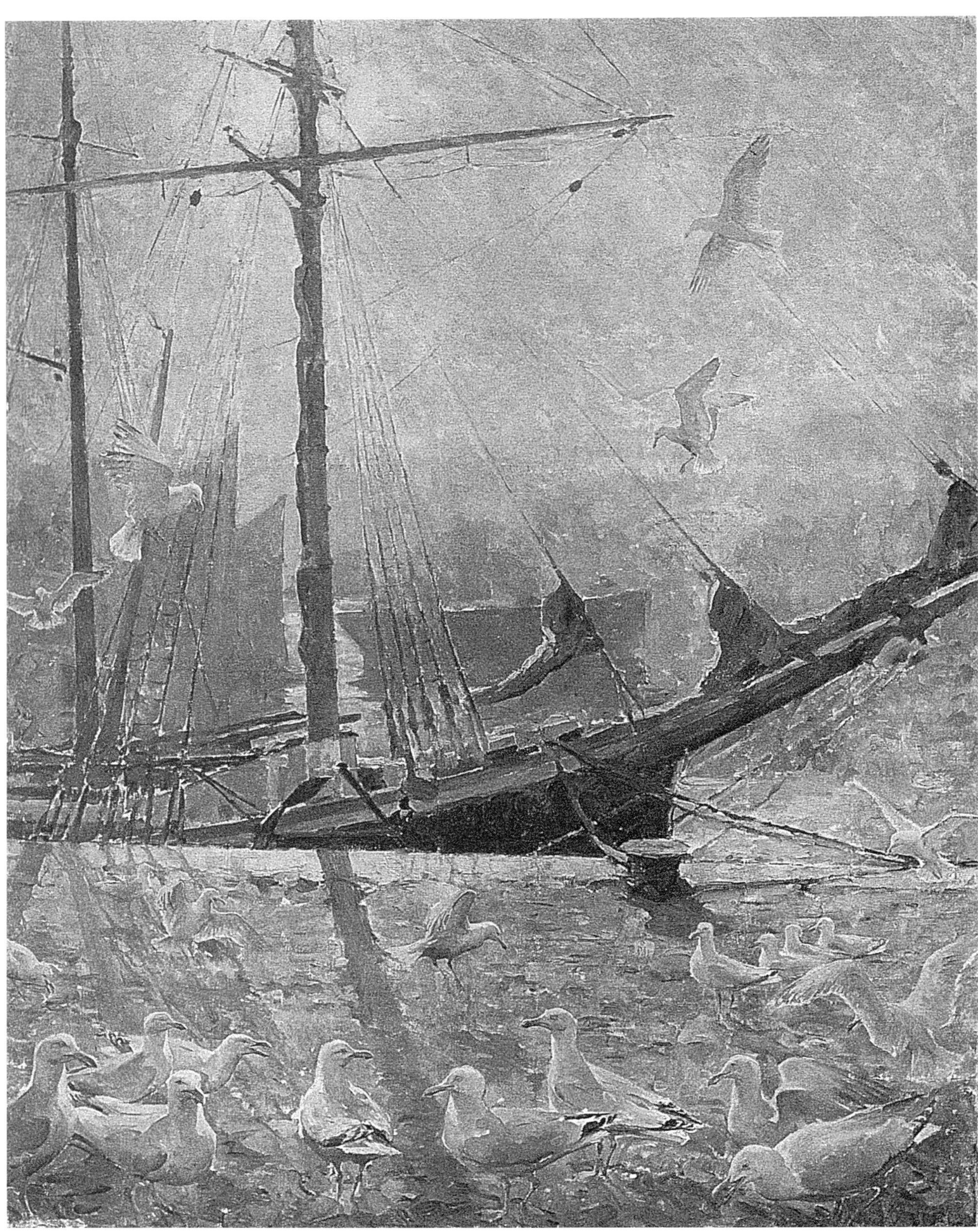

It was just as easy to reach Newlyn. St Erth was the last stop before Penzance, from where it was not far along the sea front. The Newlyn artists from the 1880s had painted the life of fishermen and their families. Stanhope Forbes's *A Fish Sale on a Cornish Beach* of 1885 is a realistic depiction in silvery tones of local people engaged in an everyday activity. Walter Langley and Frank Bramley showed the hardship the community endured, the grief of women whose husbands and sons were lost at sea. In 1899 Stanhope Forbes and his wife Elizabeth established their School of Painting, attracting new talent. Many of the younger artists were less interested in traditional Newlyn subjects. S.J. 'Lamorna' Birch was a landscape painter who settled in Lamorna, taking its name as his own. His presence and the beauty of the wooded valley leading to the sea drew others to the area, some three miles along the coast from Newlyn.

At Tregethas, Simpson was geographically and artistically between the two colonies, neither a figure painter nor a purely landscape painter. The early farm paintings are the only ones that could be described as 'Newlyn', resembling in subject and treatment the rural pictures that Stanhope Forbes and Harold Harvey were painting at the time. *Loading the Hay Cart* might be by either of them.

He would seem closer to St Ives, where several of the artists had studied at Bushey, but when he moved from Tregethas Farm it was to another barn studio at Chywoone Grove, a farm at the top of the steep hill out of Newlyn on the road to Lamorna. He took lodgings in the village at Penzer House and joined the Newlyn Society of Artists. He began painting seagulls, attracted by the birds themselves and by their movement, the pattern of wings against sea and sky. Other artists like Frank Heath included them as part of their harbour scenes, but Simpson focused on the gulls themselves.

To keep them wheeling above him he would take a bucket of dogfish offal to the harbour and get his friend C.E.Vulliamy, a student at the Forbes School, to throw handfuls into the air. He painted them squabbling over morsels thrown into the water, some gulls floating, some rising with water dripping from their feathers, a flurry of white and grey wings above the disturbed surface while other birds swing in against the dark hulls of fishing boats. Seabirds gave him greater variety of composition; they could be arranged more freely, often in a loose semi-circle that unfolds as the birds recede into the distance. 'Simpson portrayed these gulls in yelling multitudes, as large as life,' wrote Vulliamy. 'You were deafened and excited as you looked at the pictures.'

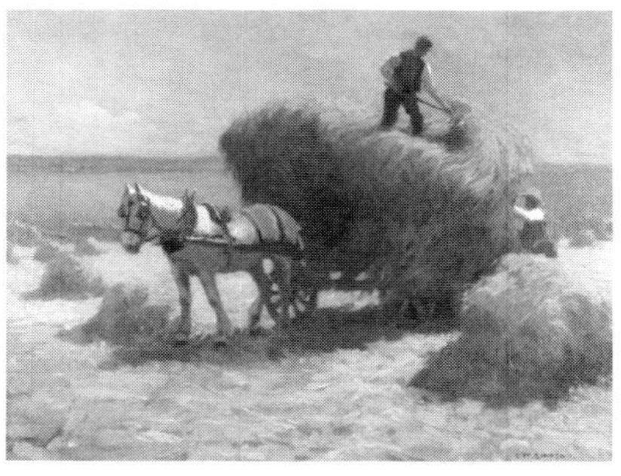

ABOVE
Loading the Haycart
Oil on canvas, 27 x 36 in
Courtesy of Lawrence Fine Art
Autioneers, Crewkerne

PAGE 22
On Newlyn Pier
RA 1946, oil on canvas, 60 x 40 in

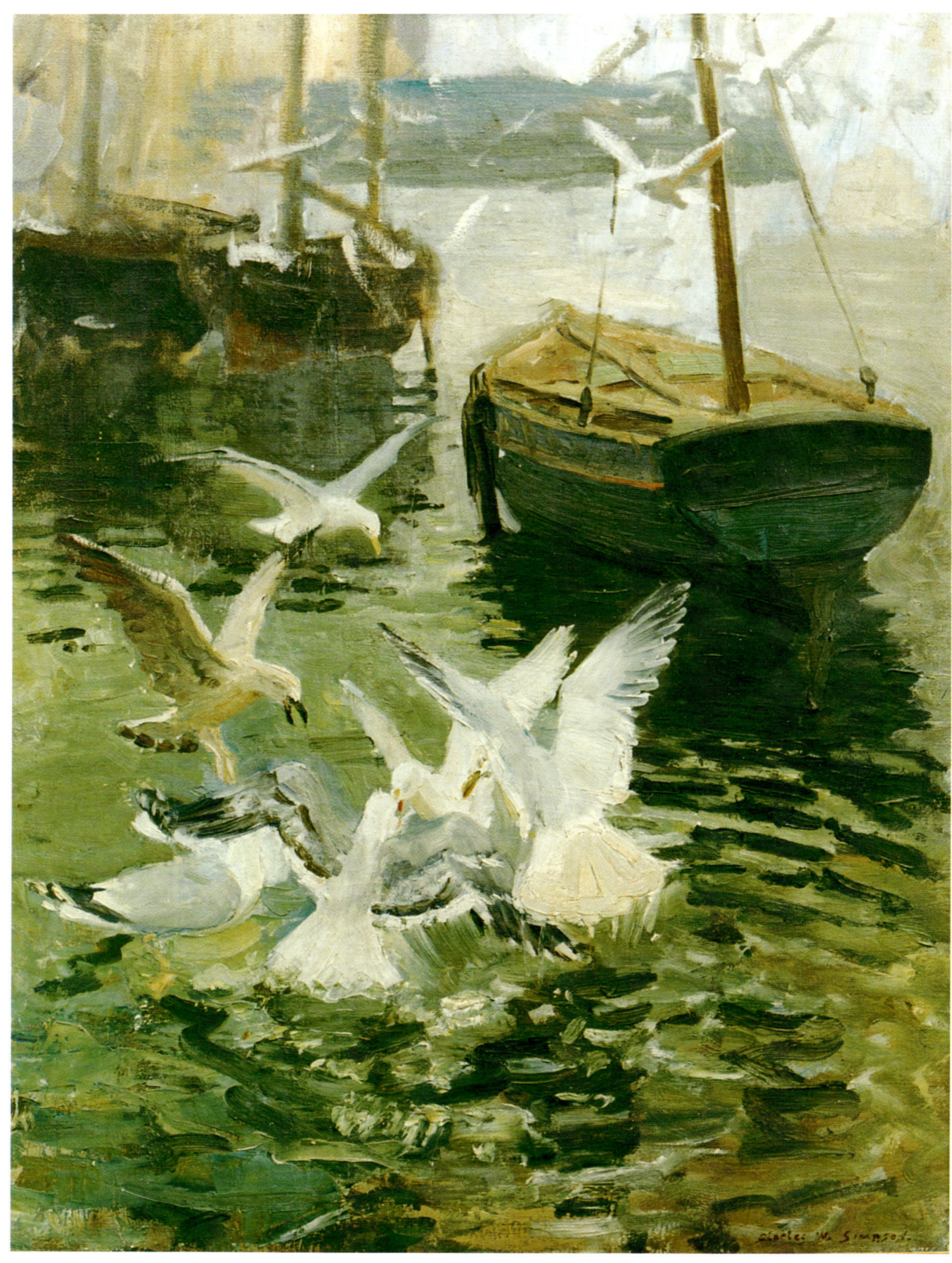

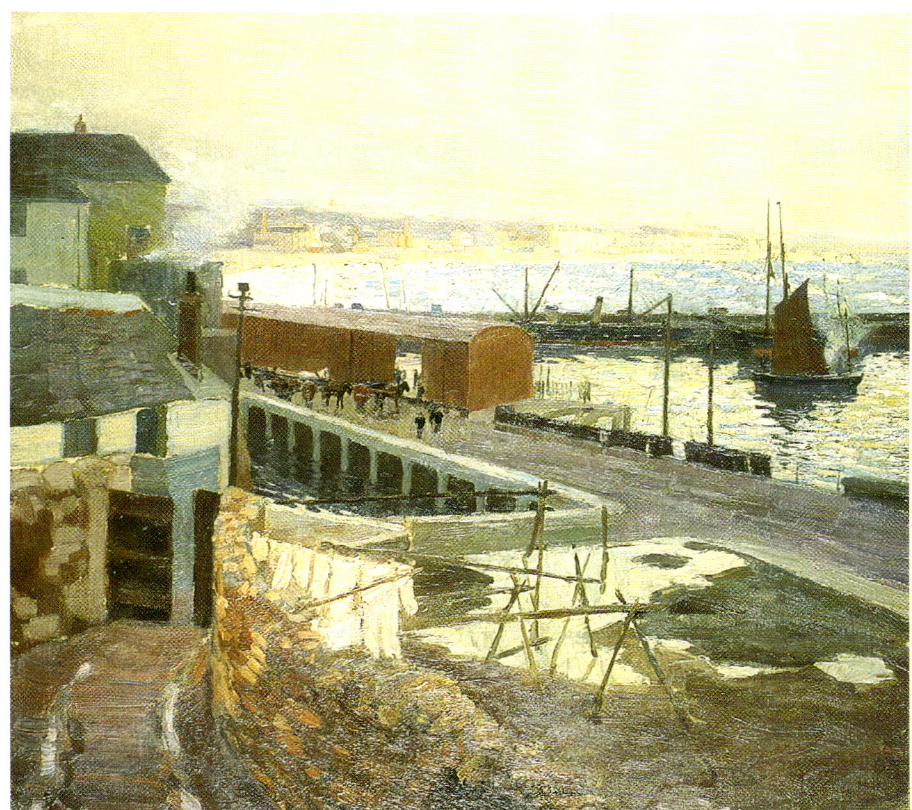

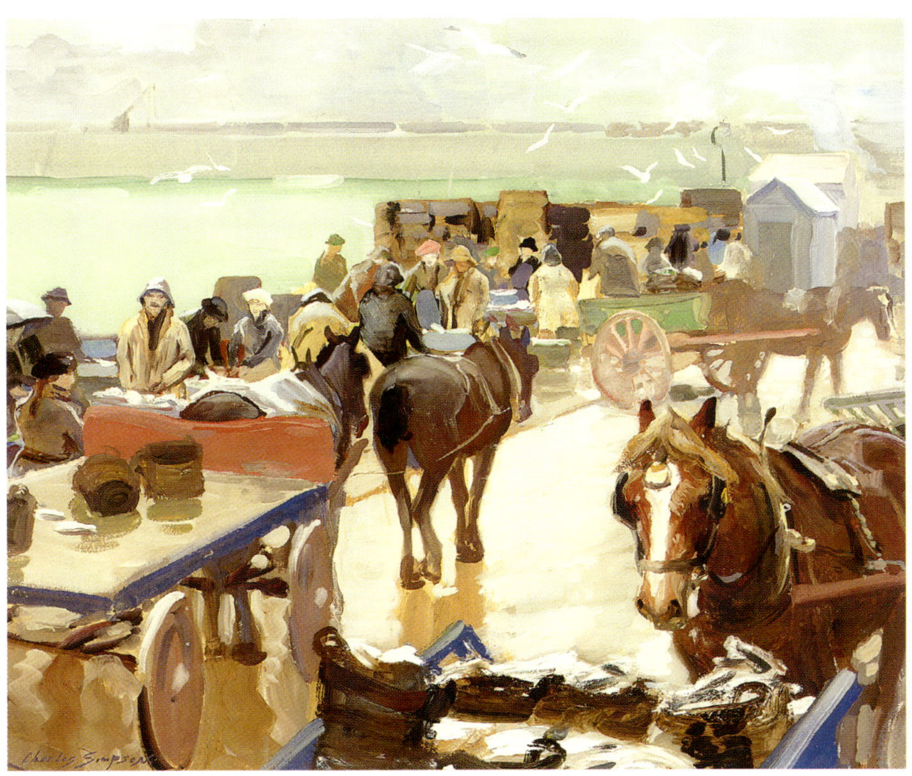

PAGE 24
Seagulls in Newlyn Harbour
c1910, oil on canvas, 40 x 30 in

LEFT
Penzance from Newlyn,
c1912, oil on canvas, 37 x 40 in
Newlyn Art Gallery on loan to Penlee
House Gallery and Museum, Penzance

BOTTOM LEFT
Newlyn Fish Market
Gouache, 26 x 30.7 in.
Courtesy of Sotheby's London

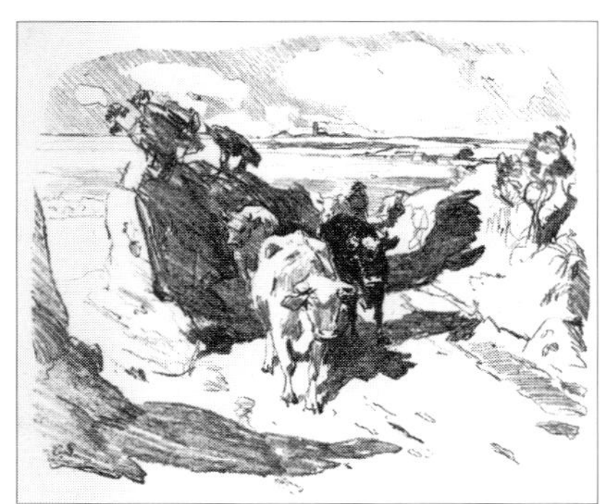

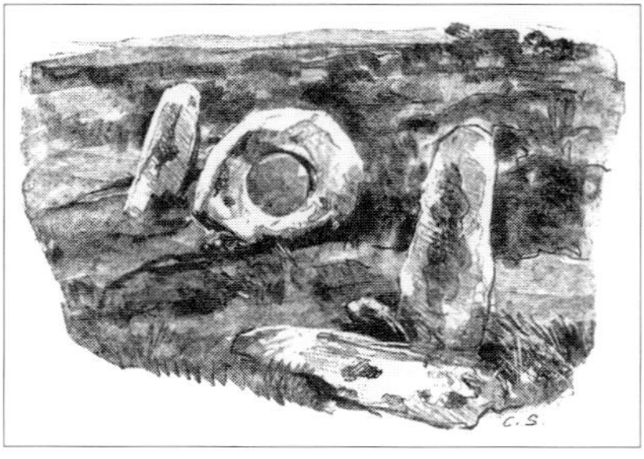

Away from the coast and harbour his other subject was the moorland, not the high moors of West Penwith but a stretch of boggy ground known as Clodgy Moor. It was about a mile from Chywoone Grove, close to the village of Sheffield. Here he built a painting hut that looked out across the marsh towards the hills and the tower of St Buryan church on the skyline. Carrying a large canvas across the exposed uplands, he often felt in danger of being lifted by the wind. The easel could be blown over, smearing the paint and losing a day's work. It had to be anchored down with ropes and heavy stones. He painted the moor in all weathers, in sunshine, rain and snow, at dawn and at sunset. He used large canvases for almost life-size cattle coming home with the evening light behind them. He worked rapidly and was liberal with his paint. Laura Knight said that 'he could be traced by the colour left on the bushes'.

Laura and Harold Knight had come to Newlyn in the autumn of 1907 from the colony of artists at Staithes in north Yorkshire. On their first morning they called on Forbes at the school and he introduced them to Ernest Procter and Dod Shaw, two of his most promising students. They must have met Charles Simpson the same day as they immediately moved into Penzer House, known as 'The Beer House' after the landlady, Mrs Beer.[1] The following year Alfred Munnings made his first visit to Cornwall, joining them at their lodgings.[2] Laura was dazzled by the personality of Munnings, his vitality, his unconventional behaviour and swagger. Simpson had acquired a reputation as a recluse, always working in his hut

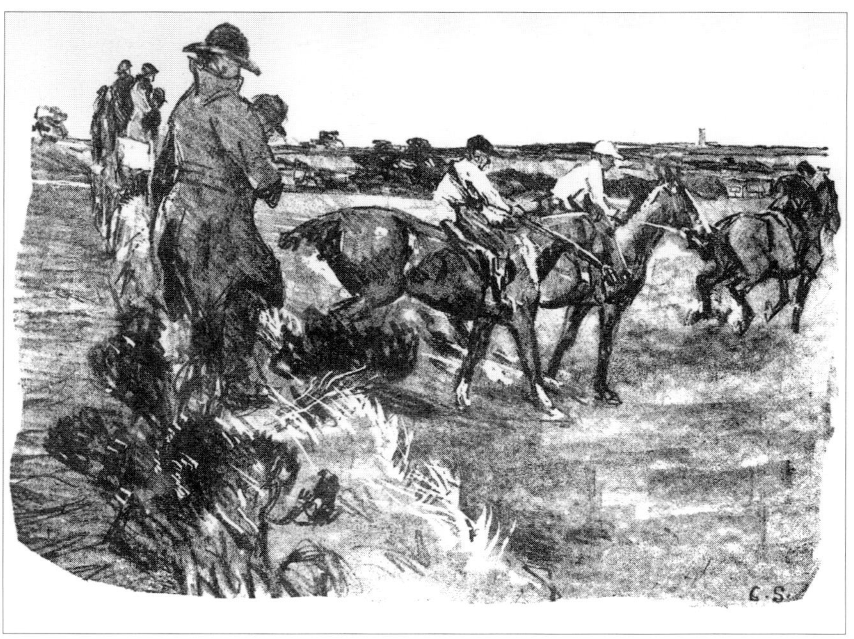

or his studio, both away from the village. He now joined in the parties of the newcomers. Munnings organised outings and events where the drink flowed and where he recited the hunting poems that he composed himself. Phyllis Gotch, the daughter of the artists Thomas and Caroline Gotch, also gave parties at Trewarveneth, the rambling house that had been the home of the Forbeses until they built Higher Faugan. She trained local girls in Greek dancing for one particular entertainment, with Laura Knight and herself as the two principals. The scene on the lawn was to be lit by torches held by Garnet Wolseley[3] in red tights and Charles Simpson in green, but it was such a damp evening that the torches wouldn't light. Simpson performed the dance of Salome, using a cushion for the head of John the Baptist. 'Such a flailing of limbs' Laura Knight had never seen.

He also became involved in *The Paper Chase*, the magazine that Elizabeth Forbes started for her students, with some outside contributions. The first edition came out in 1908. It was intended to appear quarterly but it only managed to struggle to a second number the following year. The writing was whimsical – 'We are a company of youngsters newly equipped for the road of life, pencil and notebook in hand, and knapsack on shoulder' – but the illustrations were of a higher standard, including a woodcut by C. W. Simpson in the first edition and four in the second of farm subjects, horses at the pool and cows in their stalls.[4]

Munnings was quick to fall out with people, but he and Simpson struck up a life-long friendship. Simpson admired his ability; he thought no one since Stubbs could paint a horse more truthfully and Munnings's success as an equestrian artist no doubt encouraged Simpson to emulate him. He went to stay at Swainsthorpe, the last stop on the line to Norwich, its station a raised wooden platform above the level fields. Munnings rented part of Church Farm from a relative. He had four rooms; an old couple, the yardsman and his wife who managed the dairy, lived in the kitchen end and looked after him.

The house was a long way from the road in the heart of agricultural Norfolk, an unspoilt countryside of fields and spinneys. He had a wooden studio in the meadow with cows and carthorses grazing around it. They painted together and wandered the countryside looking for subjects. In the evenings they went into Norwich, where Munnings's favourite bar was at The Maid's Head, the oldest inn in the city, with a bow window looking into the coaching yard. If they stayed there drinking until they missed the last train, they walked home across country in the moonlight, guided by the shape of the trees.

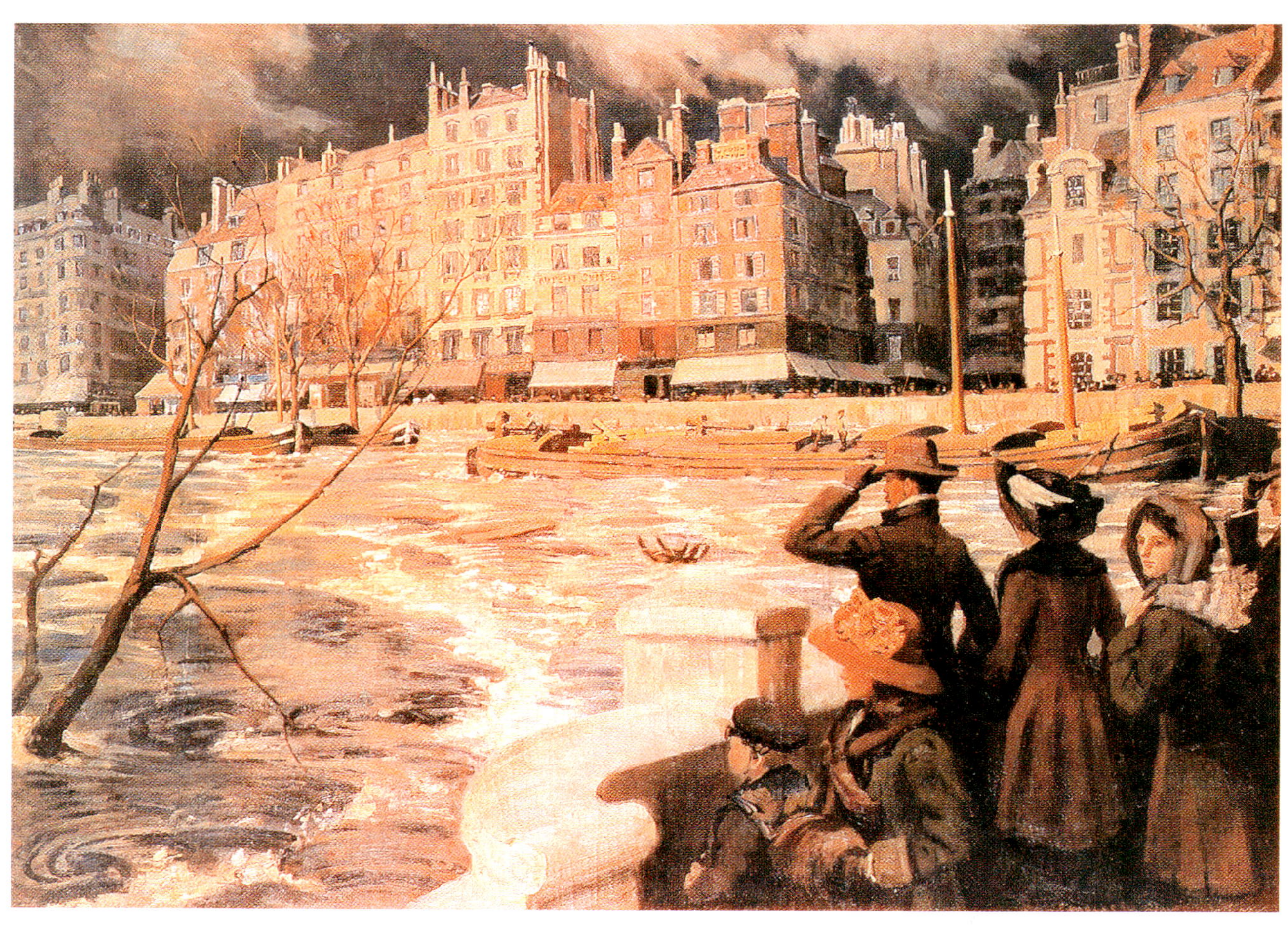

The Flooded Seine, Paris
1910, oil on canvas, 70 x 96 in
Courtesy of Guy Morrison

CHAPTER THREE

Simpson still felt a need for training and in the mild and wet January of
1910 he went to Paris. Since the 1870s a spell in one of the Paris art schools
had been regarded as a necessary part of a British artist's education. Many
of the schools, though, offered no more than basic facilities, a studio space,
a live model and mediocre teachers. The Académie Julian in the rue du
Dragon on the left bank of the Seine had better tutors, usually from the
nearby Ecole des Beaux Arts, who visited once or twice a week. The rest of
the time the students, many of whom were straight from school, were left
to work unsupervised and there was a lot of noise and horseplay. Simpson
took lodgings in the Latin Quarter, worked at the studio in the mornings
and went down to the river in the afternoon.

Strange things were happening to the Seine. It was rising rapidly,
reaching the level of the landing stages. Barges unloaded their goods at
the wharves, traffic passed over the bridges and crowds of people gathered
to stare at the swollen river. Simpson joined them, watching as workmen
hurried to carry away a load of cement that had been delivered to a lower
quay, the wheels of their carts axle-deep in muddy water. That night a
rushing sound could be heard and on the morning of 24 January the Seine
broke its banks. Simpson hastened from his lodgings. Under a dark sky,
with the rain driven by a strong wind, he saw a vast expanse of water,
rising almost to the top of the arches of the nearest bridge and submerging
the booksellers' stalls. The scene was lit by a wild light. The machinery and
steam cranes of the quays, all the activity of unloading, had disappeared.
Barges strained at their moorings, trees grew out of the water. The river
made a thunderous noise as it rushed past, yellowish in colour and bearing
wreckage on its surface, logs, barrels, the carcass of a cow. He spent the
day sketching.

On Tuesday the water continued to rise, flooding cellars and ground floors. The metro was out of use. Pumps were brought into the streets, the hose from a fire engine spouting a jet of water back into the river. People watched from upper windows. Simpson made more sketches but it had turned bitterly cold. By the next morning Paris was white with snow, while the river flowed dark and sullen. Whole streets leading to the Seine were flooded and returning to his lodgings Simpson found his way blocked as the water rose. The street lighting failed, the usually bright cafés on the boulevards were dark. 'C'est la fin du monde,' people said. There were soldiers everywhere in their blue coats, barring the way to the river and guarding the bridges. Simpson sketched from a doorway in the rue des Saints-Pères. The traffic splashed along, an omnibus showering the onlookers as the horses pranced and the driver cracked his whip. Only the Pont Neuf was open; it vibrated beneath his feet as he crossed it. In the next two days the floods spread to the right bank and the Champs- Elysées. The centre of Paris was an empty space.

Recognising the immediacy of his material, Simpson hurried back to London to organise an exhibition of his watercolours at the Graphic Gallery in the Strand. 'The Great Flood of Paris' showed over twenty pictures and sold all but three. He had not gained much from the rigidly academic tuition at the Académie Julian but in Paris he had visited museums and galleries and seen Impressionist and Post-Impressionist paintings. He had come back with a body of work that was both illustrative and decorative – and which sold well. When his exhibition closed he did not return to France or Cornwall, but stayed with his parents at Westleigh, South Farnborough, Hampshire. He had a studio some way from the house; it was also used by his sister Mary for assignations with a young officer. When their father realised what was going on, he mounted his charger and left the house at a gallop, intending to catch them together. Walter raced off on his bicycle by a different route and made good time. The Major General arrived to find Mary alone admiring the pictures.[1]

Their father had a command at Aldershot and allowed Walter to join the regiment on manoeuvres. He filled sketchbooks with drawings of soldiers on horseback, details of their uniform and equipment, the wagons and field guns and the means of attaching the horses to them. From the sketches he painted some military pictures, though it was *Milking Time* that he sent to the Royal Academy. To show at the Academy was the only way to make a reputation. He had now exhibited three times, he had had a sell-out show; he was established as an artist. His father recognised this when he commissioned him to paint a portrait group for the headquarters

Milking Time
RA 1910, oil on canvas, 26 x 30 in

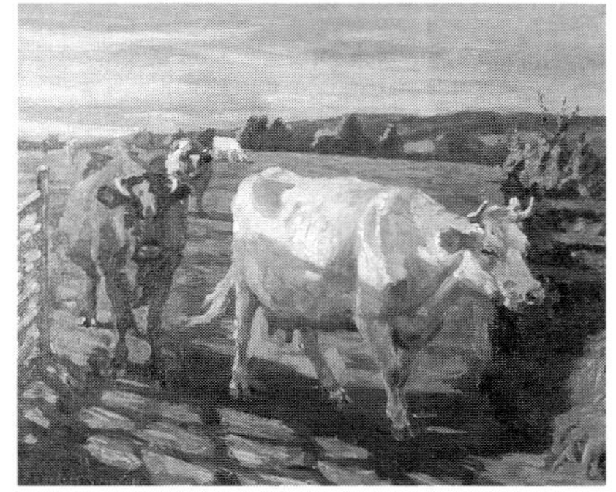

of the Lincolnshire Regiment: it shows Major General Simpson and his officers riding at the head of a brigade.

For years Walter had striven to succeed; now he had proved that he could make a career as an artist. He had worked intensively, without regard to his health, but he had never fully recovered from his head injury. When he drove himself too hard he collapsed and was unable to do anything for days. It seems that in that autumn he went off on his own in search of some sort of restoration or retreat. He wandered through Sussex, and south of Pulborough he was looking for birds at Greatham Brooks when he came across an abandoned cottage. It stood in water meadows close to the river Arun, which flooded in winter. The door was unlatched; he pushed it open and went inside. The ground floor was damp but the two upstairs rooms were snug, with the thatch hanging down over the small windows. He furnished one as a bedroom and living room and used the larger as a studio. A labourer from the farm brought him milk and eggs each morning, leaving them on the doorstep, and there was an inn a mile away.

In the valley carts were bringing in the last of the harvest before the storm broke. The gale lashed the willows and swept the surface of the river. Afterwards he stood concealed by the bridge and saw the flocks of curlew and wild duck overhead. At night he watched the swans flying inland, ghostly in the moonlight. He sketched the ducks and herons, the redshank and dunlin. As the river rose, the sheep were moved from the fields; the cattle gathered on patches of dry ground. In November, as autumn faded into winter, he left the derelict cottage standing above its own reflection in the floodwater. The melancholy cry of the curlew rang out across the marshes.

He was in Newlyn for the winter, at Polwin House; his landlady Mrs James provided him with rooms and his meals, did his washing and gave him motherly care, all for 35/- a week. He kept the studio at Chywoone Grove, where Alfred Munnings stayed on a visit before the end of the year. At one of the parties there Munnings was blamed for getting some of the students seriously drunk. It was from Chywoone the following spring that Simpson sent three paintings to the Royal Academy, all of which were accepted. They represented a change of subject from the farming pictures that he had previously shown and resembled the work of no one else in Newlyn. *Winter on a Cornish Moor* was painted from the hut at Clodgy; the other two were *The Pond* and *Ducks on the Water*. These were his first exhibited paintings of one of his favourite subjects. To some of the academicians 'duck should only be mentioned when roast', but Simpson

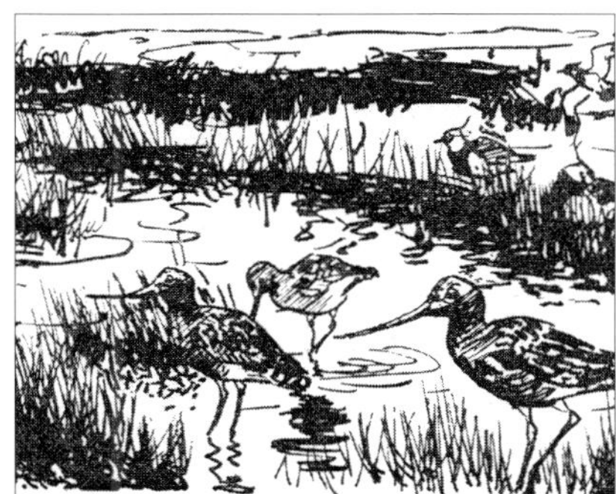

Wading Birds
Illustration from *Son of a Gun*

delighted in their shape, so neat and tidy, so self-contained and delicate, so various in colour. After the floods in France and Sussex he delighted too in painting light on water.

The influence of Paris rather than Newlyn now appeared in his work. He always denied that he was an impressionist, but he understood the theory and took from it what he wanted. To him, impressionism was a matter of light and colour. Instead of drawing a line around an object, the impressionist defines it by light, losing much of the detail if necessary. Instead of using flat colour mixed on the palette, he uses all the colours of the spectrum, allowing the eye to mix them when standing back from the canvas. The result is increased brightness, the paint appearing less 'muddy'. Shadows are not black or grey, but include the complementary colour of the object in shade. In paintings before 1910 Simpson used white for the foam on a wave; after that date he usually painted foam with prismatic colours.

It was the custom for the artists to show their Academy entries at the Passmore Edwards Gallery in Newlyn before sending them off to London by rail. Simpson became more involved with the society, being elected 'subscriber' with Garnet Wolseley in March at a meeting of the committee chaired by Walter Langley. He was one of twelve members present at the following general meeting which voted for a donation to Mrs Forbes's Fund, set up to help with the cost of the full-time nursing that she required. She had returned from treatment in London and Italy for 'tuberculosis', though in fact she had cancer. In April he was one of the two witnesses at the wedding of Harold Harvey and Gertrude Bodinnar at St Peter's Church.[2]

In June, 1911, at the start of the Forbes School of Art summer term, he left Newlyn for Sussex. At the cottage in the water meadows of Greatham Brooks the floods had receded and the fields were golden with buttercups. Yellow irises on the riverbank attracted crowds of dragonflies, cattle splashed in the stream and trampled the rushes. A cornet player performed outside the inn, a fair passed through and he met a tramp who had grown up in the cottage. The old man travelled the countryside finding work where he could, but was always drawn back to the place in a cycle like that of the migrating birds. The vagrant described the winters that he remembered as a boy, when the snow came half-way up the windows and at night he would lie awake terrified by the beating of the wings of immense flocks of geese wheeling above the house. The shepherd returned with his flock. He lived in a hut in the fields to be close to them, and Simpson sat with him all one night to watch the sun rise over the downs.

He found that there were things he could not express in his painting,

even if his love of nature and creatures of the wild was implicit in them.
He began to write to convey his feeling for places haunted by memories
of the past and his sense of the transience of life, such a brief span in the
immensity of the universe. He saw parallels with music, the rhythm of the
seasons being part of a vast cosmic symphony. He wrote a long essay on the
influence of Beethoven's deafness on his late compositions.

He returned to Newlyn at the end of the summer and in October was
elected 'hanger' at the gallery with Walter Langley and Harold Harvey.
In the next year, 1912, he was on the committee which sent a message of
sympathy to Stanhope Forbes. Elizabeth Forbes had died on 16 March at
the age of fifty-two. Simpson was very moved by her death and filled many
pages of a notebook with drafts of an elegy written in memory of her.[3]

He was best man at the wedding of Ernest Procter and Dod Shaw at
the church of St Leon de Pol in the village of Paul above Mousehole. The
couple were expected to have brilliant careers, but other friends were still
struggling for recognition. 'Tommy' Thompson painted gloomy pictures
of moors beneath grey skies. Nobody bought them and he survived by
teaching drawing two days a week at the Penzance boys' secondary school,
while still attending Forbes's classes. C.E. Vulliamy was uncertain whether
he wanted to be a painter or writer. He was half French and half Welsh (his
first name was Colwyn), English-speaking except when under stress.

Amongst the students there was much talk of romance, of relationships
formed and broken off or marriages made. Simpson's name had never been
linked with any young woman and it was generally assumed that he had
no interest. He told Tommy Thompson that at the age of twenty-seven he
had never kissed a girl. Tommy was keen on Kathleen Earle, always known
as Kay, a bright and promising student at the school, and Simpson said he
would like to try it with her, purely out of scientific interest. Tommy said
that if he did he would knock him down.

One fine afternoon in May Simpson was going to call on Vulliamy at
Harbour View Terrace. He was planning a concert in his studio and he
wanted Vulliamy to play the piano. As he approached he saw 'a gorgeous-
looking girl in a large black and white straw hat' coming away from the
house. The next day he was wiping the condensation from the big glass
window of his studio when she passed below. She looked up and thinking
that he was waving to her, she waved back. He rushed down to explain
that he would not dream of waving to a lady to whom he had not been
introduced. But he took the opportunity of inviting her to his concert.

Her name was Ruth Alison.

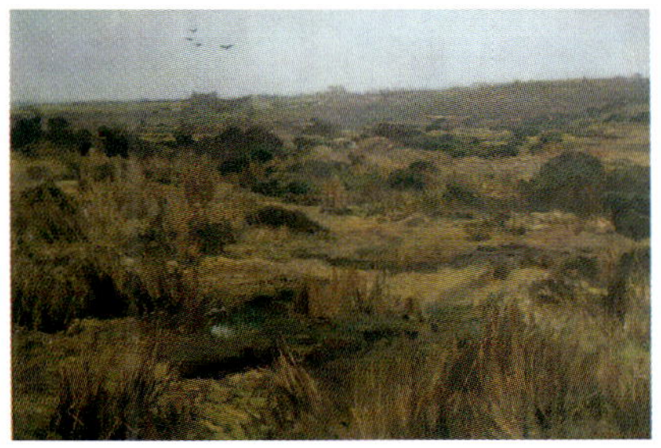

Clodgy Moor
Oil on canvas, 26 x 39 in
Courtesy of the Lander Gallery, Truro

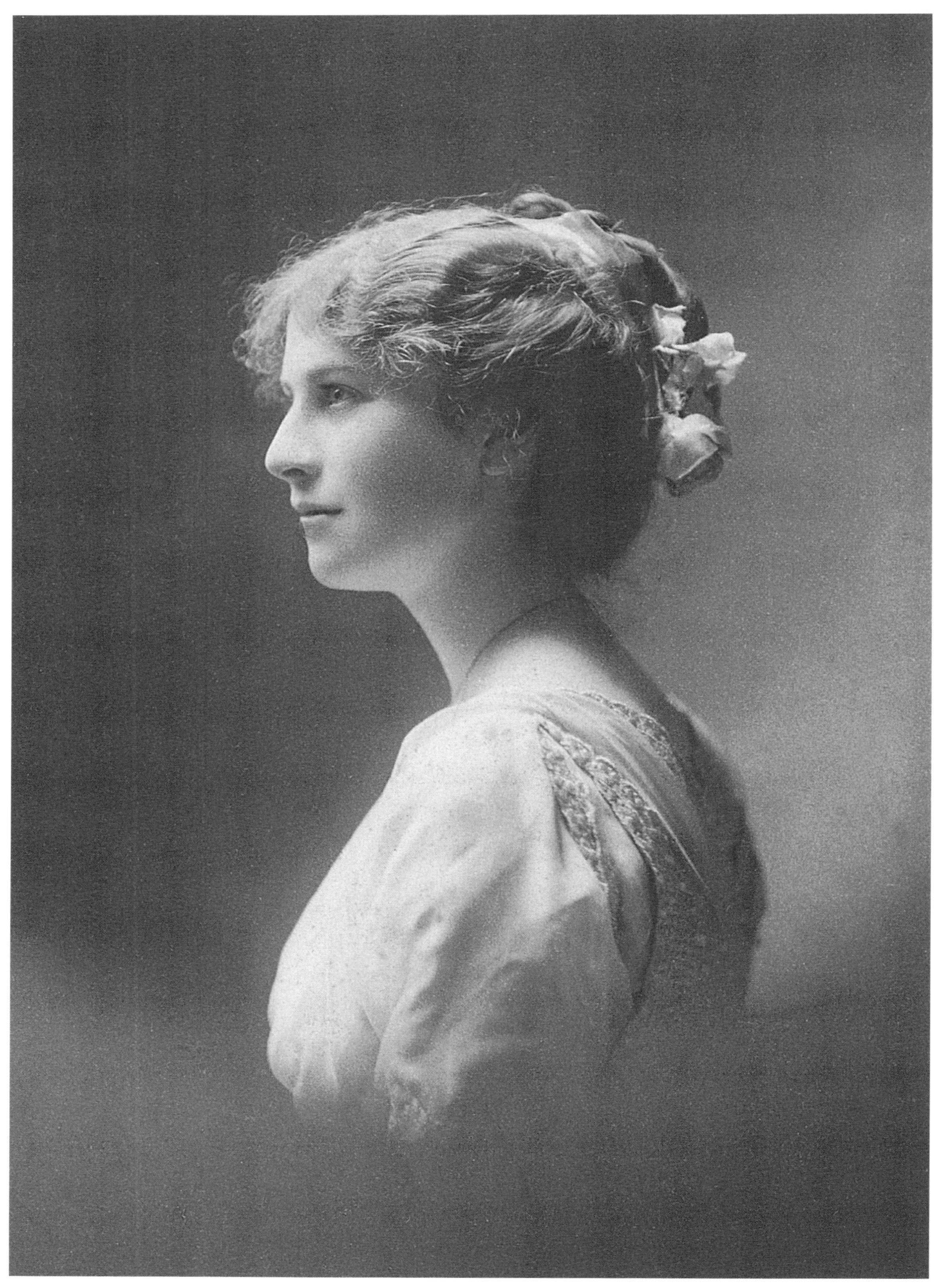

Ruth Alison: 'A Great and Wonderful Love'

A few days earlier Ruth had left her home, Dunain Lodge, York Road, Harrogate, and with her younger sister Rose had caught the morning train to London. They went to the Royal Academy before meeting Ruth's fiancé Ralph, who was the brother of her friend Lorna Dewhirst and who worked in London while hoping to qualify as an architect. He took them to his boat club at Hammersmith, where they had tea in an upstairs room opening on to a veranda overhanging the river. They went for a sail, tacking up to Chiswick in a stiff breeze. In the evening they went to the *Merrie England* show at Earl's Court. The next morning at Paddington the guard found them a smoker with two corner seats. Ralph arrived with his sister Lorna. Tommy Thompson, who would not be in Newlyn that summer, came to see off Kathleen Earle. The train left, leaving two disconsolate males on the platform, while Ruth and Rose, Lorna and Kay set out for the summer term at the Forbes School of Painting.

At twenty-two, Ruth had battled with her parents to gain the life she wanted. She was the daughter of Alister and Ada Alison and was born on 28 September 1889 in Newcastle, her mother's home town. Her father worked for the Royal Exchange Assurance company and travelled daily from Harrogate to his office in Leeds. A severe and dour-looking man from a Scottish family, he had his two daughters educated at Wycombe Abbey School in Bedfordshire and brought them up to be marriageable young ladies. They caused him a lot of anxiety. Rose attracted the most unsuitable men and had to be rescued from several scrapes. Ruth was more amenable, quieter and less flirtatious in manner, but had become engaged to Ralph Dewhirst against her father's wishes. He was not happy about her attending art classes in a distant part of the country but had allowed her to spend the previous summer term at the Forbes School. Freed from the constraints of home, she had enjoyed student life, the picnics in Trevelloe Woods or

PAGE 34
Ruth Alison as a young woman
Photograph

at Lamorna Cove with Kay Earle, Tommy Thompson and C.E. Vulliamy, even though she and Kay had to live at Penalverne, a girls' boarding school in Penzance. Here they kept school hours and were always under the watchful eye of the headmistress, Miss Hare. But now the four girls were to lodge together at the Old Manor. It was so much more exciting to be in the centre of Newlyn. With doors and windows opening straight on to the street, students and artists would drop in as they passed up the hill.

Ruth accepted Simpson's invitation to his first studio concert and sat by the window looking out over Mount's Bay. She listened to Vulliamy and Miss Frayer playing Beethoven duets and watched the moon rise over the sea. Afterwards she and Simpson went for a walk along the quayside, with the tide lapping against the walls, the moonlight shining across the water and the strains of Beethoven still in her ears. She felt she was in heaven.

When she wrote to her mother on 20 May she could not conceal her excitement. At ten o'clock the previous evening there had been a cry of 'What ho!' outside and she pulled the curtains. Three heads in a row were looking in, Vulliamy, fat Jonsson the Swede and 'a sweet artist called Simpson. He is awfully clever and has a picture of ducks on the line at the Academy this year. He had another wonderful huge moorland picture accepted too, but at the last they said they could find no room for it. A great shame. He is quite young too, only 28 and is now doing a marvellous 8ft canvas of life-sized seagulls and blue sea and sunny cliffs.'

She knew that she was in love, and he with her. But it placed her in a terrible dilemma. She was engaged to Ralph and she was convinced that Simpson would ask her to marry him before she was free to say yes. When she had seen Ralph in London she felt that they no longer had much in common. Seeing so little of each other, they had grown apart and she convinced herself that he probably felt the same. But she couldn't write to break off the engagement as he was taking his finals at the end of June. She would have to wait until the exams were over before dropping her bombshell. Although she no longer loved him, she was fond of Ralph and didn't want to hurt him.

She told her father not to worry about her moonlit walks as she was quite capable of looking after herself. She described Mr Simpson as she had to her mother, correcting his age to twenty-seven and adding those details that would appeal to Alister Alison: that he had made two hundred pounds in two months with his sketches, that his father was 'a colonel or general' in the army, in command of Mauritius. She told him – but not to tell mother because if she knew it would get back to Mrs Dewhirst – that

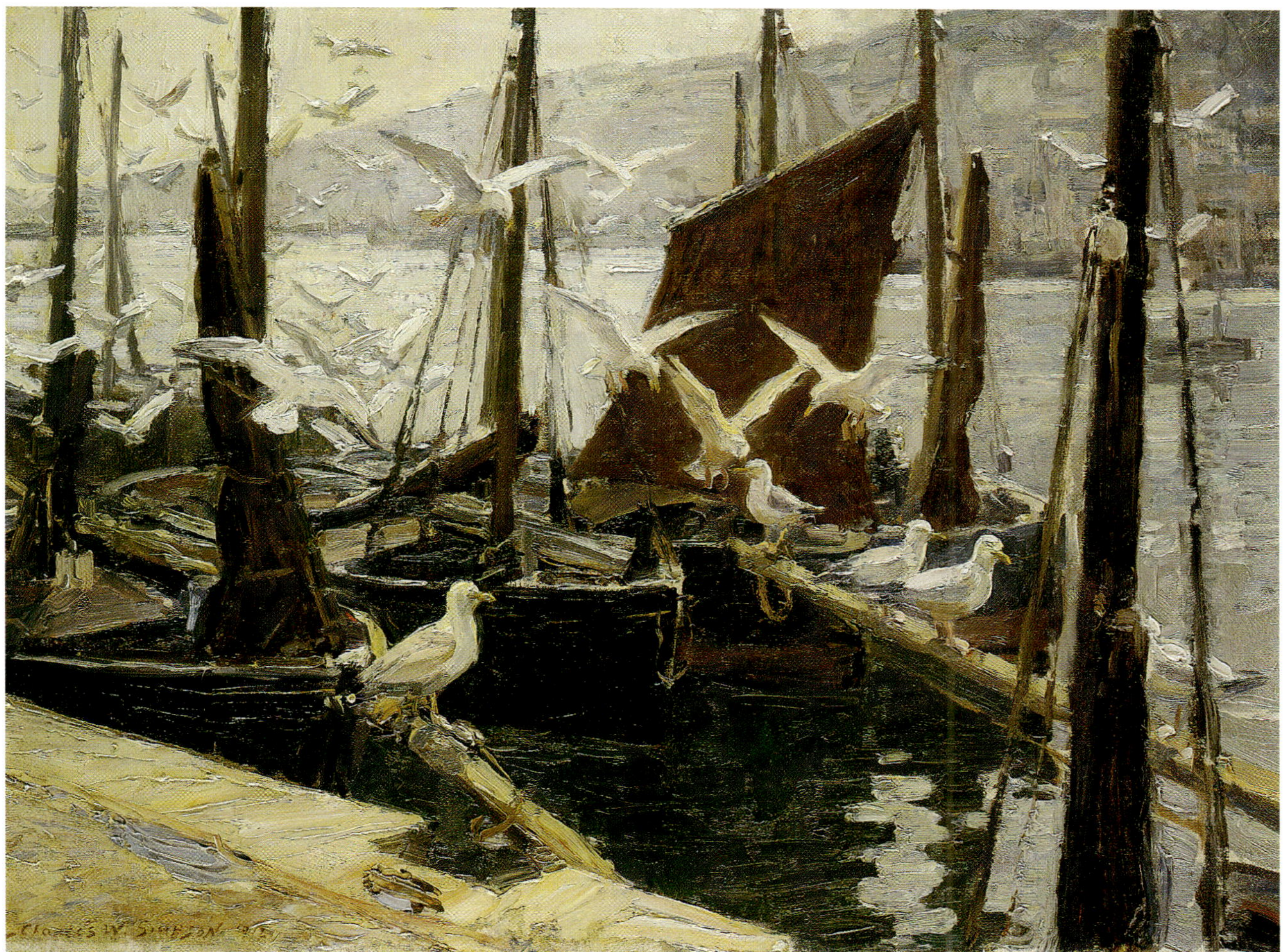

Gulls on the Quayside, Newlyn
1912, oil on canvas, 30 x 40 in
Reproduced by kind permission
of David Messum

she was going to finish with Ralph: 'doubtless you and mother will shriek
for joy.' Then she let out her secret. 'I *may* (I only say *may*) bring you this
very C.W. Simpson Esq as a son-in-law – in the future – who knows? I only
know that he is extremely interested in me and hardly ever off the doorstep
when work is over. He's been in twice today! And will probably look in
again. He is nice-looking, tall (6ft) and slim and an artist to his fingertips…
What he sees in me heaven knows. It would be a liberal education to marry
a man like that… Pretty cool of me to talk like this, when I've only known
the man a bare week.'

Not surprisingly, this letter did little to allay Mr Alison's anxiety and
he wrote back urging caution, fearing that she wanted 'to be on with the
new before she was off with the old'. Ruth tore up his letter in case Rose
should see it. Events were moving fast. She wrote an astonishingly frank
letter to her father again. 'Yesterday we went another picnic to the cave
in Trevelloe Woods and he (Mr Simpson) became rather [heavily scored

out] Well! I can't describe it except that I felt electricity in the air all the time, tho' he's not a bit of a flirt and hates flirting. Anyway I was simply terrified of having a proposal from him before I had finished with Ralph.' On the long walk home, when the air became more electrical than ever, Ruth pulled herself together and told him all about Ralph. 'He was nice and sympathetic and gave me lots of very good advice.' It was agreed that she would tell him as soon as she had written to Ralph in three weeks' time and he made it clear that he would ask the important question as soon as she was free.

One wet evening Charles Simpson and two American students, 'Pete' Peters and another known as the Elephant (who was keen on Lorna) sat around the fire telling ghost stories. Simp – as Ruth now called him – had a thrilling voice and made them all shiver with his tales of horror. When the Elephant left Newlyn and came to say goodbye they ate biscuits and oranges and played *Old Maid* and *Introduced, Proposed, Engaged*, till Simp and Ruth were the last ones left in the game. She had the four kings and he had the four queens. 'Oh – gasp – we're married!' he exclaimed, to the mirth of everyone else. Ruth found it hard to remember that he wasn't a student but a very accomplished and clever artist. 'He's just an ordinary jolly boy,' she thought as she watched Rose throwing biscuits for him to catch in his mouth. C.W. Simpson behaving so foolishly!

On a fine Saturday after morning 'crit', the weekly commentary that Stanhope Forbes gave on students' work, they went to the beach with their lunch and swam and sunbathed all afternoon. Rose and Kay fetched their tea and supper and they remained there until 8.30, by which time they were hungry again. 'The useful Simp' invited them back to his place to see what Mrs James could do for them. They jumped at the idea as they would get no more from their landlady, Miss Leeson. His sitting room at Polwin House was high up over the bay. The table was lit by candles with pink shades and stood before the window with the blue twilight beyond. Mrs James produced a meal of mackerel, poached eggs in sauce and fruit with clotted cream. Then they had cups of cocoa. Unfortunately for Ruth, Simp had insisted on her trying his stout before they ate, and after the fish she was terrified that she was going to be sick in his beautiful room.

The Old Manor became a centre of interest and gossip for the whole community. Simpson hired a jingle to take them all in style to Penzance Fair and they went on every merry-go-round, switchback and helter-skelter. He bought a huge lump of nougat that his penknife couldn't cut so they twisted off pieces and got very sticky; he bought a bottle of lemonade for

them to wash their hands. Ruth and Simp went alone to the West
of England Cattle Show, which came to Penzance every seven years.

Ruth was excited and worried, sleeping little and suffering from
headaches as the time approached for her to post her letter to Ralph.
By chance it crossed his first letter since the exams, a nice ordinary letter
which made it clear that he loved her as much as ever and assumed that
she felt the same. It made her feel terrible. Lorna was very worried about
her brother and sent a telegram asking if he would like her to come and
stay, but he wired back that he didn't want anyone. When he wrote to
Lorna it was clear that he was utterly miserable and he thought that on
top of everything he had failed his exam.

Amongst all this emotional turmoil Ruth tried to make progress with
her painting. She sent in some pictures for the summer exhibition at the
Passmore Edwards Gallery. As she said, it was useful being so pally with
the hanging committee. Simpson hung her paintings, two by Lorna and
two by Kay Earle. Ruth did a portrait of Kay in a green hat, sitting on the
edge of a table and smoking a cigarette. Simpson was very complimentary
about it and advised her to concentrate on portraiture. The next morning
she had a good 'crit' from Forbes for her head of an old man. 'Yes, it's
quite good – very good – excellent,' he said. 'Yes, I really think you are
beginning to learn now.'

Ruth herself felt that she was getting on. She thought she had done
one or two decent studies. The other students considered her very quick;
she thought she would soon be the best at the school. She told her parents
that she was really determined to be a proper artist, someone they could
be proud of. Simp helped her and she learned a lot from the artists he
introduced her to. They had dinner with the Munnings, Alfred and his
beautiful young wife Florence who had also been a student at the Forbes
School. Keen for her parents to know that an artist could earn a lot of
money, she told them that Munnings made about £2,000 a year. She
found it very instructive looking at his work and hearing Mrs Knight and
Simpson comment on it. It was good to be in a grown-up set, she was tired
of silly kids – meaning Rose and Lorna.

The silly kids had been taken up by Mr Miller, a man of means who
was providing endless expensive entertainments for them, especially for
Rose. He took them in a motor to Kynance Cove, treating them to tea.
Ruth dropped out of these excursions, preferring to have lunch with Simp
on the beach or in the fields. They were sitting under a fuchsia hedge
above the granite quarry when there was a sudden storm and they huddled

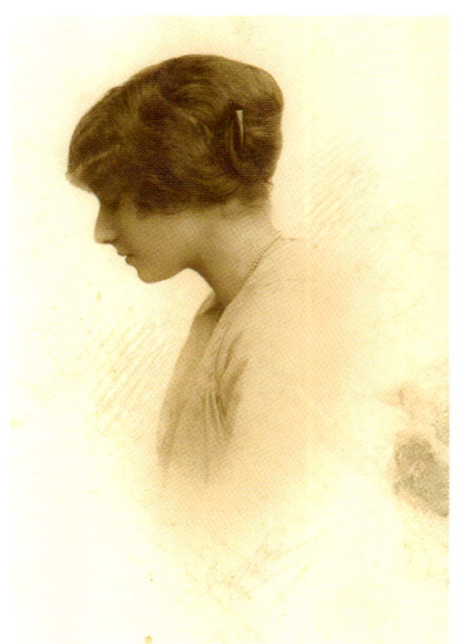

Profile of Ruth Alison
Photograph, WCAA

together under her Burberry for shelter. After tea she would work until suppertime. One evening she arrived back and found all the others had gone to the theatre in Penzance, so Simp took her up to his digs and they had a lobster supper.

For a dance that he gave, the 'kids' prepared a cabaret. Rose and Lorna, Pete the American and Bunny Shaw, the brother of Dod, were a Russian corps de ballet, coached in their dances by Laura Knight. At a charity concert in Lamorna, Stanhope Forbes's friend Walter Barnes played the violin and Simpson booked him for his next Wednesday concert. Alfred Munnings entertained with comic hunting recitations and a fat clergyman sang folk songs. Mr Forbes was in the audience with his son Alec. His former pupil and present secretary Maudie Palmer, whom he would marry in 1915, was also there, as were the Graftons and the Knights.

As the end of term approached, Ruth was reluctant to return to Yorkshire. The other girls were going home, but she intended to stay on in Newlyn until the winter term began. A letter from her mother came as a shock. Her parents were not happy about her being at the Old Manor on her own. 'I consider it curious to say the least that you think me not old enough or not sufficiently well-balanced to live by myself,' she replied. 'I have been living here the entire summer minus a chaperone (and looking after three others).' She discerned the hand of her father in the letter. 'Will you please tell him from me with my love that his ideas on the subject of grown-up daughters are antiquated… This is most emphatically *not* the censorious world of Harrogate… I want to be independent, as I really think I should be allowed to be.'

However, she went home in September, determined that it would be for no more than the two weeks' break between terms. She travelled with Rose, who was accompanied as far as Bristol by her latest beau. They parted dramatically, the young man on the platform kissing her hand and holding on to it as long as possible as the train gathered speed. At Leeds station she was met by one of her Yorkshire young men.

As soon as she could Ruth wrote her first letter to Walter, as she now addressed him. 'I expected that when here I should be feeling that everything that happened in Newlyn this summer must be a wonderful dream and this my real everyday existence. Instead I find it quite the other way about. This is most unreal, the proper me belongs to Newlyn.' Her mother came to her room when she was going to bed and wanted to talk. To Ruth's surprise, she understood exactly how her daughter felt and was so much in sympathy with her that Ruth was ashamed to have misjudged her. 'She was wonderful, she is pleased that I am going to live the life that I intend, it is what she would have loved herself.' She had no objection to Ruth staying on her own at the Old Manor and would like to spend Christmas with her. She suggested a quiet wedding in Newlyn because of the Ralph affair. She would give Ruth £50 a year and wished it were more. The only problem was Dad, but she thought he would give no trouble when the time came.

In Newlyn Walter told Gertrude and Harold Harvey of their engagement, knowing the news would soon spread and put an end to all conjecture. In Harrogate it became known that Ruth had ended her engagement to Ralph. It was uncanny the way she kept seeing his mother, in the street where they cut each other dead – though Ruth's knees were trembling – and in the theatre where turning around she saw Mrs Dewhirst three rows behind her. She was staring at her and bowed coldly. Ralph wrote her a letter beginning 'dearest'; it annoyed Walter as he thought he was the only one with the right to call her that. She sent him muffins and crème de menthe to cheer him up and Walter sent her fuchsias to remind her of the time they sat under the hedge beneath her Burberry in the rain.

When the new term began at the School of Painting and Ruth hadn't returned he thought of asking Stanhope Forbes to write to Mr Alison, enquiring why she was missing. Forbes was concerned that his numbers were down, a lot of the men having gone to Paris. But Mr Alison gave in

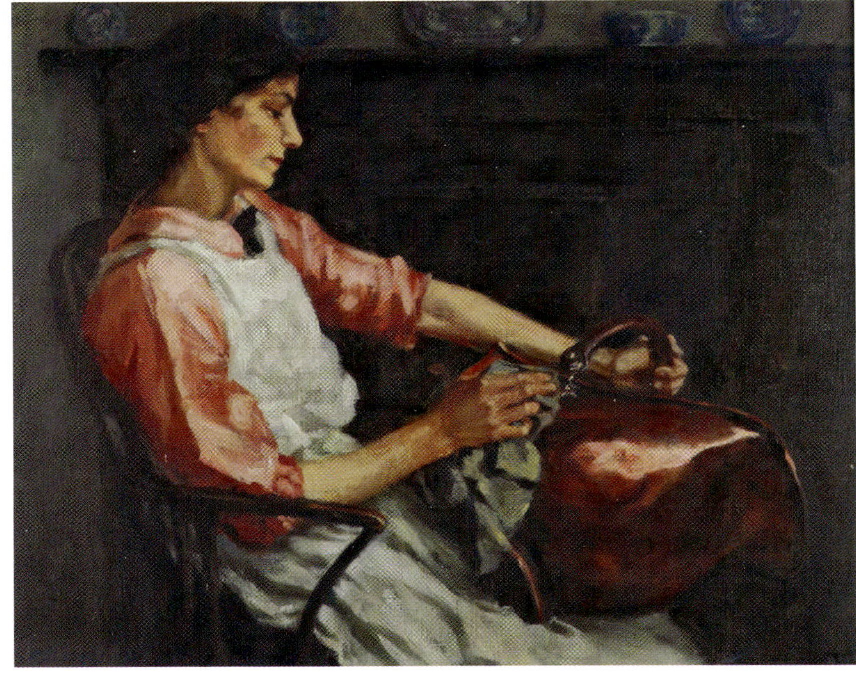

Sophie (Sophie Bodinnar)
Ruth Alison
1913, oil on canvas, 24 x 30 in
Photograph by Venture, Truro

to pressure and Ruth went back to Miss Leeson as her only lodger, though with Mrs Grafton as her chaperone. The Graftons were an American couple, both painters, living in Newlyn. When they were called back to the States because of the illness of Mrs Grafton's mother, Gertrude Harvey took over the position. There was a farewell dinner for the Graftons and Munnings made a speech. In it he referred to Walter, saying that he 'always knew that if Simpson fell in love it would be a great and wonderful love'. Walter used to be a messy fellow in paint-splattered clothes and never changed for the evening. Ruth had already smartened him up. Ernest Procter predicted that Ruth would rule the roost. A large crowd saw the Graftons off at Penzance station.

The Procters had just returned from a summer in France. Walter and Ruth had lunch with them and saw the collection of watercolours they had brought back. Ruth thought one of Dod's 'knocked all his into a cocked hat'. Tommy Thompson, having recovered from being thrown over by Kathleen Earle, was also back in Newlyn. During the summer Kay had answered an advertisement by a Yorkshire silk manufacturer for a poster designer and had met him in London with a portfolio of her work. Alec Walker was twenty-three years old; his father had given him a mill, where he produced Vigil silk. He was so enthused by Kay and her account of Newlyn life that he immediately travelled down with her to see it for himself.[1] Walter and Ruth also lunched with John Birch and his wife Houghton at Flagstaff Cottage overlooking the cove at Lamorna, followed by tea with the Leaders, another artist couple who lived at the head of the valley. If Lamorna was full of talented people, so was St Ives and they visited artists' studios there. The seagulls around the harbour were 'as tame as chickens' and it was difficult to tear Walter away. He returned in the week to make more studies of them. He was working this autumn on two big seagull paintings and was preparing watercolours for his next show. He sold one for five guineas that he thought too rough to keep. The people who bought it wanted one of ducks for the same price, so the next morning he dashed up to Chywoone Grove and produced a superb painting. He wouldn't let them have it for less than fifteen guineas. They refused and he was happy to keep it for his collection.

'Oh! Mother,' wrote Ruth, 'he is a *splendid* man. I find more in him to respect and admire as well as love every day… He is looking so well and happy too at present and seems to me to get better looking every day… He is so simple and boyish with me that I keep forgetting how awfully clever he is and order him about and scold him if he's untidy in his dress.'

Walter was interested in photography and he had photos of Ruth in various poses and costumes taken by a Newlyn photographer, Miss Thorpe, in return for a sketch. Ruth painted Miss Thorpe with her Aberdeen terrier in her lap; Vulliamy told Walter that he had no idea Ruth could paint so well. She had taken over Dod Procter's studio, and it now contained only one landscape, all the rest were portraits. She painted *The Milkmaid*, showing a handsome young woman holding a milking stool under one arm and with a churn at her side; it was widely praised.[2] She started a portrait of Walter, Vulliamy sat for her and she promised to paint her father when her parents came for Christmas. They were to meet Harold and Gertrude Harvey on Christmas Eve and she arranged some games of bridge for them with Tommy ('lately belonging to K.Earle'). She was dismayed though that they were bringing 'the poor desolated Rose…She will be mouching around with nothing to do all day.'

In the event Christmas passed well, but in the New Year and back in Harrogate the Alison parents had another crisis of confidence. A girl who was engaged should have a relative with her; her father wanted her to return. Ruth was in despair. She was working on Walter's portrait and she would be home at Easter anyway until the marriage. Walter wrote to Mr Alison to say that his aunt would come to take the place of a near relative on Ruth's side and the matter was settled.

Ruth thought that the last painting she did as a student was her best. Sophie Bodinnar was the sister of Gertrude Harvey; they came from a family of ten children born in Newlyn. The girls were strikingly good-looking and mixed socially with the students and artists, going to their parties and concerts. As a child and again as an adolescent, Sophie had been painted by T.C. Gotch.[3] Ruth posed her in a pink blouse against a black fireplace, sitting in a wooden armchair and polishing a copper coal scuttle. 'The copper really is well painted, though I says it as shouldn't, and the whole thing is looking very well… Walter's very pleased with it.' If she had submitted it to a 'crit', Forbes could only have been pleased with it as well, for it did everything that he taught: the lit figure against a dark background, the effects of light reflected from different surfaces.

Walter too was working well. He always drove himself hard, at times to the point of exhaustion and collapse. Although he was known for painting easily and rapidly, he had days of depression. But in the spring of 1913 with his marriage approaching, he felt at the height of his powers and was planning to enter a large picture in the Paris Salon for the first time, as well as preparing for the Royal Academy. In addition a gallery in New Zealand wanted some of his work.

'It's nice to be so successful isn't it?' Ruth wrote to her mother.

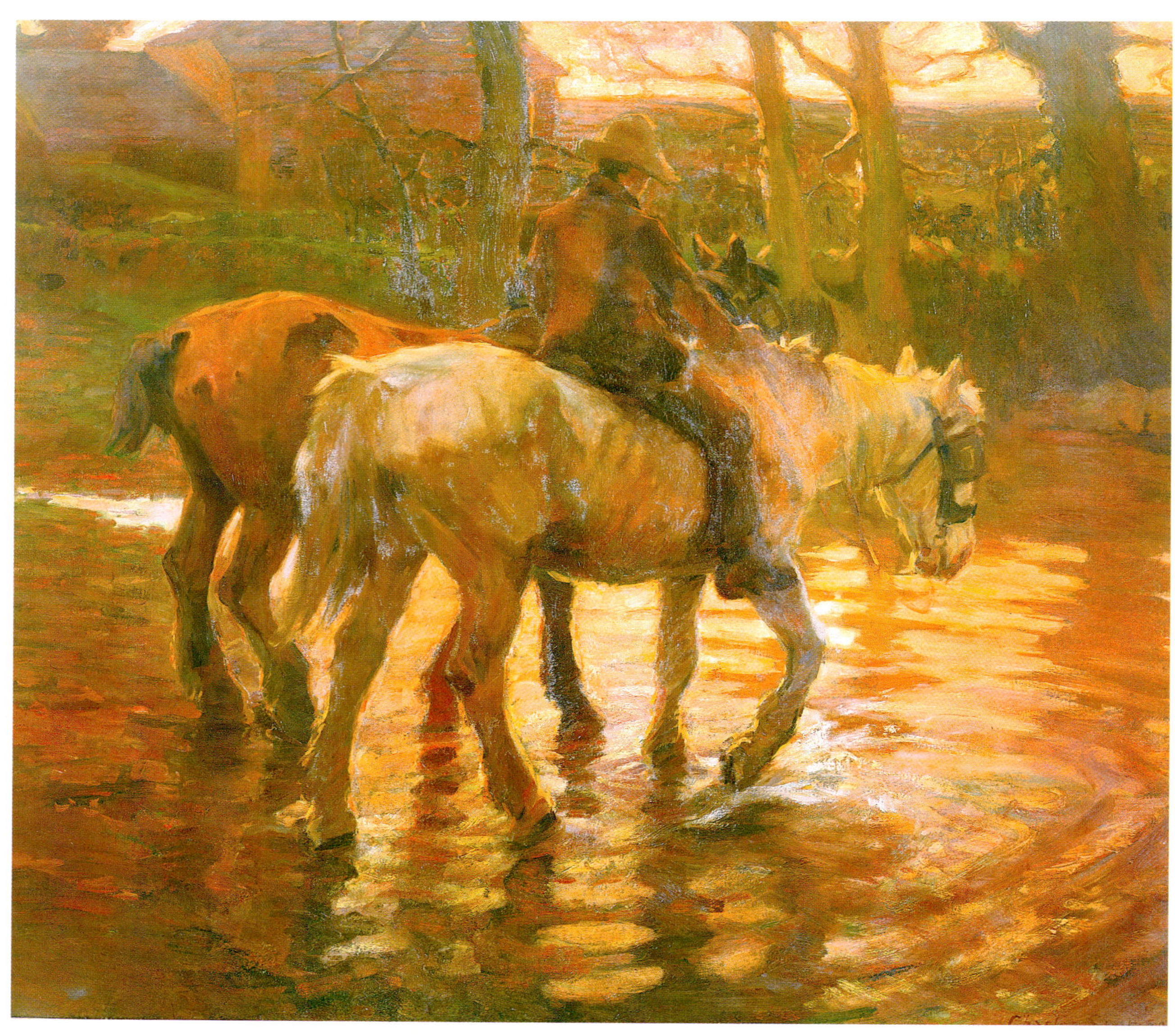

Autumn Sunset
RA 1913, oil on canvas, 72 x 84 in
Reproduced by kind permission
of David Messum

When Ruth left the Old Manor in March, Walter felt that their separation was quite unnecessary. He wanted an early wedding and he wanted it in London, around the time of the opening of the Royal Academy Exhibition when many of their artist friends could be present. Mr Alison wanted the wedding later in the year at Harrogate, but for Walter that was where Ralph's family and friends lived. 'It's our wedding,' he insisted and he left for London to make his own arrangements.

He thought it wise to have a medical check-up and the doctor pronounced him fit, a first-class life insurance risk. But the ear specialist diagnosed 'nerve deafness' which extended into the whole nervous system and which caused the pain and noises in his head. He could have an operation in which three small bones of the ear were removed to stop the buzzing, but it could cause complete deafness and was not recommended. While in London he enjoyed Kearton's film of wild animals in Africa and went to the Empire to see the bioscope of the Grand National, meeting Alfred Munnings there. They spent an afternoon together at the National Gallery and Munnings was in good form. The suffragettes were active in the city and although he supported their aims he disapproved of militancy, believing that the extremists made it less likely that women would get the vote. He warned Mrs Alison, who had given financial support to Mrs Pankhurst, that the police could obtain the secret list of backers and prosecute them. But Ada Alison had already switched her donations to a more moderate group.

He felt nervous about going to Harrogate and asked Ruth to be considerate, not taking him into large groups of people or introducing him to many of her friends who would have known Ralph. They had a secret plan. Walter was expected at Dunain Lodge for lunch. He took a late train the evening before, booked into the Station Hotel and Ruth came to him there after breakfast the next day. They had the morning alone together. He presented his future parents-in-law with a large cow picture and then felt it would dwarf everything else in their dining room. He also thought it might upset guests who were afraid of cows, and offered to change it if they wished.

His mother and youngest sister returned from Mauritius for the wedding and
Walter, annoyed that Mr Alison would not allow Ruth to accompany him, went
to Southampton to meet them. At 6.30 in the morning he saw the *Kenilworth
Castle* arrive, a great grey steamer with red funnels. He joined them for breakfast
on board before they all returned to London on the boat train. His mother had
a commission from his father to buy jewellery for Ruth, up to about £50 and
preferably diamonds. He would give them an allowance of £200 a year for the
first years of their marriage. His mother gave them chairs, and other gifts arrived
from family and friends, a silver teapot from Ruth's Aunt Maud, a dinner service
from Uncle Harry, cutlery, candlesticks and an appalling mayonnaise mixer.
The present that touched them most was a pendant from Harold and Gertrude
Harvey that was way beyond what they could really afford.

Walter asked Ruth to have the 'bands' read in Harrogate and she pointed out
that they were banns, not bands to bind them together. She was very busy shopping
for her trousseau – 'nice undies, very interesting and exciting!' – and having fittings
for her dress. Judy and Rose were the bridesmaids and Rose created a panic by
missing appointments and seeming to leave it too late to get her dress made in time.

Who to invite to the wedding was a problem; they couldn't ask the whole
of Newlyn. They drew up their list: Stanhope Forbes, the Birches, Leaders,
Knights, Harveys, Heaths, Sidgwicks, Hughes, Rheams and Garniers. If he
met any at the varnishing day at the Academy he would ask them then. He
had entered three paintings, including *Autumn Sunset*, and couldn't wait for
the opening, going instead to the entrance where rejected pictures could be
collected. There was nothing for him so he assumed that they were all accepted.
He spoke to an old carpenter who said that he personally had hung the big gull
painting in a centre position in Room 3 just above the line. A day or two later
Forbes sent him a note saying 'I found both your pictures well hung, a little
high but nicely centred.' He hadn't noticed the third. If they didn't sell, Walter
planned to place them in the Anglo-German exhibition at the Crystal Palace.

The wedding party assembled at the Cleveland Court Hotel in Lancaster Gate.
On the first evening the young people went to the theatre while Mrs Simpson and
Mrs Alison, meeting for the first time, stayed in the hotel for a long talk. The next
night they all had dinner together and the wedding took place on Thursday 8 May
1913, Walter's twenty-eighth birthday, at St Mary Abbots Church in Kensington.
That morning Ruth had received a letter from her husband-to-be, giving her precise
instructions on how she was to behave during the service; she was not to speak to
him in the vestry. Vulliamy, feeling that he lowered the tone of the occasion in his
bowler hat, blue suit and yellow socks, ushered in the guests; they had been ordered

to arrive promptly at two o'clock for the half-hour of organ music that Walter had chosen from Beethoven's Fifth Symphony. Ruth walked down the aisle at the *Finale*, wearing the veil that her mother had worn at her wedding. The recital continued after the signing of the register with movements from the Ninth Symphony. The *adagio e molto cantabile* had been played as a piano duet at the concert in his studio when they first met. The horn passages in C minor sounded well and the organ drowned the voices of those tiresome guests who wanted to talk.

After the ceremony the married couple went straight back to the hotel and had tea in their room. In the evening Ruth put on her wedding dress again and they went to the Criterion for dinner. Walter bought himself a half-bottle of ancient port covered in cobwebs. They stayed on at the Cleveland Court for their honeymoon. 'I love being married,' Ruth wrote to her mother. The only hitch at the wedding was when the photographer refused to wait for them and left. They had to set up the wedding photographs again, but without the bouquet.

They went to Rumpelmeyer's, famous for its iced Viennese coffee, but Walter spoiled his by accidentally putting salt on it. To make up for this expensive mistake they went to Selfridge's, where he had an enormous chocolate ice-cream soda for 6d. Walter fixed a show with the Baillie Gallery. He had his teeth seen to in return for a sketch and was also having treatment four times a week for his damaged ear. Ruth had herself vaccinated, as Newlyn was full of chicken pox and measles. They spent a few days with Walter's relatives the Fairbrothers in Guildford, where they played billiards and Walter abused a pianola. They were longing now to get back to Newlyn but he was waiting to collect two paintings. He sold the watercolour at the Royal Academy for £25 and made altogether over £60 on his honeymoon.

Walter had little interest in having a house of his own, unlike several of their friends in Lamorna, the Heaths at Menwinnion, the Hughes at Chyangwheal and the Napers at Trewoofe, all of whom had recently bought land from Colonel Paynter of Boskenna, the estate that owned the western side of the valley, and built homes in which they would remain for the rest of their lives. Walter told Ruth before they married that he would want to go on living in his digs at Polwin House. 'My goodness!' thought Ruth. 'That's the life for me.' Mrs James would look after them and they would be free to paint together. Ruth hated housekeeping; Elizabeth Forbes had never done any housekeeping but stuck to her work.

Back in Newlyn Ruth too stuck to her work, painting portraits of Rose and Judy, her two bridesmaids who had come to stay. Rose had had an operation for appendicitis but recovered well, standing at an easel for hours. She put on weight, weighing nine and a half stones to Ruth's eight. She stayed on an extra week so that the portrait could be finished. Judy did Ruth's darning for her so that she could concentrate on her painting.

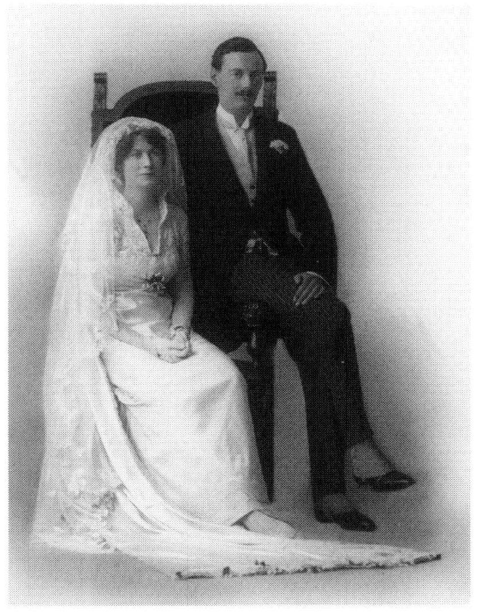

The wedding of Charles Simpson and Ruth Alison, May 1913

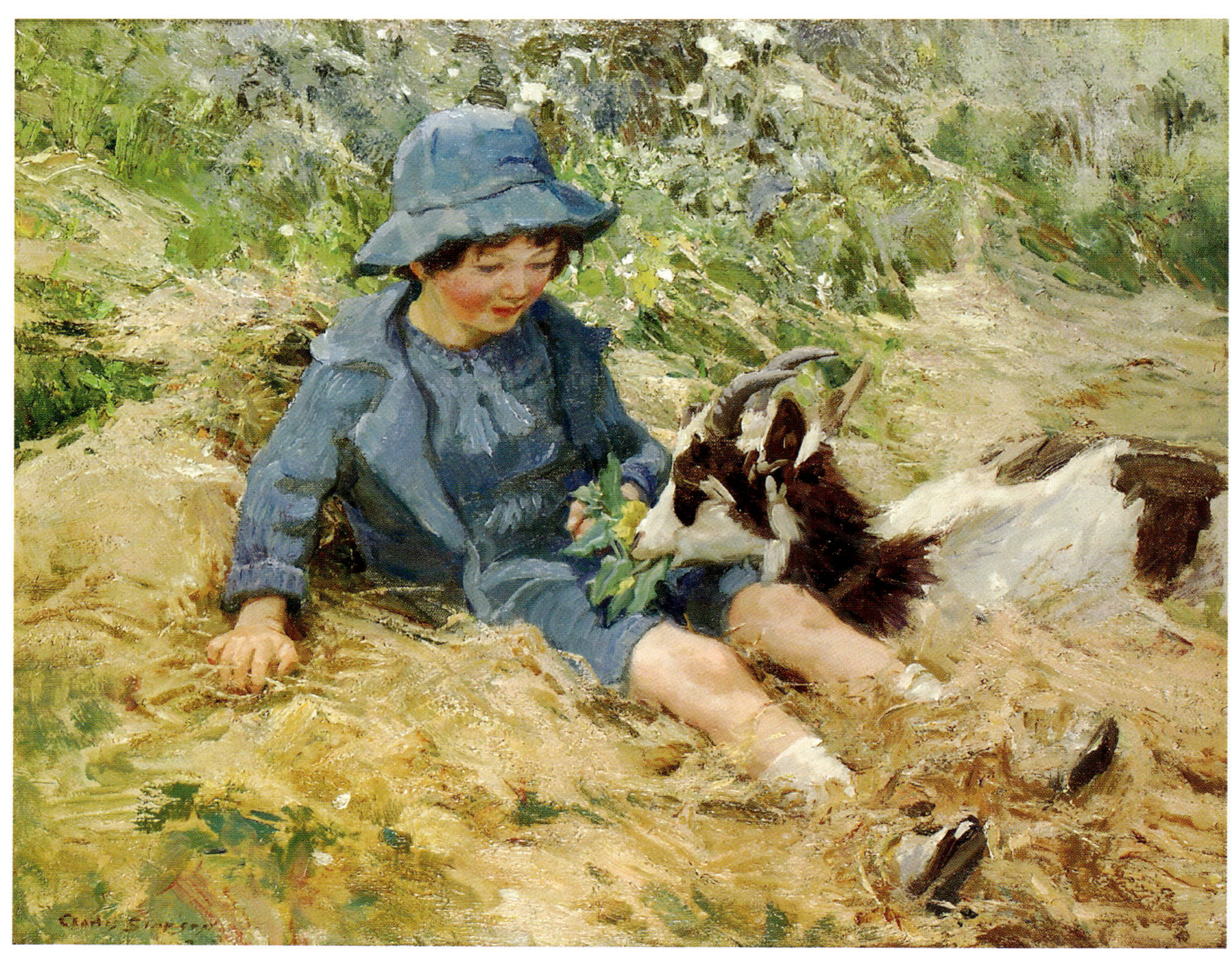

Leonora and the Pet Goat
RA1920, oil on canvas, 29 x 37 in
The Grundy Art Gallery, Blackpool

Leonora: Little Gonwin and Lamorna

In October Ruth wrote to her parents with interesting news. She was fairly certain that they would be grandparents before next summer. A year earlier she had heard that 'Dod Shaw as was, poor little thing, is going to indulge in an infant soon – in the spring. She is only 22 and it seems rather young to have to start such a serious business, doesn't it? Besides they are not very well off… Also she is a remarkably talented painter and I fear that <u>that</u> will be entirely knocked on the head for ages when the baby comes.'

If Ruth felt that her ambition to be a really good painter would now be set back for a few years, she did not show it. 'I'm quite all right and very cheerful and excited!' she told her parents. Two weeks later she was staying at the Portland Hotel in London, where Walter was seeing to the framing of his pictures for the 'Ducks and other Farm Studies' exhibition in November at the Baillie Gallery. She told her mother that she had twice the energy

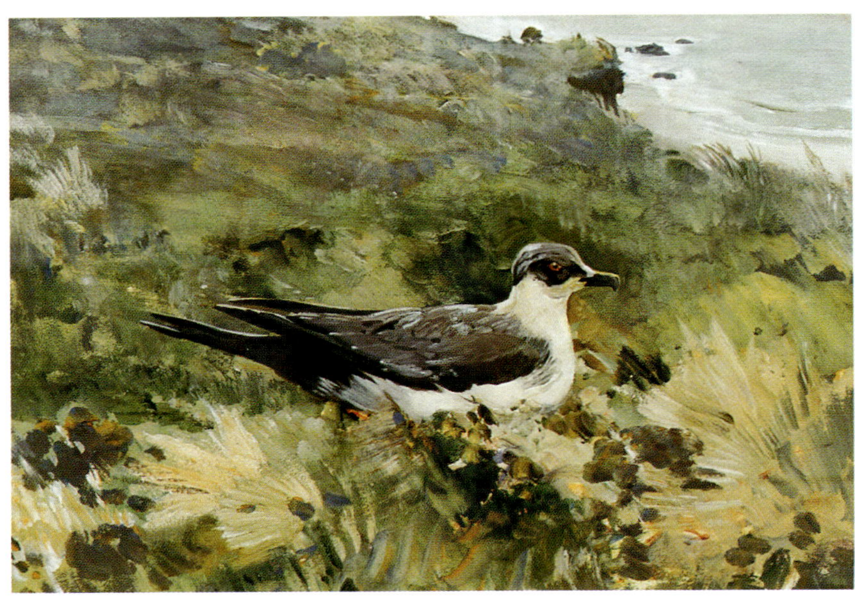

Arctic skua, from the *Wild Bird Series*
1910–1920, oil on card, 20 x 30 in

that she had in the summer, though she felt sick at intervals. She would be attended by the same lady doctor and nurse as Dod Procter. Her mother sent her a trunk of baby clothes, most of which she had made and embroidered herself. Ruth was grateful for the work it saved her and promised to keep them for Rose, 'providing I do not go on indulging in a new infant every year for the next ten years'. It seemed quite possible, she reflected ruefully. She went for walks each morning and lay down in the afternoon. 'It seems a feeble existence, doesn't it?' In January she was excited to feel the baby move for the first time. 'I believe it's going to be a hefty little beggar. It gave quite a powerful kick for its tender age.' They both hoped for a boy and already called it Peter. They couldn't settle on a name if it should be a girl.

With a family soon to support, Walter was looking for other opportunities. They went to London again to meet a Lieutenant Beavor who had written a book about his experiences on the Turkish side in the Balkan War, which the publishers wouldn't take without illustrations. They lunched together, got on well and saw the publishers Nelson, who agreed in principle to produce the book with fifteen illustrations by Charles Simpson. Beavor was now an aviator – Ruth hoped that he wouldn't crash before the project was completed – and he visited them in Newlyn to give details of the soldiers' uniforms and the Balkan landscape. Simpson used grisaille for the pictures – *The Russian Menace, Trapped by Russians in an Iron Ring, The Serbian Retreat into Albania* – but it seems that the book was never published. However, in March he was elected to the Royal Society of British Artists, one of twelve chosen out of fifteen candidates. He had the support of the president, Frank Brangwyn.

Ruth and Walter's daughter was born at Polwin House on 17 June 1914 and they called her Leonora after his mother. The Munnings called to offer their congratulations and to see the new baby. Florence questioned Ruth closely, wanting to know every detail of the birth. Then with a cry of 'I couldn't stand it!' rushed from the room. A month later she committed suicide.

'Blote', as her friends unkindly called her, had made a disastrous choice in marrying Alfred. His earthy qualities that appealed so much to Laura Knight were repugnant to her. She was delicate and fragile, seemingly cold and reserved. She was unhappy in her marriage. Colonel Paynter's land agent, Gilbert Evans, gave her sympathy and understanding and they became very close before he left for Africa with his regiment. At a fancy dress ball at Trewarveneth, currently the home of the Garniers, the merriment was cut short by a drunken Munnings shouting at Florence and calling her a bloody whore. She was possibly pregnant. She left in tears for Cliff House, the hotel in Lamorna where they stayed. She went down to breakfast the next morning and then returned to her room, where she took cyanide. One of the first to arrive was Laura Knight, who tried to save her but when the doctor came he pronounced her dead. As soon as the inquest was over the Knights and the Harveys joined the Napers on holiday at their painting hut by the side of Dozmary Pool on Bodmin Moor. Alfred Munnings went to stay with Ruth and Walter Simpson. 'It was not a proper marriage,' he told Walter. 'It had never been consummated.'

He joined them not at Polwin House, for that was in the centre of Newlyn and he needed to avoid people, but at the more secluded spot that they had moved to, a 'splendid bargain' discovered by Nora Simpson when she and Dolly had visited. Little Gonwin was a small farm of seven acres near Carbis Bay, leased at £20 per annum.[1] Walter and Ruth could no longer pretend they were students in digs now they had a child. They had to say goodbye to Mrs James and all the comforts she provided and Ruth became responsible for their own four-bedroomed house. One afternoon Simpson and Munnings were playing chess in the sitting room, while Ruth entertained friends at the far end. A visitor joined the ladies and immediately asked, 'What was it that Blote took?' She then realised that Munnings was in the room and was overcome with embarrassment and distress. He went over to her and comforted her, before returning to the game. 'It was most gracefully done,' said Walter.

From Little Gonwin, Simpson was able to walk with his black spaniel Nell along Porth Kidney Sands to the mouth of the river Hayle and the salt marshes of Lelant. On the other side of the water were the 'towans' or sand dunes and out in the bay was Godrevy Island with its lighthouse. It was a paradise for bird-life. He could approach close to redshank and dunlin and sometimes through his field glasses he saw less common birds, goldeneye ducks and great northern divers. Once on an open stretch of sand he saw a water rail, far away from its natural haunt of reeds and sedges. His favourite time for watching birds was in the early hours of the morning, often sheltering under one of the railway bridges. From Lelant he looked straight into the rising sun that shone on the mud flats. It cast shadows of the birds, mallard and teal, the light catching the edge of a bill or back, moulding and transfiguring plovers and sanderling. He saw patterns everywhere in the mud and shallows. At twilight great flocks of curlew would fly in, congregating on the shoreline.

There was a ferry across the river and he made friends with the ferryman, Tom Pomeroy.[2] Tom had a ramshackle hut on the beach where the hulks

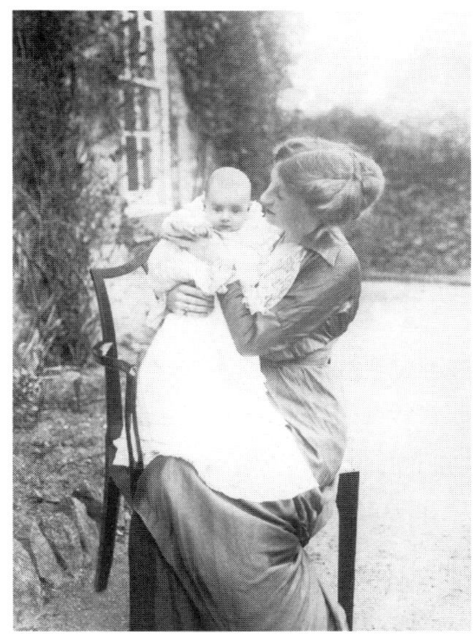

Ruth holding Leonora
at Little Gonwin, Carbis Bay
1914, photograph, WCAA

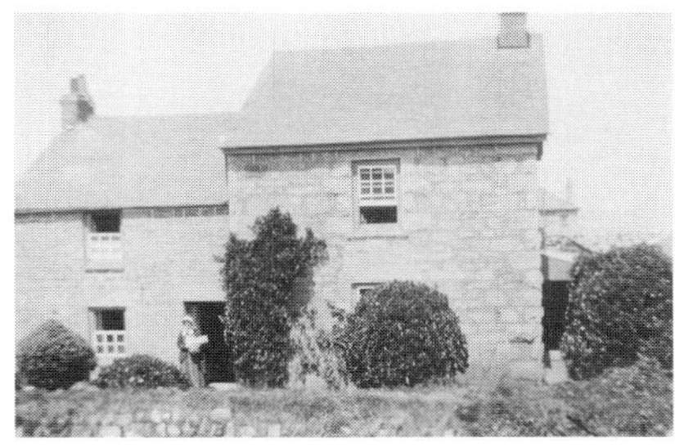

Ruth at the door of Little Gonwin
1915, photograph, WCAA

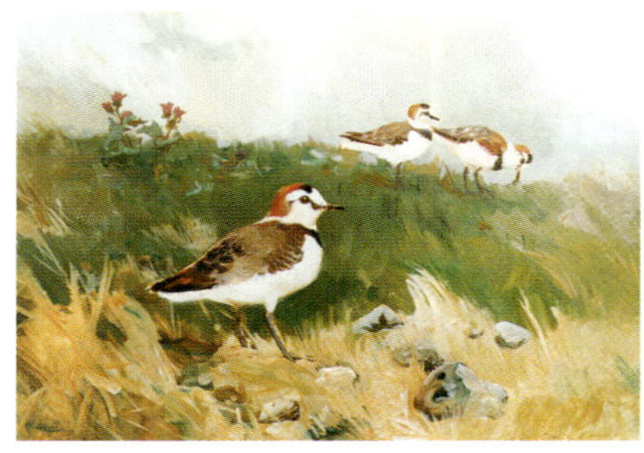

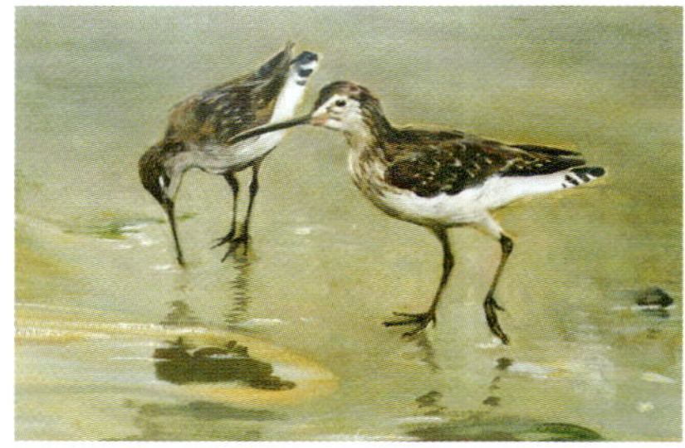

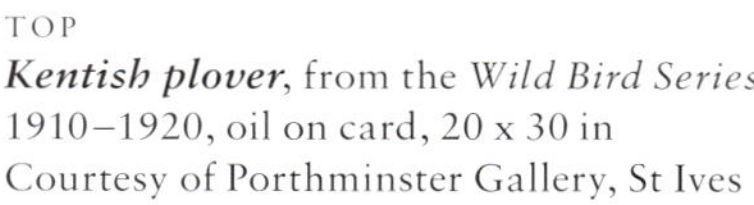

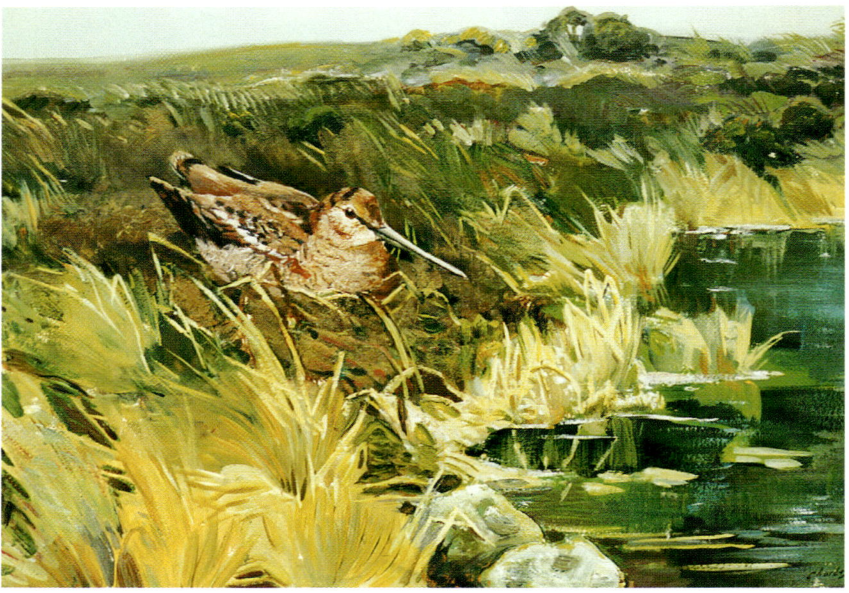

of old boats were left to decay. Here in bad weather a few men would take shelter, longshoremen, fishermen and wildfowlers. The air thick with tobacco smoke and the fug from a seal-oil stove, they discussed the birds, the weather and local topics. The war with Germany seemed far away.

But war could not be ignored for long as the situation on the Western Front worsened. Many of Simpson's contemporaries joined the army and suffered heavy casualties. Frank Heath was gassed and brought home to convalesce; Benjamin Leader and Alec Forbes were both killed in France. There was no question of Simpson's fitness for military service and he still visited specialists in London. But he looked a strong and healthy man and he felt the anomaly of his situation. He was intensely patriotic and made several attempts to enlist but was always rejected. He did what he could, donating a picture for sale through the St Ives Arts Club in aid of the Red Cross, sending parcels of tobacco and cigarettes to the troops. The accident that had allowed him to become a painter now possibly saved his life.

In the middle of the war they left Little Gonwin for Lamorna where most of their friends lived, the Knights having moved from Newlyn to Oakhill at the head of the valley. Bodriggy was a fine house built in 1913 by Algernon Newton, the landscape painter and member of the family that established Winsor and Newton, the company supplying artists' materials. It had a large garden alongside the stream that rushed beneath trees and over boulders to the cove. Here Simpson joined the coast-watchers who patrolled the cliffs night and day on the lookout for enemy activity. 'What a coast-watcher is Mrs Simpson,' remarked Birch sarcastically when Ruth,

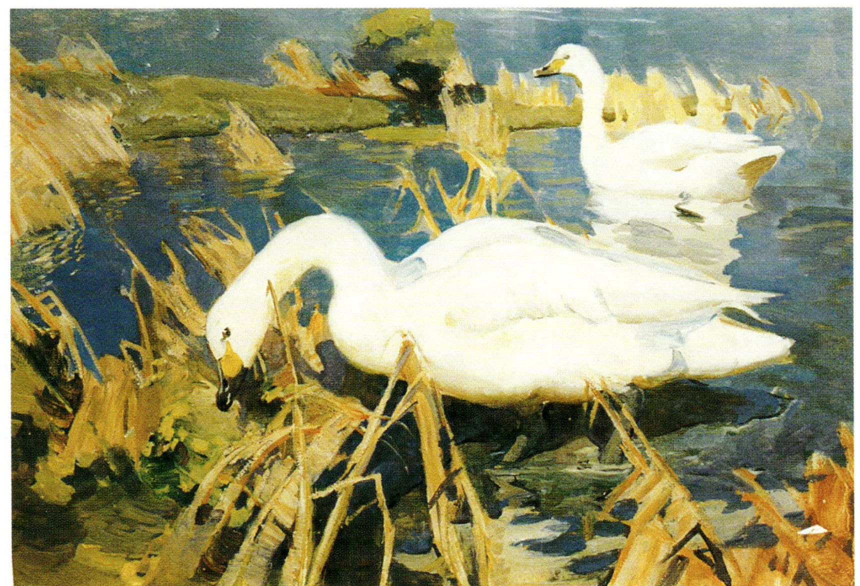

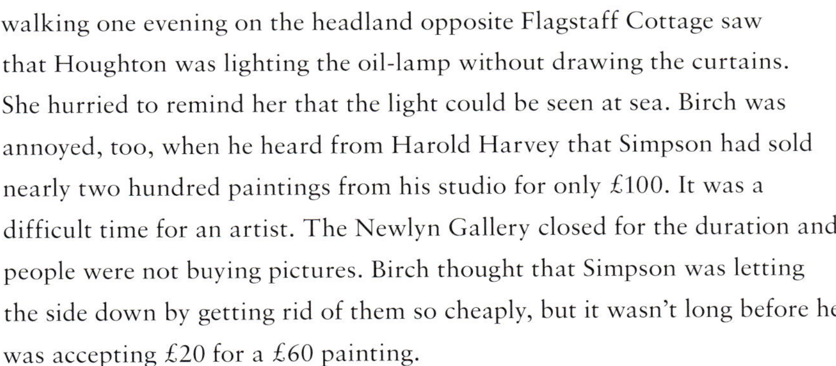

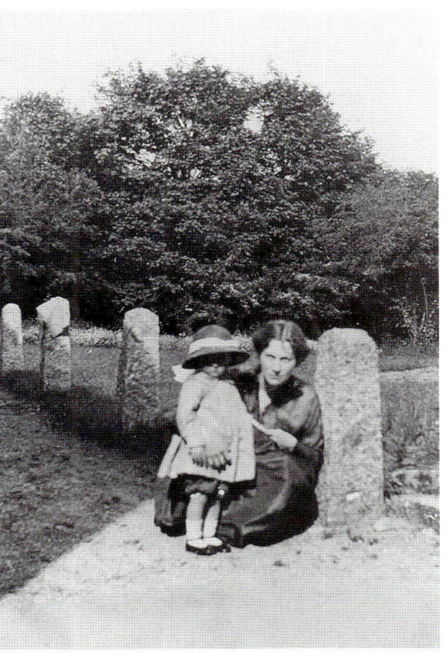

Ruth with Leonora at Bodriggy, Lamorna
1916, photograph

Bewick's swan, from the *Wild Bird Series*
1910–1920, oil on card, 20 x 30 in
Courtesy of Porthminster Gallery, St Ives

walking one evening on the headland opposite Flagstaff Cottage saw
that Houghton was lighting the oil-lamp without drawing the curtains.
She hurried to remind her that the light could be seen at sea. Birch was
annoyed, too, when he heard from Harold Harvey that Simpson had sold
nearly two hundred paintings from his studio for only £100. It was a
difficult time for an artist. The Newlyn Gallery closed for the duration and
people were not buying pictures. Birch thought that Simpson was letting
the side down by getting rid of them so cheaply, but it wasn't long before he
was accepting £20 for a £60 painting.

Food was rationed, though in Lamorna the rations could be supplemented
with fish and rabbits. One evening Laura Knight went to several farms trying
to buy eggs and managed to get only one. Walking back in the dusk through
the paddock where the Napers kept a donkey, she tripped over a dead branch
and fell, breaking her leg. She was within calling distance of the house and
Harold fetched help from Walter and Ruth, who were about to sit down to a
whole leg of lamb, which they had to abandon. Simpson rushed into The Wink,
astonishing the regulars at the Lamorna inn by crying in a high, singsong voice,
'I need a bottle of brandy, Mrs Knight has broken her leg!' Other friends arrived
and sent a man on a bicycle to get the Penzance doctor. They lit cigarettes
for Laura and John Birch held her hand. He told her it was one of the most
picturesque scenes he had ever seen: 'the lanterns on the ground lighting up
the crowd, the donkey's head hanging over the fence… the trees overhead black
against a Prussian blue sky.' When they carried her back into Oakhill there were
about twenty people in the kitchen, finishing off Walter's bottle of brandy.

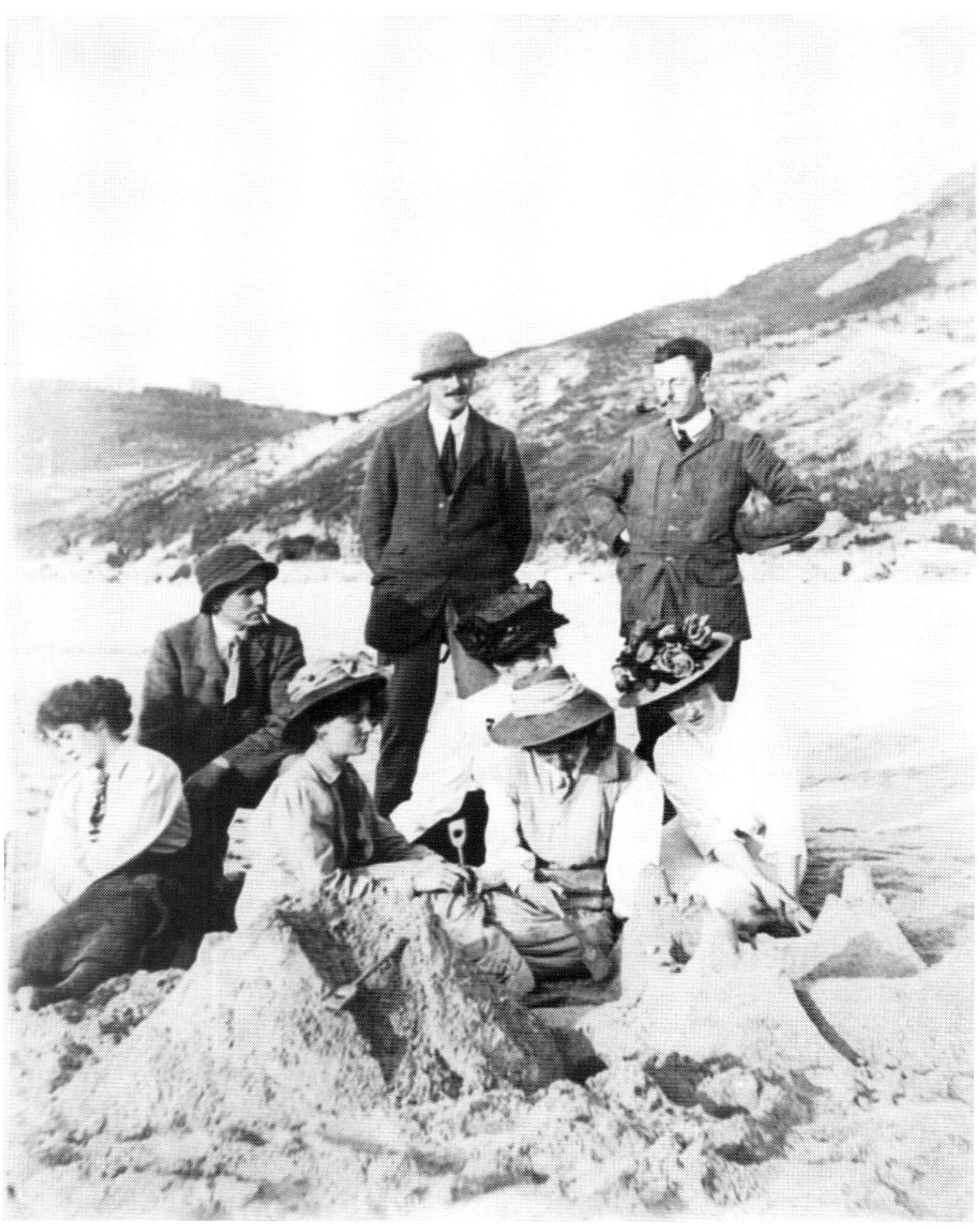

St Ives: The School of Painting

Lamorna Birch was particularly incensed when Simpson lowered his prices because he already had a source of income. Walter and Ruth had started taking students at the Shore Studio on the Wharf at St Ives, overlooking the harbour. Simpson was looking for any new openings and in September thought he might try paintings of children. He went along to Porthminster Beach with a sketchbook and found the usually crowded beach deserted except for three girls digging a sandpit: it was the first day back at school after the holidays. One of the girls was Jennifer Rowe; she lived in London but when the Zeppelin raids began on the city in 1916 her mother took her to stay with their Cornish relatives in the coastguard cottages. On this morning she went to play as usual and joined the other girls; she did not know them or why they were not at school. Although it was illegal to draw or paint within two miles of the coast, Simpson made some sketches and asked Mrs Rowe if Jennifer could come to the studio. She sat for three paintings – once or twice he gave her half a crown – and they were exhibited in Bond Street the following year.

Laura Knight's paintings of children playing on a beach are celebrations of childhood, full of colour and joie de vivre. *The Sandpit – on Porthminster Beach, St Ives* is not quite so simple. Jennifer sits on the edge, a striking figure in her green stocking cap and matching cardigan over a pink dress. The other girls wear satin dresses and are low in the pit. The smart Londoner contrasts with the old-fashioned Cornish girls, and there is tension between them. Jennifer seems to rise as the others sink into the sand and out of the picture, against a background of tumultuous waves. It's an uneasy painting about the new and the old, about changing times. Another picture has semi-naked youths playing games on the beach, the same young men whose lithe bodies might soon be shattered in battle. *The Injured Seagull*, its wings broken, becomes a symbol of the times.

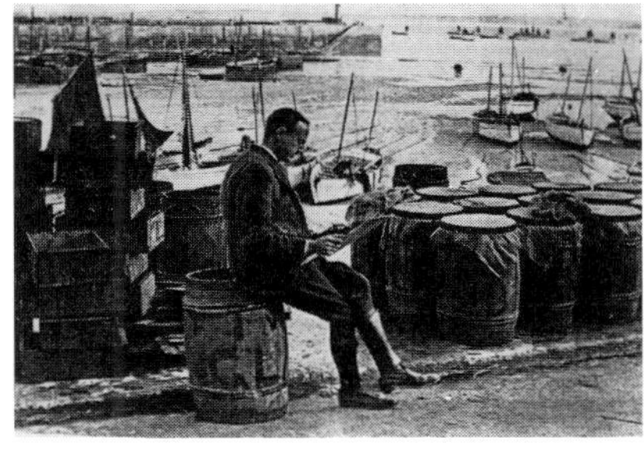

ABOVE
Charles Simpson sketching on the
Wharf outside the Shore Studio, St Ives
Eve Ladies Pictorial, 5 Dec 1923

PAGE 54
On the beach at Sennen Cove; Charles and
Ruth Simpson on the right, Dod and Ernest
Procter on the far left. Others include Cicely
Tennyson Jesse and Ella Naper
Photograph, WCAA

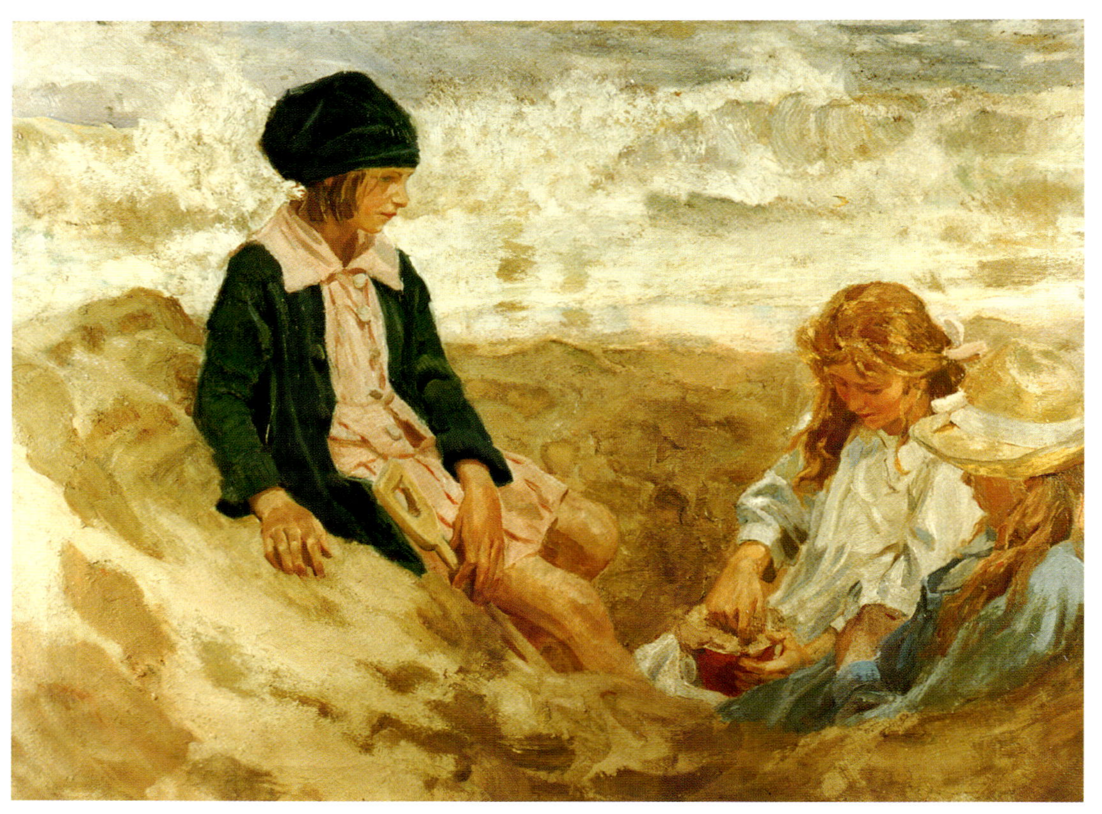

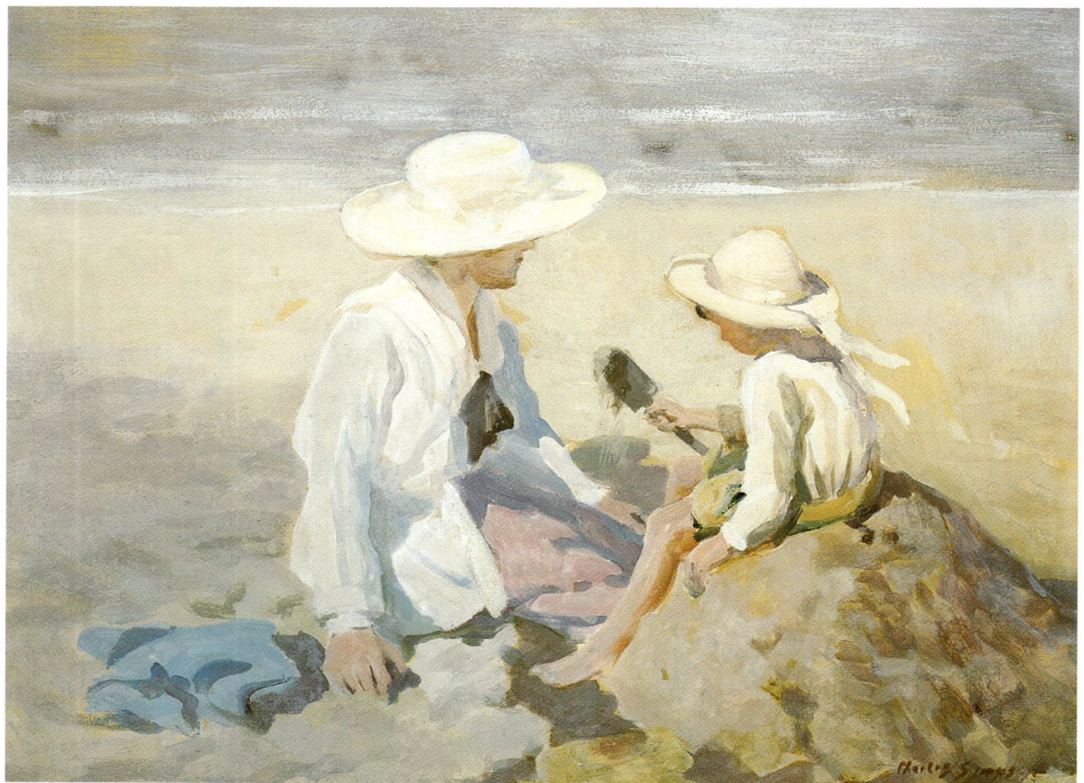

In the Shore Studio he painted his only self-portrait. He stands with soldierly bearing at his easel, brushes and palette in hand, the habitual cigarette drooping from his lips. The harbour is seen through the window behind him, with Smeaton's Pier projecting disconcertingly from the right-hand side in a mirror image. For the portrait of Ruth, done at the same time, he posed her in the large black and white hat that she had been wearing when he first saw her. It makes a dramatic effect, with its black and white striped ribbon tied in a large bow and its brim sweeping right out of the picture. The face below is tenderly and carefully painted, in contrast to the loose brush-strokes of the black coat and frilly white blouse, the vermilion scarf knotted at the neck the only splash of colour.

From a few pupils in 1916, the St Ives School of Art grew into a successful business. It was attractive to parents who did not want their daughters exposed to the impersonality and danger of a large city, especially in wartime. As in Newlyn, there were plenty of lodgings available, rooms from 12/6 and full board from three guineas. Simpson was an inspiring teacher and Ruth had already shown herself capable of taking responsibility for young charges. If pupils could not have rooms alone, they could become resident students at Loyalty Cottage, the house at Carthew Terrace high above Porthmeor beach that the Simpsons moved to at the end of 1917 or early in 1918. The school was much less rigid than the Forbes School and was open throughout the year without any division into regular terms. Students had the personal attention of Walter or Ruth in the mornings and could continue work there at all other times. They took over the Piazza Studios, numbers four and five, for lessons. The top studio overlooked Porthmeor Beach facing the Atlantic and the prospectus drew attention to its wide view of the sea and coast. Its windows were constructed for the special purpose of marine painting in rough weather, though landscape classes were held outside when it was fine. Models posed daily for the figure classes.

Ruth taught the art of portraiture as distinct from figure studies. A sad opportunity arose for portrait painters as a result of the war. Parents who had lost sons on the battlefield often wanted more than a photograph to remember them by and Ruth had several commissions. They sent a photo of their son, usually an officer in uniform, and details of the colour of his hair and eyes. One father touchingly insisted that his boy's skin should look very fresh. 'He had a lovely complexion,' he wrote. Ruth charged five guineas for these portraits; she sometimes let her students fill in the background. Walter painted a posthumous portrait of Charles Naper's brother Frank, killed in France in 1917.

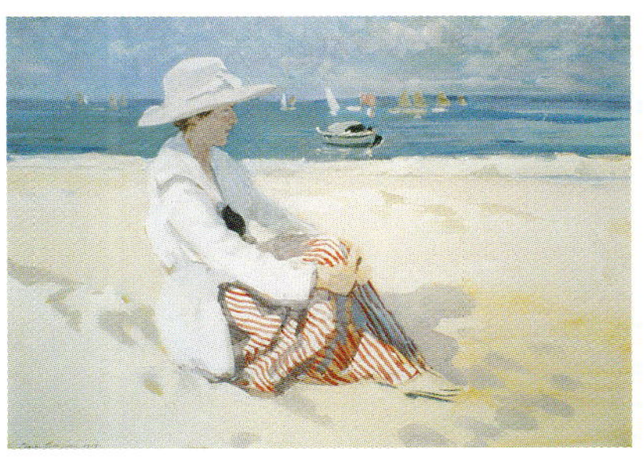

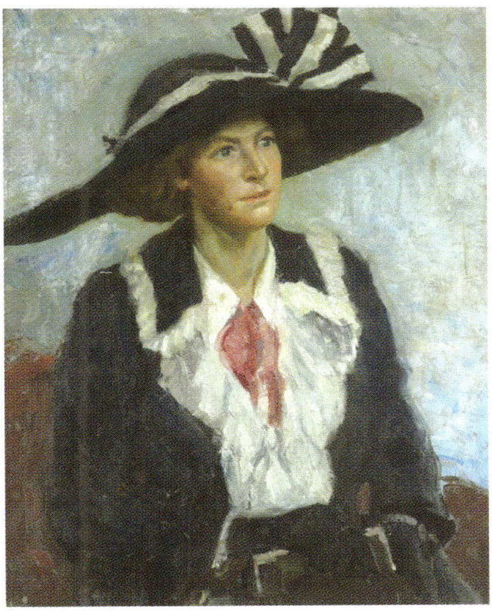

TOP
On the Beach
Oil on board, 21 x 29 in
Christchurch Art Gallery,
Te Puna o Waiwhetu, New Zealand

ABOVE
Portrait of Ruth
c1918, oil on canvas, 30 x 24 in
Photograph by Venture, Truro

PAGE 56 TOP
The Sandpit – on Porthminster Beach, St Ives
1916, oil on canvas, 30 x 40 in

PAGE 56 BOTTOM
The Sandcastle
Ruth and Leonora on the beach
c1919, tempera, 21 x 29 in
Image courtesy of Penlee House Gallery
and Museum, Penzance

The object of the school was 'to teach all branches of painting and drawing, and illustration work with a view to reproduction'. Simpson gave instruction in the cutting of woodblocks and specially prepared linoleum for coloured prints. Another feature of the school was the study of animals and birds and the training of memory to record rapid impressions. It also offered correspondence courses in landscape and animal painting at a guinea per month for monthly criticisms, postage included. The normal fees were a guinea per week for a minimum of four weeks, or private tuition at three guineas per week.

Throughout the war years Simpson sent to the Royal Academy, pictures of ducks or water or St Ives beaches. He was in London when the war ended and Munnings arranged an armistice dinner at the Chelsea Arts Club, the dining room patriotically decorated for the occasion. It was a riotous affair and the celebrations continued for several days. One evening towards midnight when everyone had had a lot to drink Simpson started to wrestle with Algernon Talmage and threw him. Then he threw the critic Paul Konody and went for Munnings. They were locked in each other's arms and fell to the ground, fighting like mad. Munnings drew his arm back, aimed a blow at Simpson and missed. His fist struck the coalscuttle and he broke a bone in his hand. It was in splints for months.

A St Ives resident remembered Simpson at this time and like many people assumed he was an officer returned from the war. Soldiers were allowed to keep their uniforms as long as they took off all badges and buttons. 'I saw him with an officer's jacket on. It was obvious to me that he was saving on clothing. He was wearing a pair of shorts as well. That was Simpson.'[1]

In 1919 the Cuningham sisters, Phyllis and Vera, joined the school for a while and Simpson painted several oil sketches of them. Vera was a wild young woman whose father had turned her out of his house because she was a bad influence on her older sisters. He gave her a small allowance and she shared a flat near Oxford Circus with three other art students, though after a few weeks at the Central School of Art she decided that the school had nothing to teach her. She looks quite demure in Simpson's paintings. In *A Wet Day* she sits on the sand beside her sister, sheltering inside a beach tent and gazing out at the rain-swept sea. They reverse their positions in *Resting – on the Beach at St Ives*. Vera in a long pink dress stretches out in the deck chair, quietly reading a book on her lap, while Phyllis daydreams. Beyond them is empty yellow sand and blue sea. They appear again walking along the beach with high waves behind them and in another painting the two young women, now wearing coats left unbuttoned and falling loosely over the same dresses, lean against the side of an open boat at low tide in St Ives harbour. The charm of these pictures is in the casual stylishness of the girls in the St Ives setting and in their spontaneity, having the freedom of rapid sketches rather than finished paintings.[2] Simpson also used tempera with its smooth surface for beach studies, such as the painting on board of Leonora, toy spade in hand, sitting on top of a sandcastle while Ruth in a large white sunhat sits beside her. They had a joint exhibition that year at James Lanham's gallery in St Ives, where Walter showed his local paintings. *Snowballing* catches the wintry feeling of St Ives harbour as two groups of boys hurl snowballs at each other. In the seven-foot-long canvas *The End of the Holidays* a handsome young couple walk arm-in-arm along the edge of the sea. Ruth showed portraits, including *Lady in Black* and *The Lustre Jar,* in which the girl's face is lit by the reflection from the lustre.

They exhibited together again the following year in Plymouth, 'one of the most striking collections of modern work ever shown in a provincial gallery'.[3] At the end of the war Walter's parents had retired to Strathcar at Tavistock in Devon, where the Major General became a county councillor and magistrate, and when visiting them Walter painted in the area. He called the show *The Freedom of Dartmoor*; there were scenes of winter on the moors, with huddled groups of ponies, of foxhunting and otter hunting with the Dartmoor Otter Hounds. Another joint exhibition was at the Grieves Art Gallery in London. Simpson showed eighteen screens, decorated panels mounted in simple frames.

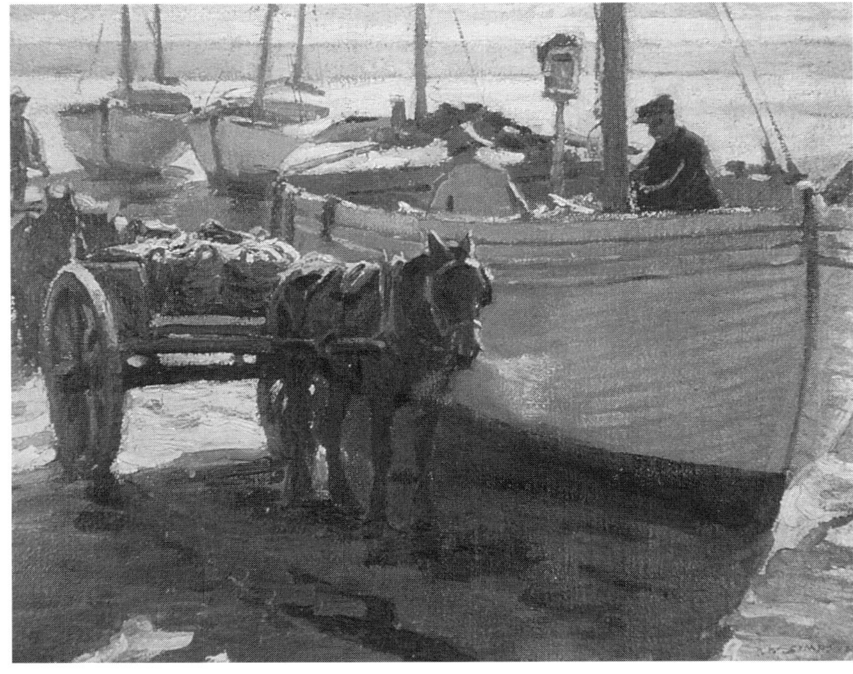

Landing Herrings
Oil on canvas, 24 x 30 in
Christchurch Art Gallery, Te Puna o Waiwhetu,
New Zealand

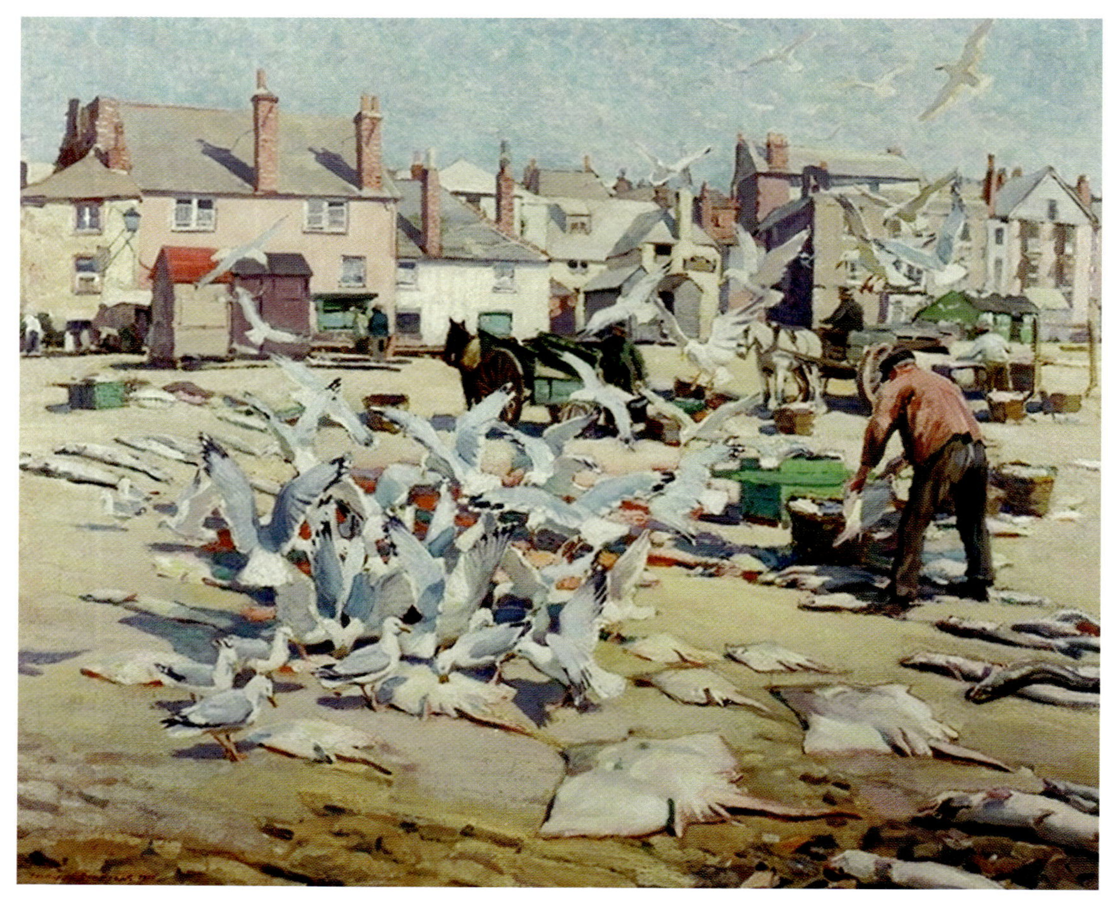

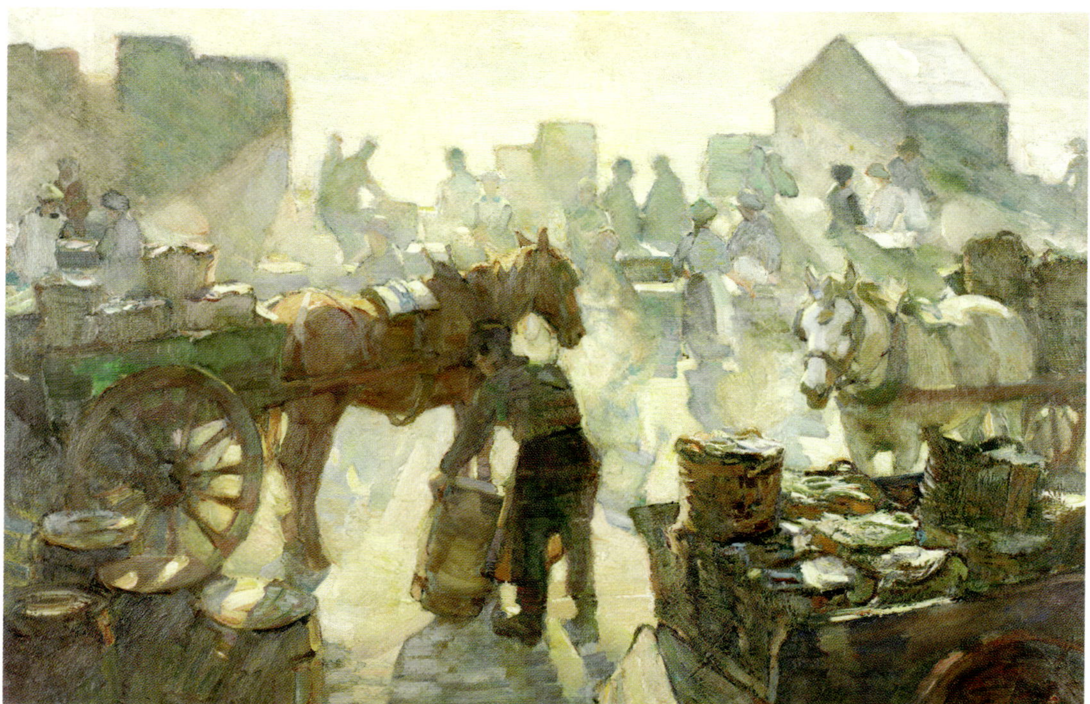

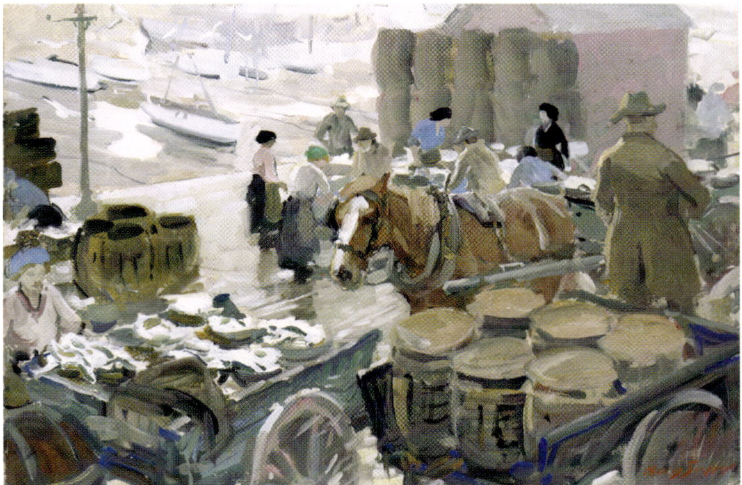

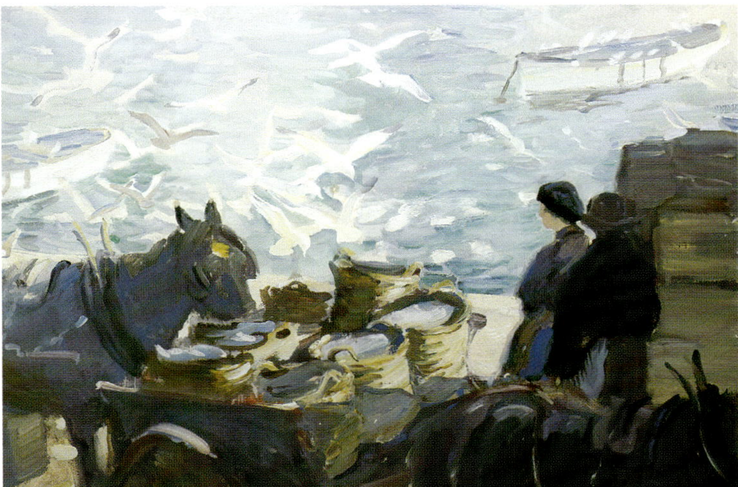

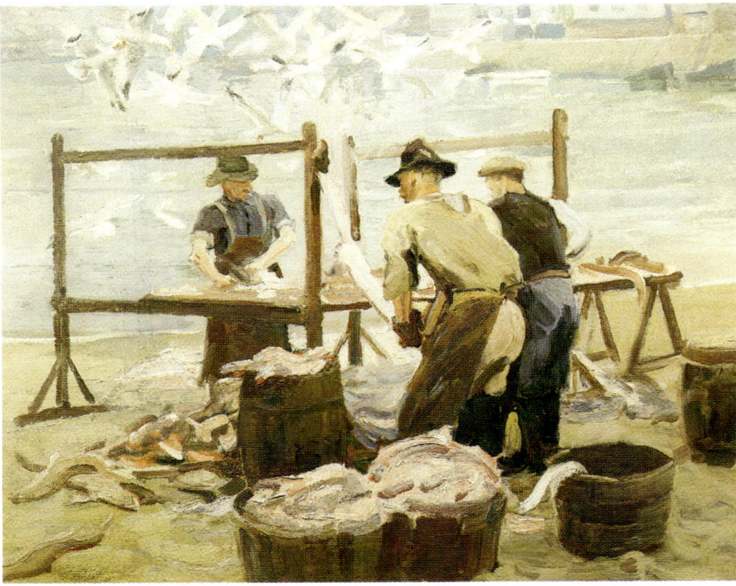

PAGE 60 TOP
The Line Fishing Season
Oil on canvas, 40 x 48 in
Plymouth City Museum and Art Gallery

PAGE 60 BOTTOM
The Herring Season: from my
Studio Window
RA 1924, oil on canvas, 48 x 72 in
Laing Art Gallery, Newcastle upon Tyne

LEFT
On the Quay: the Herring Season, St Ives
Gouache on board, 21 x 31 in
Dunedin Art Gallery, New Zealand

BELOW LEFT
The Herring Season
1923, gouache 22 x 31 in
Reproduced by kind permission
of David Messum

BOTTOM LEFT
Skinning Dogfish
Oil on canvas, 24 x 30 in
Reproduced by kind permission
of David Messum

They had titles like *Fishers of the Deep, Teal, Goldeneye Duck, Green Plover, Moonrise, Wild Swans, Curlew* and *Blue Water*. In some he experimented with a cloisonné style in which all the shapes were outlined in black, filled in with blocks of colour. Prices ranged from eight guineas to forty pounds; they suited contemporary taste and sold well.

When Kathleen Slatter, a seventeen-year-old student from Rhodesia, came to the school in 1921, she was met at St Ives station by Simpson's father. He took her to Loyalty Cottage on the back of his son's motorcycle, her trunk sticking out of the sidecar. She and another young woman lodged with the Simpsons. Most of the students were female, but a few ex-servicemen joined the classes. One of these was George Fagan Bradshaw, who against the odds had survived the war as a submarine commander. A career naval officer, he continued in the service after the armistice until he was court-martialled when his submarine sank in Portsmouth Harbour. He was on leave at the time, the vessel sank because of a design fault and he was acquitted, but he was so sickened by his treatment that he left the Navy. He was thirty-three and unemployed, but hoped to turn his hobby of painting ships and seascapes into a new career. He chose the Simpsons' school because St Ives was associated with marine artists like Julius Olsson and Louis Grier. The attractive student and the war hero immediately fell in love and Kathleen and George were married the following year. Bradshaw made such rapid progress as an artist that he was soon helping out in the school, while his business sense made

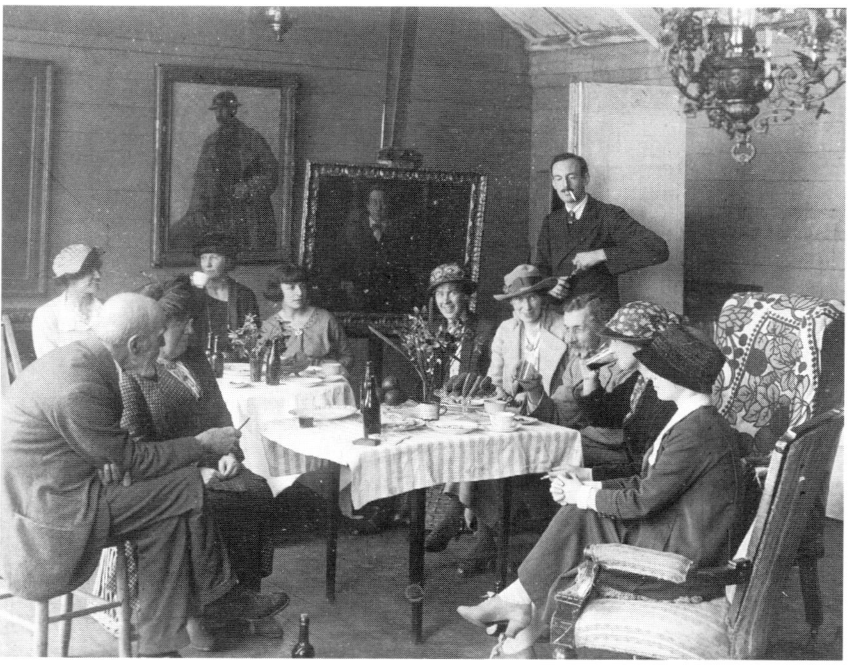

A luncheon party in the Piazza Studios, 1921. Seated around the tables are Ruth Simpson, Eleanor and Robert Hughes and Ella Naper. Kathleen Slatter is at the far end, with Professor and Mrs Sidgwick on the left. Photograph, WCAA

him useful as a manager. The prospectus added after the proprietors' names
'assisted by Lieut-Commander G.F. Bradshaw R.N.'

Kathleen described life at the school. At lunchtime a table in the studio was
covered in a blue and white cloth, with a vase of anemones and a bowl of fruit,
and the Simpsons provided a simple picnic meal. Sometimes they entertained
friends from Lamorna. The photograph of a luncheon party in 1921 shows
Simpson, cigarette hanging from the side of his mouth, drawing the cork from
a bottle, while sitting around the table before him are Ruth, Eleanor and
Robert Hughes and Ella Naper. Kathleen Slatter is at the end of the table and
Professor Sidgwick and his wife Cicely are on the left. Ruth's portrait of *The
American*, the actor Charles Rollo Peters, rests on the easel and *The Company
Commander* hangs on the wall, her life-size portrait of an officer in trench
coat and shrapnel helmet. Walter might still surprise his guests with some
boyish prank; after a lobster meal he once pushed the feelers up his nostrils.
They enjoyed entertaining and Leonora recalled the happy parties and dances
they had in the studio and at Loyalty Cottage when she was a child.

It had become a popular tradition every March to open the studios to
the public on Show Day, when works could be seen before they were sent to
the Royal Academy. On Show Day in 1922 Simpson exhibited a portrait of
Kathleen Bradshaw, in profile and wearing a blue dress, and Ruth showed
a portrait of George Bradshaw in naval uniform. A reviewer in the *St Ives
Times* described Ruth's painting as 'a valiant attempt at an extremely difficult
problem of rendering quietly the recurring spots of gold in the uniform'.
Borlase Smart in the same newspaper thought it her best work yet and felt that
she had overcome the difficulty of portraying the dark uniform against a dark
background 'with much mastery'. The Shore Studio was visited that year by
the former prime minister Herbert Asquith. He called at two other studios,
those of Alfred Hartley, the etcher, and Borlase Smart; he expressed the hope
that the town council would preserve the old-world buildings.

Simpson himself made a conscious effort to preserve a record of the fishing
industry in St Ives. From the Shore Studio in 1923 he painted a series of
twenty-two pictures showing all the activity taking place on the Wharf. They
illustrate the working day of the port, starting with the empty quay before
the arrival of the boats and going on to show the whole process of landing,
packing and transporting the fish. The titles give an idea of the operations:
Waiting for the Gurries, Herring Packers, Landing Herrings.[4] The herrings
were packed in barrels for export to Italy, the work being done mostly by
women. The berets they wear provide splashes of colour amongst the flurry
of gulls. The fish for sale are laid out on the sand, figures casting long blue

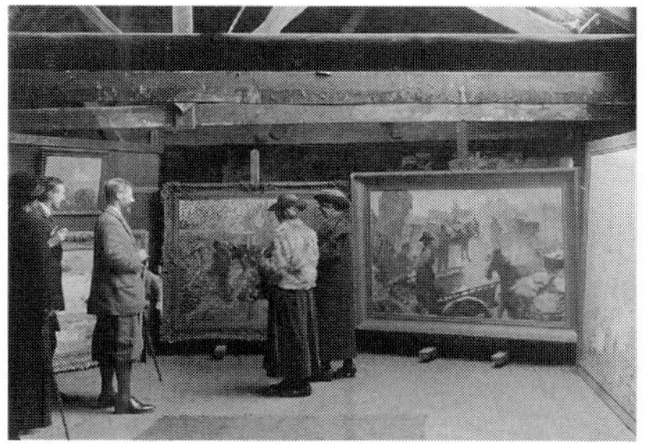

Lamorna Birch admires two of Simpson's
paintings in the Piazza Studios

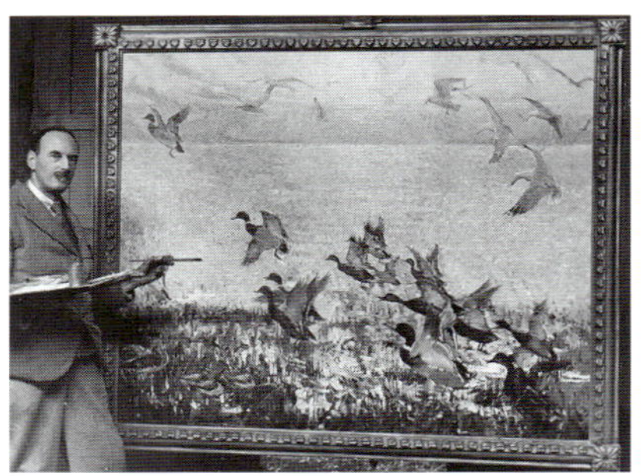

Charles Simpson with **Sunrise on the Estuary**, exhibited at the Royal Academy, 1926

The Flight of Wild Duck
RA 1922, oil on canvas, 60 x 72 in
Silver Medal, Paris Salon 1923
Courtesy of Chomé Fine Art, Bath

Roseate tern; **Long tailed duck**
from the *Wild Bird Series*
1910–1920, oil on card, 20 x 30 in
Roseate tern Courtesy of Porthminster
Gallery, St Ives

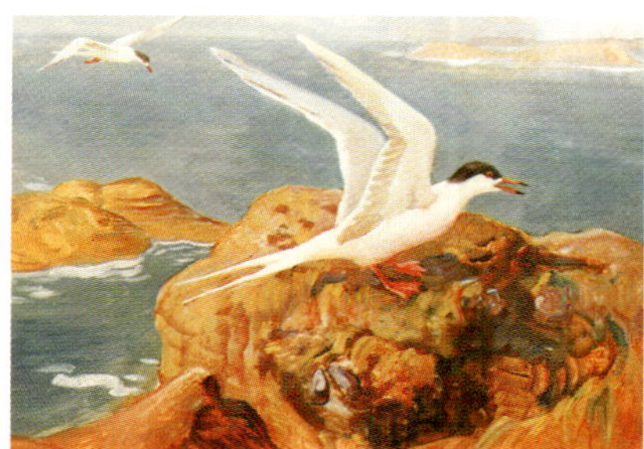

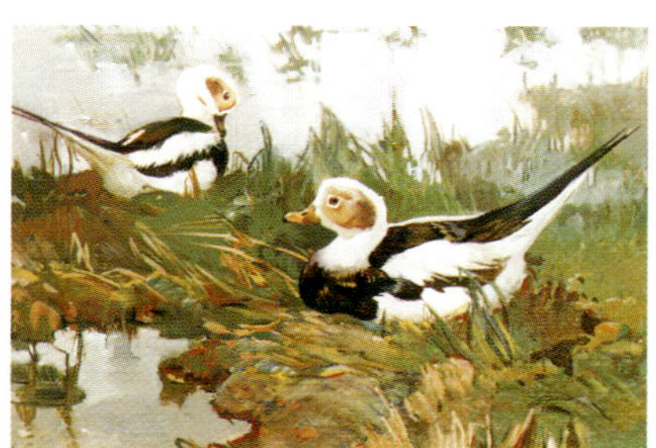

shadows in the early morning light. Agents for the buyers wait on horseback or on carts. The series ends with *A Cornish Nocturne*, in which one man still works among the barrels in the glow of a street lamp while a knot of people gaze in reverie across the still water as the high tide reaches the slipway. Like the earlier record of the Paris floods it was intended as a documentary – the *St Ives Times* called it 'a sort of cinema story of the fisherman and his fish' – but it had a decorative quality as well. It gave atmosphere rather than detail and was more effective than any photography of the time. *The Herring Season: from my Studio Window* was exhibited at the Royal Academy in 1924. The sun is breaking through the mist on to a scene of bustling activity, men and women ghostly against the haze and outlined in colour as they handle barrels of fish and load the waiting carts.

On the Hayle salt marshes he painted some of his most impressionist pictures, large canvases like *Sunrise on the Estuary*, again looking straight into the light that glistens on the water as the ducks rise in alarm, detail lost in half-silhouette. At the bottom right of the picture they are about to take off. As they rise to the top left they are in different positions of flight, like a Muybridge photograph of a sequence of movements. *The Flight of Wild Duck* was first seen at the 1922 Show Day. 'Mr Charles Simpson has one of the pictures of the year so far as St Ives is concerned,' reported *The St Ives Times*, mistaking sunrise for sunset. 'The golden light of a setting sun warms up

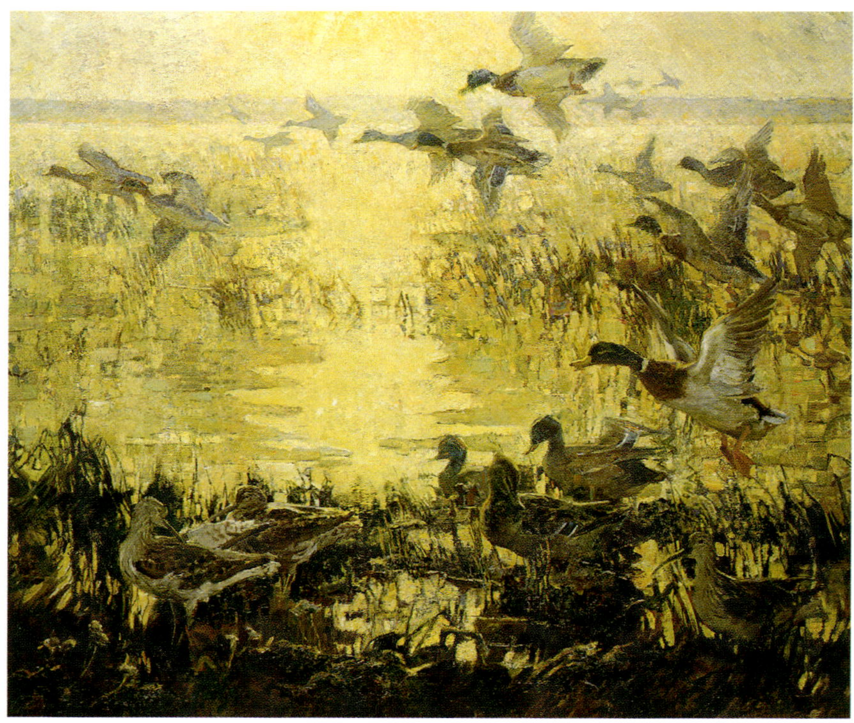

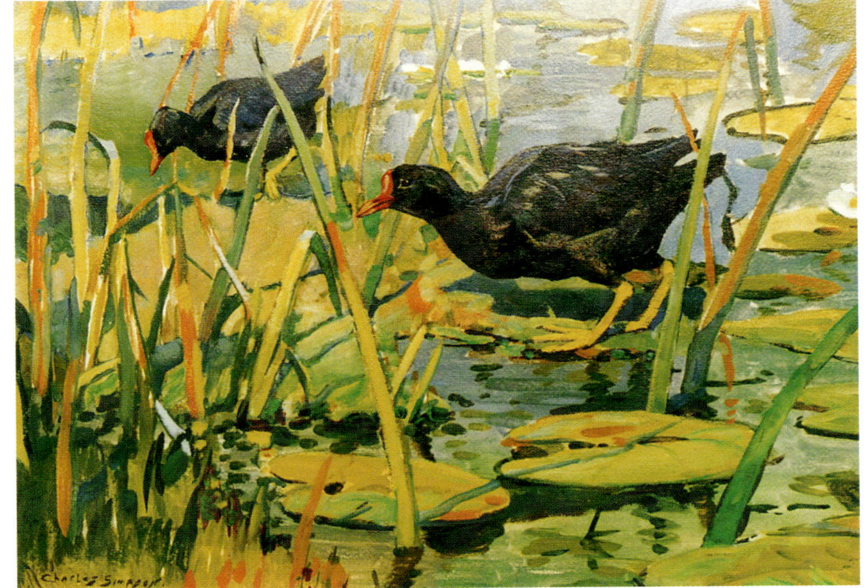

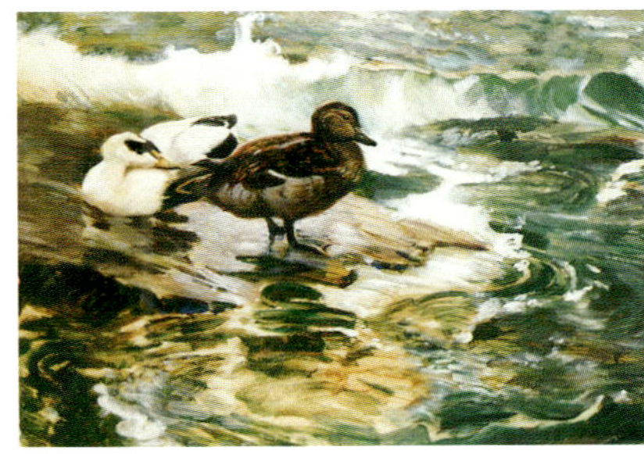

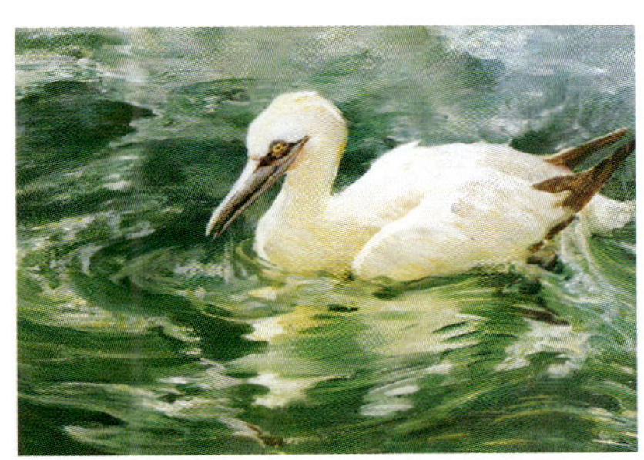

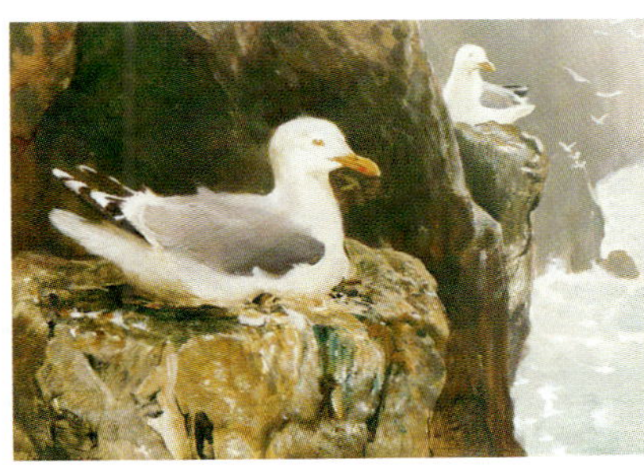

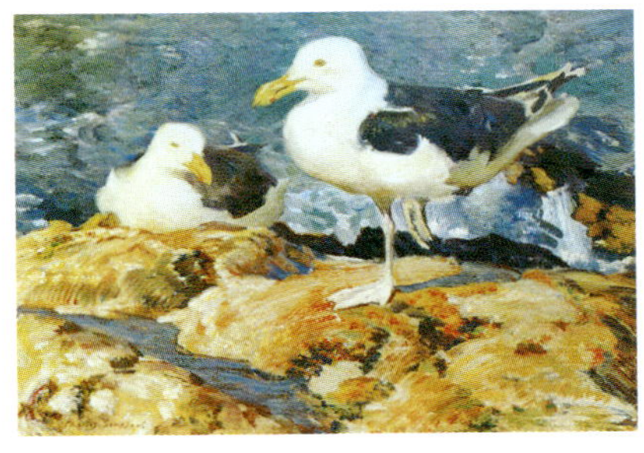

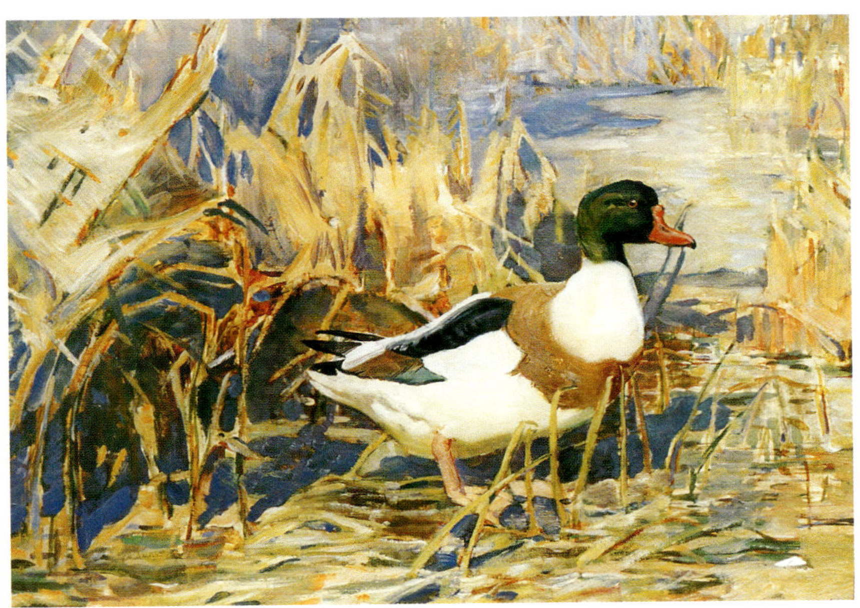

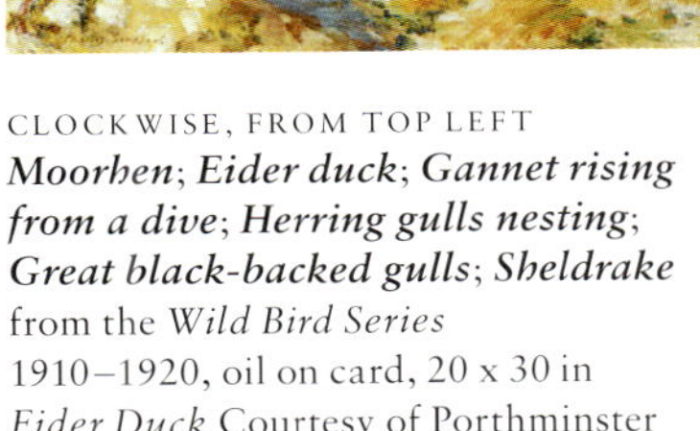

a scene of bird life on a reedy marsh. A flight of ducks is in the air, preparatory to settling… The warm colour is striking their plumage in a series of tints of half-tone beauty. The feeling of motion is wonderfully expressed.' It was exhibited at the Royal Academy and won a Silver Medal at the Paris Salon the following year. 'C'est une émouvante symphonie naturiste,' commented the *Revue du Vrai et du Beau*. *Duck Shooting – the Punt Gunner*, similar in subject and composition, won a Gold Medal at the exhibition of sporting pictures held in Paris in conjunction with the Olympic Games of 1924. These great paintings are all concerned with the transfiguring effect of light, how

CLOCKWISE, FROM TOP LEFT
Moorhen; *Eider duck*; *Gannet rising from a dive*; *Herring gulls nesting*; *Great black-backed gulls*; *Sheldrake* from the *Wild Bird Series* 1910–1920, oil on card, 20 x 30 in *Eider Duck* Courtesy of Porthminster Gallery, St Ives

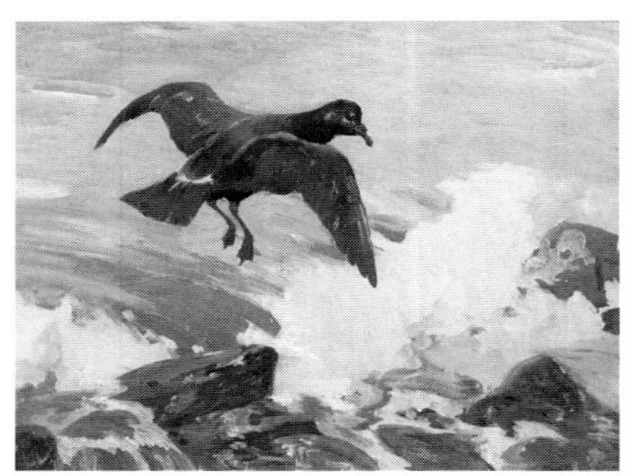

Storm petrel from the *Wild Bird Series*
1910–1920, oil on card, 20 x 30 in
Courtesy of Porthminster Gallery, St Ives

green plover seem to sparkle through a film of violet, how the reflection of the sun from the water outlines the mallards with deep orange and crimson.

Over the course of a decade, between 1910 and 1920, Simpson produced the remarkable Wild Bird Series, some eighty paintings in either gouache or oil on card about 20 x 30 inches in size. At an early stage he hoped to publish them as a book – another idea was for a series of zoo paintings – but he was unable to interest a publisher. He continued to paint them with an exhibition in mind. He believed that the danger for a painter of birds was the naturalist standing behind his shoulder, wanting a coloured map of the bird that would show its species. This is what he would seem to be doing in ornithological studies, but they are always more than guides to recognition in their subtle colouring and sensitively painted settings. There is no attempt to prettify; the seabirds are predatory, their beaks vicious, their eyes reflecting what Simpson called the mystery and terror of all wildlife. The most decorative are those with more than a single bird, such as the pair of moorhens swimming amongst reeds or the puffins flying in formation over the waves, the repetition of the wings conveying rapid movement. These birds are *in* their natural surroundings rather than *on* them. The series was shown in St Ives, in Plymouth and at the Laing Art Gallery, Newcastle; Simpson produced a pamphlet, printed by James Lanham of St Ives, to accompany the exhibitions. They were all painted, he wrote, on the north-west coast of Cornwall during the spring migration. The text reveals the same detailed observation as the paintings, with the addition of information that could not be shown in a picture, the whirr of sound as guillemots and razorbills rush through the air, the long lazy wing-strokes of cormorants and shags. He describes how gannets circle at great height, mark the fish below and hurl themselves downwards, casting up a column of spray as they strike the water. Once they come up they need a wind to lift them from the surface and one still day in a sheltered cove hundreds of gannets were dragged under the waves, unable to rise while others plunged to join them in a scene of wholesale destruction. Disasters, whether human or in nature, always preyed upon his mind.

He used James Lanham again for a more ambitious project. In 1922 he published *A Pastorale*, his account of the months he spent on the Sussex marshes and which he thought of as 'a simple melody on a rustic theme'.[5] The de luxe edition of seventy-five copies, numbered and signed, has fifty-one pages of text interleaved with woodcuts and linocuts protected by tissue paper, the whole bound with silk thread in a soft leather cover. The woodcuts, quite primitive in style, are of the thatched cottage and of the birds: curlew, whooper swans and Brent geese. It had little commercial prospect but was very close to his heart. It expressed the philosophy that underlay his painting, that a

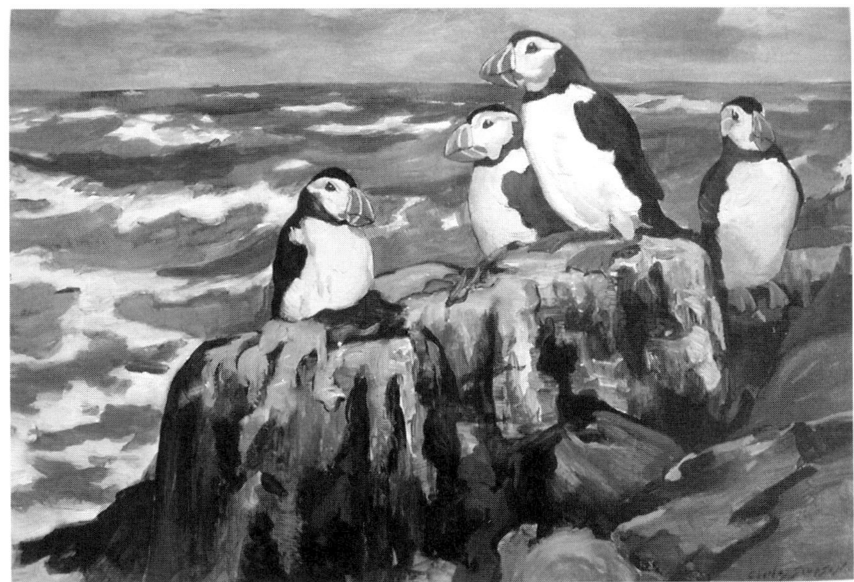

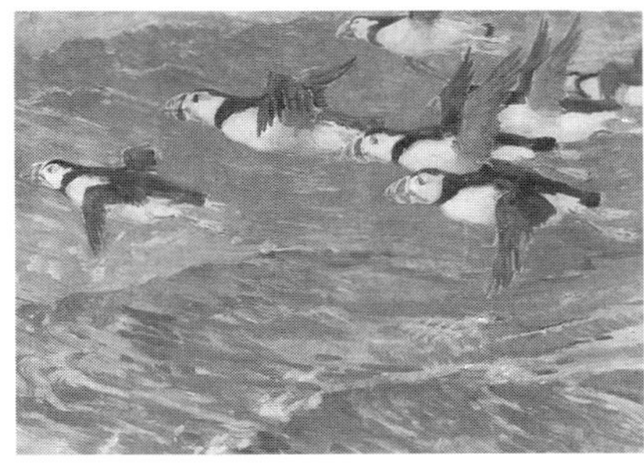

Puffins from the *Wild Bird Series*
1910–1920, oil on card, 20 x 30 in

gull silhouetted against the surf or a pair of mallards amongst the reeds have beauty in so far as they suggest the larger unity of which they are a part. The whole cosmos is seen in its smallest details.

He sent a copy to his uncle John St Loe Strachey, editor and owner of *The Spectator* and cousin of Lytton. He complimented Walter on his enterprise, thought he could set up a little fine-art printing business and was glad he had 'a second string to his bow'. He made an exception and gave it a review, written by his brother Harry. The reviewer for *The Observer* praised the beautiful woodcuts; he thought 'his prose is not as good as his woodblocks but it has passages of rare observation and is sensitively alive to the changes of natural life'. Norman Garstin admired his initiative but found some of the illustrations too slight. Simpson himself feared that his meditations were too elusive, but he saw himself from now on as a writer as well as a painter.

As his fortieth year approached he considered his future. He was the leading figure in the St Ives art colony and his school was flourishing.[6] But he felt restless, that it was time for a change of scene and subject. He asked Strachey to enquire if there were any vacancies at the Royal College of Art. The director William Rothenstein replied that he had nothing to offer that would be worth his while, though he knew and liked his work. He applied for the post of Director of the Glasgow School of Art. His uncle wrote a glowing reference but he was not appointed. He had already had commissions for racehorse paintings and thought it would be easier to secure work if he was based in the capital. But when he moved to London the immediate reason was to see the rodeo at Wembley Stadium.

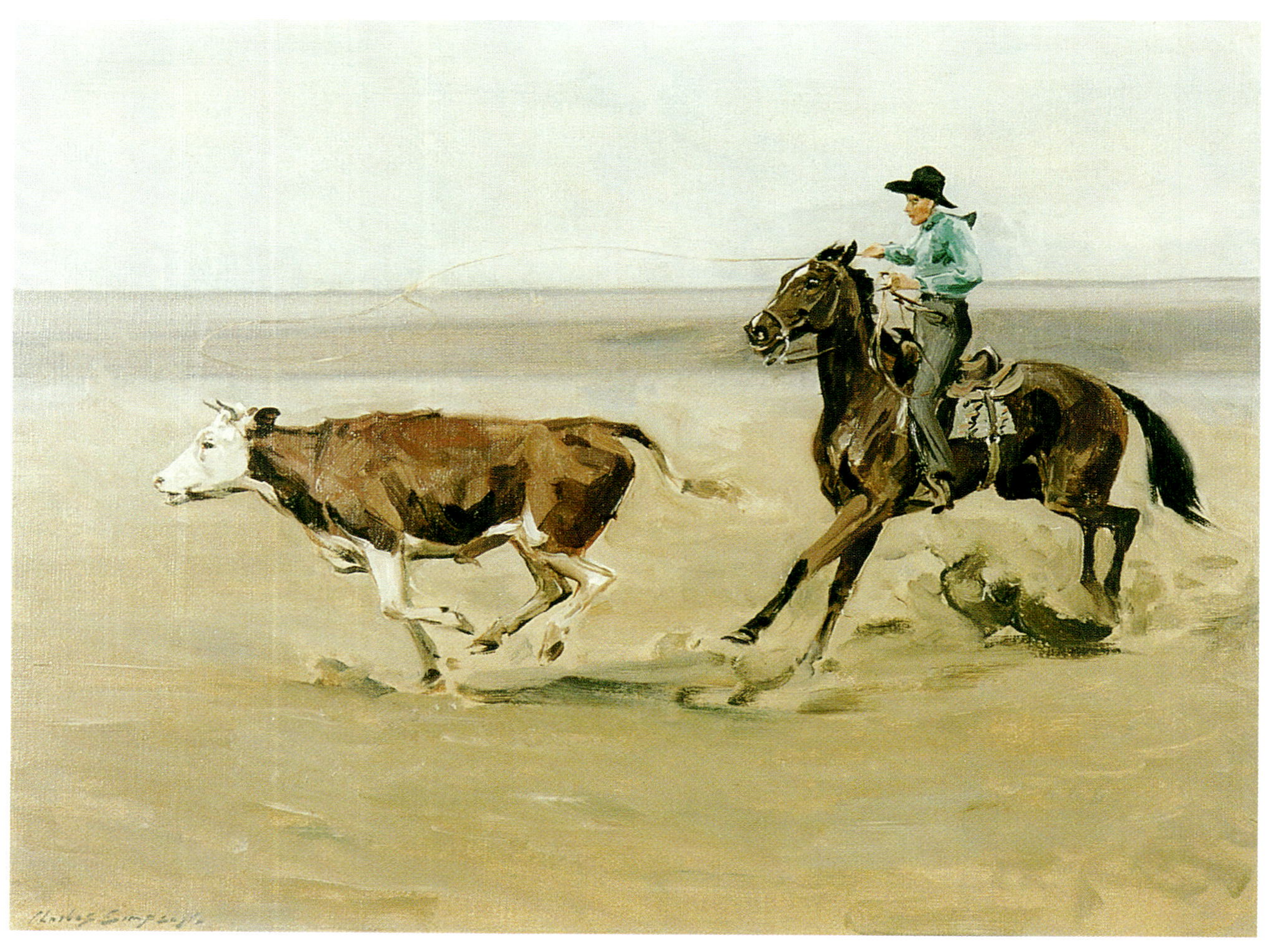

The Rodeo
1924, oil on canvas, 18 x 24 in
Courtesy of Chomé Fine Art, Bath

The rodeo had begun in the competitions for riding wild horses and roping steers in Texas and New Mexico. Tex Austin saw its possibilities as an entertainment and took it as a show throughout the United States. In 1924 he chartered a boat and loaded it with wild cattle, 'spoilt hosses, all bad, a herd of cowboys and a fancy selection of cowgirls'. Into the hold went saddles, chaps, hay, corn, oats and six-shooters. The Great International Contest at Wembley drew huge crowds and vast amounts of publicity. 'Nothing as far as I remember has ever given London such a theme to talk about as the rodeo,' said the writer on equine matters R.B. Cunninghame Graham. 'The greatest triumph of America over England since the revolution,' reported the *Dallas Morning News*.

Simpson gained permission to sketch in the arena and spent the greater part of three weeks at the stadium from early morning until midnight. It was not without some risk to life and limb. He had to be ready to leap out of the way of a stampeding steer or wild bronco and scramble up the wire fence, his drawing and painting materials tied to his waist by a string. The show gave him a continuous rush of excitement, conveyed in dramatic sketches of animals in movement, bucking and rearing, and the poise of riders as they balanced on their mounts. There were scenes of bronco riding, steer roping, riding and wrestling, known as 'bulldogging'. Captain Tom Hickman of the Texas Rangers, a riding armoury with his four six-shooters and a Winchester carbine, led the judges. The cowboys and cowgirls were in colourful costumes, check shirts of black and green with scarlet neckties, shining leather belts with heavy buckles and sheepskin chaps decorated with coloured wool. Their names were just as colourful: Nowata Slim, Buck Lucas, Skeeter Bill Robbins. They squatted in cowboy fashion along the wire fence waiting their turn to ride, chewing gum or a quid of tobacco. They competed for prizes and made light of their injuries,

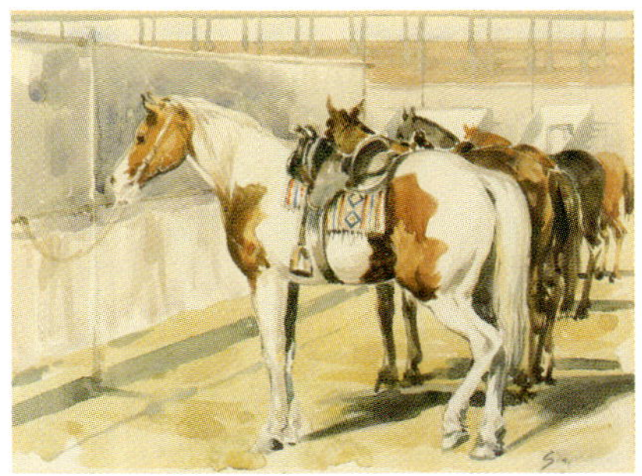

The Rodeo: a Pinto
Oil on canvas, 18 x 24 in
Courtesy of Adobe Gallery, Santa Fe,
New Mexico, USA

the girls as much as the men. Anita Studwick was rolled on by her horse and carried out of the ring with a broken collarbone. Olive Tegland, half-stunned by a blow from her horse's head, swayed back and forth in the saddle like a rag doll.

To show that it was a genuine test of skill, the audience was invited to have a go. The casualties brought in by the stretcher party were so great one evening that the gangway 'looked like the communication trench in a battle'. Cavalrymen, jockeys, even a clergyman were all thrown. Simpson described how an Australian, Snowy Thompson, took up the challenge, with a large sum of money wagered on his success. 'The arc lights shone on his blue silk shirt with its gaudy Union Jack. Thompson looked a little perturbed – somebody whispered the horse was a devil… The animal's vicious grunts and the ring of its hoofs on the ground…must have scared the life out of him… The horse was 'pitching' and the concussion of each landing, with a terrific jerk of its quarters, seemed enough to throw the rider out of the arena. And finally Thompson went, like a shuttle-cock from a racquet, up into the air and down on his head.' Only one amateur succeeded, a seaman from the British Navy. As daylight faded the floodlights gave eeriness to the scenes of trick riding and the evening ended with the wild horse race around the arena, while the band of the Royal Fusiliers played the national anthem.

Simpson caught the atmosphere in his rapid sketches and one hundred and twenty-five pictures were exhibited at The Arlington Gallery. The show was so popular that it had to be extended for another month. One of the visitors was John Lane, who offered to publish them as a book at The Bodley Head. Simpson wrote a text in which he said that the rodeo had left him with 'an impression of something quite above and beyond the thrills of its contests, the pageantry of its scenes, or the fine sense of open air and freedom that its ensemble conveyed – it has left an impression of something classic, belonging to all time'. *El Rodeo*, with over one hundred illustrations, came out before the end of the year. The book played a part in changing American perceptions of their own culture. The rodeo had been looked down on in the States; it was too Wild West, crude and boisterous. Americans were surprised that the cold and aloof English should consider it a classic performance, fit subject for an artist. It made some of them reconsider their indigenous art instead of always looking to Europe. Simpson made many friends among the riders, giving them sketches and keeping in touch. One of the cowhands wrote from America to say that the old gang asked after him and to thank him for 'the swell way you handled

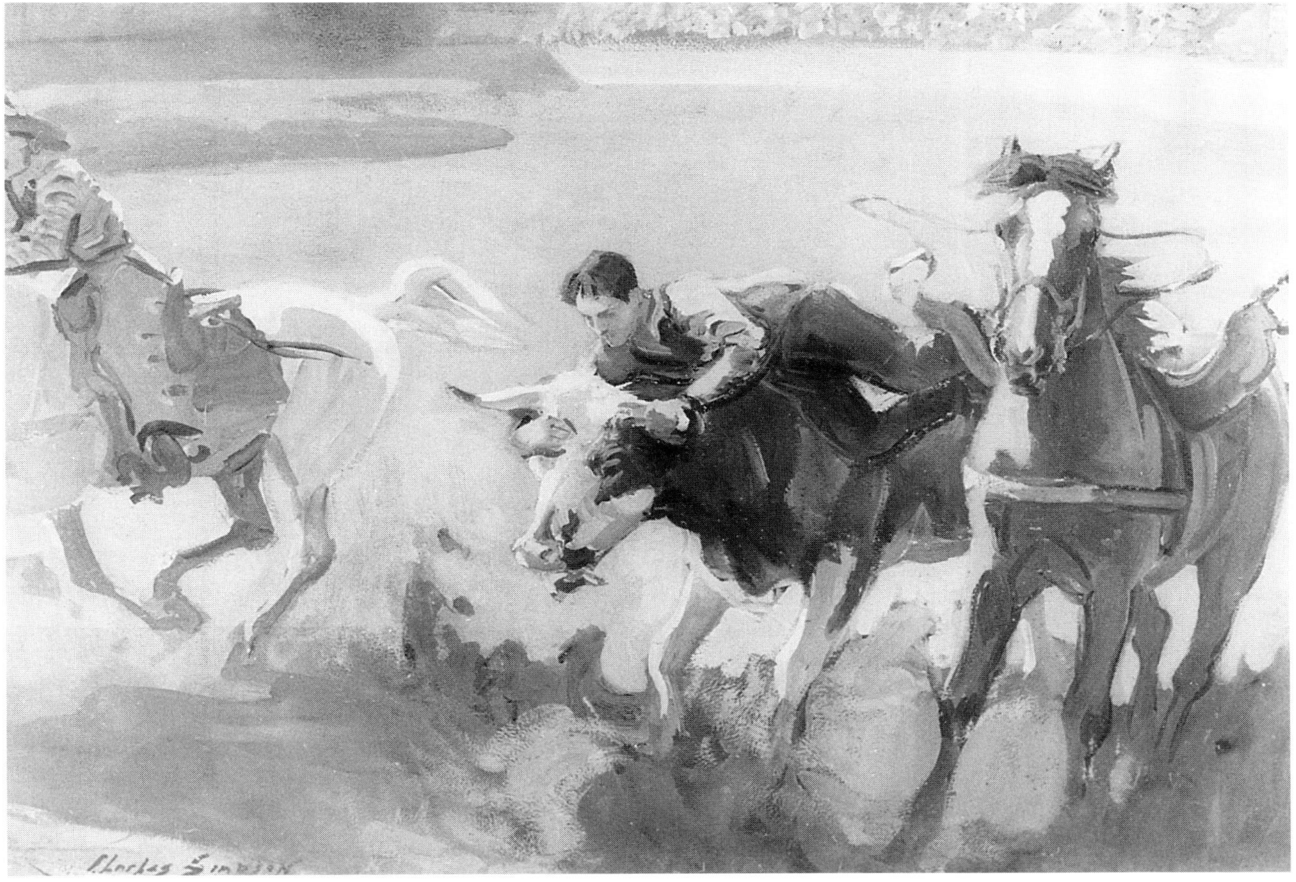

Steer Wrestling – a rapid impression
Illustration from *El Rodeo*
Courtesy of David Lay Auctions

your account of our show'. Tom Hickman told him the rodeo had opened up many new opportunities for the boys and girls. It changed Simpson's life as well. John Lane immediately commissioned a book on the Leicestershire hunts and he went off to spend the winter of 1924–1925 in and around Melton Mowbray.

Charles Simpson in his forties seemed to become a different person. As a young man his preferred company was that of a vagrant outside The Labouring Man on a summer's evening, an old shepherd in the Sussex water meadows or a ferryman on the Hayle estuary. He was happiest alone with a pair of field glasses on the cliff tops near Land's End, watching the migrating birds, or if he wanted companionship he chose the society of fellow artists. For twenty years he had lived in quiet country places or in the art colonies of Newlyn and St Ives. Now he was based in London and for the next decade took pleasure in knowing and being the guest of wealthy landowners like Major Burnaby, Master of the Quorn, and Sir Arthur Hazelrigg, Lord Lieutenant of Leicestershire. He made the transition with ease. His painting too altered. He had painted the subjects

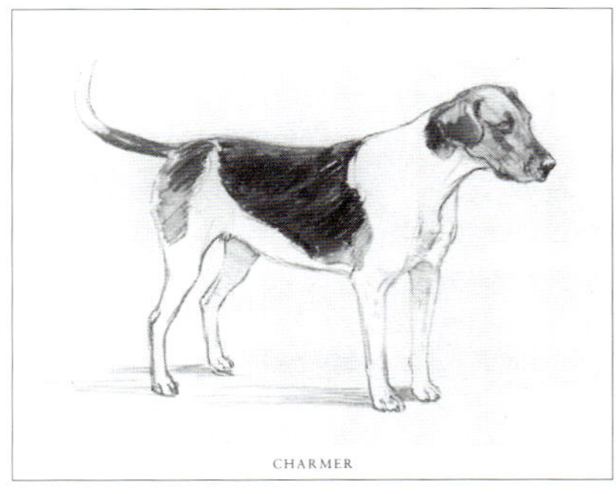

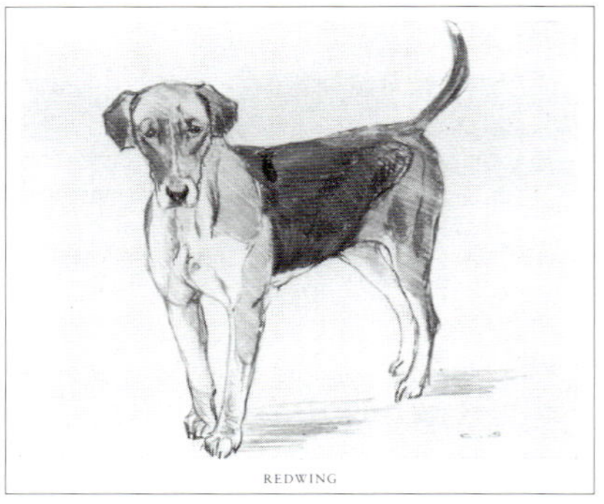

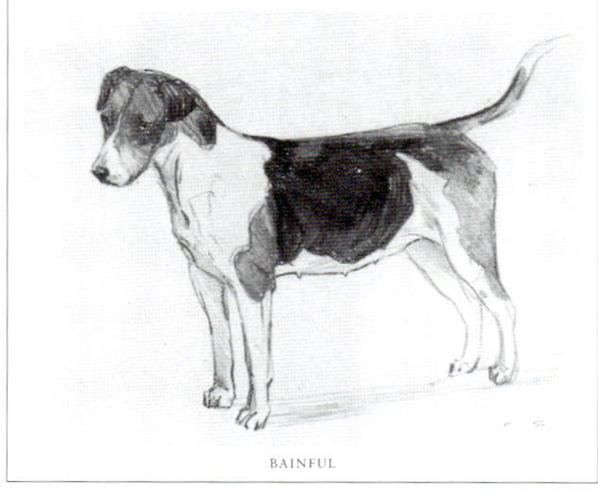

The Quorn in Belvoir Vale
Gouache, 20 x 30 in
The frontispiece to *Leicestershire and Its Hunts*
Courtesy of Chomé Fine Art

Charmer, Redwing & Bainful:
three hounds from the Quorn bitch pack
Pencil illustrations from *Leicestershire*
and Its Hunts

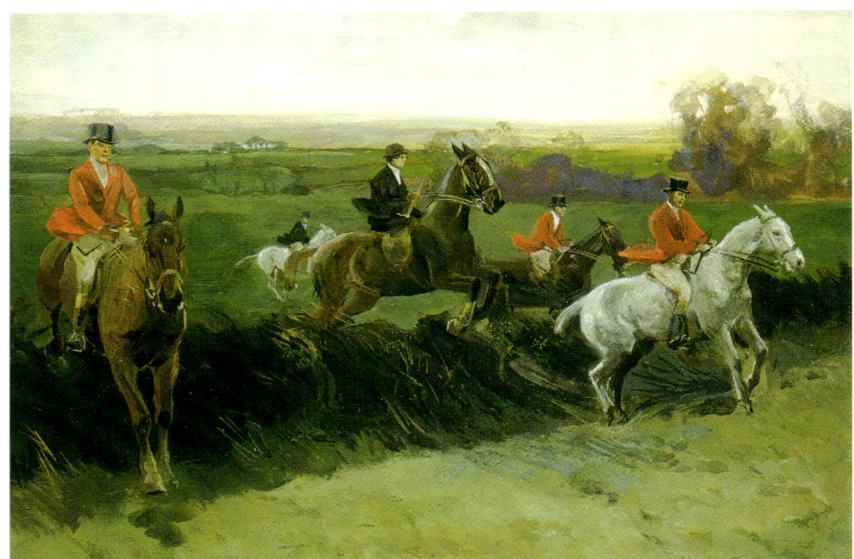

that mattered to him, his family and friends, the timeless moors, farmyard cattle and seabirds, in a broadly impressionist style. He now painted realistic scenes of foxhunting. Even his appearance changed. The slim young man put on weight, his face widened as his hair receded, his chest broadened, his middle spread.

He did an enormous amount of research, in libraries and on the ground. He read up all the extensive hunting literature as well as the history, geography and geology of Leicestershire. He explored the 'countries' of the three hunts, the Monday and Friday meets of the Quorn, the Tuesday and Saturday meets of the Cottesmore and the Wednesday meet of the Belvoir. He described the scene at one of the meets: the grooms arrive in a quiet village, each leading a horse with clipped flanks and shining saddlery. Bit-rings jingle and scuds of foam are flecked on the roadside grass. A few sportsmen of the old school hack to the meet; there's an immaculately attired veteran with a glinting eyeglass, two young girls, a few children on ponies. The cars arrive, a Rolls-Royce, Humbers and Daimlers, and the riders mount, the men in hunting pink with coat-tails, white breeches and top hats, the ladies riding side-saddle in dark blue habits with white cravats. A cry of 'Hounds! Gentlemen, please!' and the pack comes round the corner of the village street. The hunt moves off to the fields. And Simpson follows them on his motorcycle, an outlandish figure in leather helmet and goggles. He affronted some of the hunt masters, especially when through his knowledge of the terrain and the ways of the fox he arrived ahead of the field. But he was accepted into their society. With his military appearance and social ease he was generally taken for an army officer who had been injured in the war and so could be excused some eccentricity.

Leicestershire and Its Hunts is a large, expansive volume, written for readers in sympathy with the subject and with time on their hands. It's a celebration of Old England and the great days of hard riders and hard drinkers. There is regret for the past and a patronising view of the present. At the George Hotel in Melton Mowbray, which once rang with the 'view halloas' of the huntsmen, the guests are now commercial travellers and people who don't know that Belvoir is pronounced Beevor. It's a celebration of the English countryside, a litany of the names of hill and valley, field and spinney, hedge and brook. They would chime in the memories of sportsmen, each name recalling the story of some chase or feat of endurance, some fox gone to earth or caught. 'Only the man who rides straight,' wrote the reviewer in *The Morning Post*, 'knows that beauty of memorial which makes every English meadow, hill or covert a sort of holy of holies.'

The book was published in 1926 at 31s 6d, with twenty-eight illustrations in colour and fifty-five in black and white. There was also a de luxe edition suitable for the libraries of great country houses, printed on

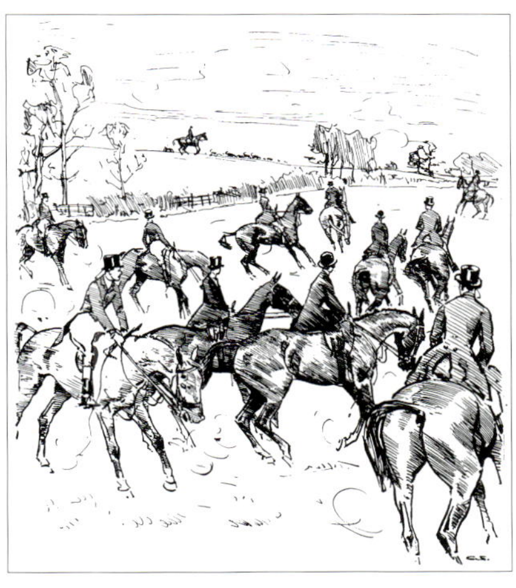

ABOVE
Riders ahead of the hounds
Illustration from *Wit and Wisdom of the Shires*

BELOW
Some of the Fernie bitch pack: Sempstress, Gainful, Saucy, Toilet, Secret and Tranquil
Illustration from *The Harboro' Country*

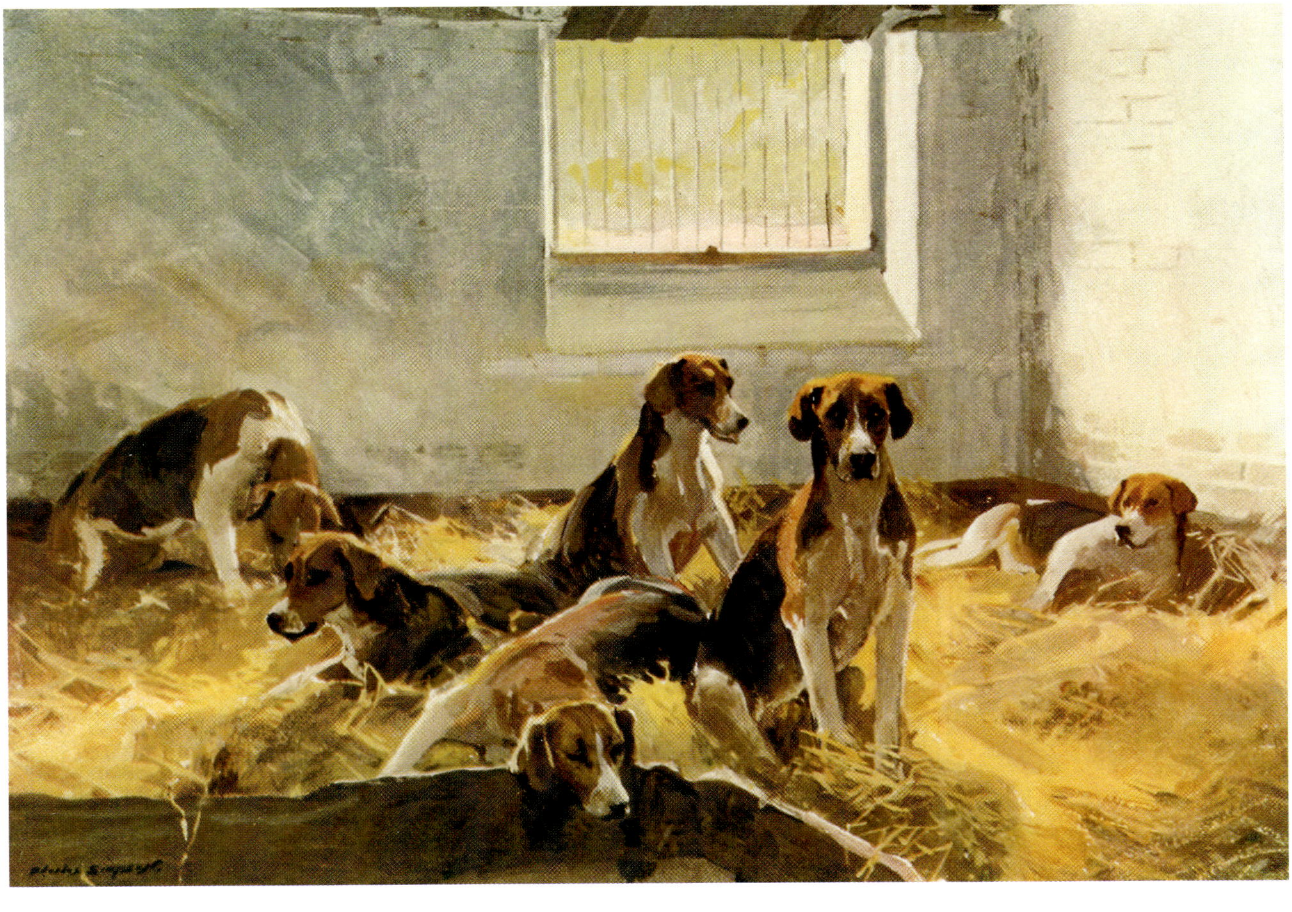

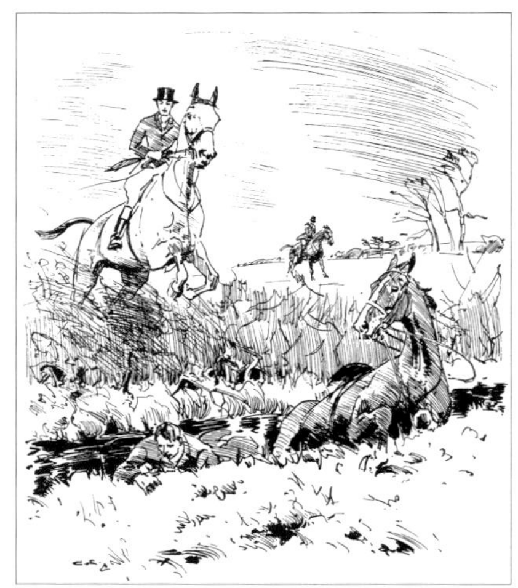

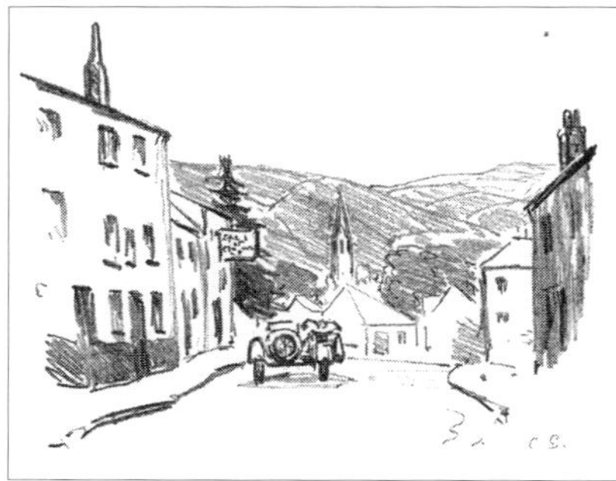

hand-made paper and limited to seventy-five numbered and signed copies. It was warmly received and had enthusiastic notices in the press, even the *New Statesman* finding it 'full of stirring reminiscences of ancient runs, amusing and exemplary sketches of by-gone sportsmen, and appreciation of horses, hounds, and country sights and sounds'. 'Few hunting books have afforded me greater pleasure,' wrote another reviewer, convinced that the author had hunted in the county all his life. 'Full of delight… a feast of good things.' Only Vulliamy wondered whether the subject was worth all the work that had gone into it, but 'hunting and hunting people are incomprehensible to me'.

Simpson's collaboration with Vulliamy, *Unknown Cornwall*, had come out in 1925, while he was working in Leicestershire. Vulliamy had finally decided he was a writer rather than a painter and the book was one in a series of 'unknown' counties, exploring the lesser-known aspects of Kent, Sussex or Surrey. It too was published by John Lane at The Bodley Head. Simpson had made the illustrations before leaving for London, thirty in colour, fifteen in monochrome and sixty-seven in pen and ink, pencil or crayon. They travelled together on the Royal Enfield with sidecar attached and shared the same feelings for places, archaeological sites where past and present seem one and moors where 'time suffers a contraction'. Simpson's illustrations are again more evocative than the photographs in guidebooks of the period. In the picture of Goss Moor the road stretches away into the distance beyond the Iron Bridge of the railway and there's not a single car in sight, only a white wooden signpost at the crossroads. The motorbike and sidecar is the only vehicle parked in the main street of Lostwithiel. Besides the drawings made especially for the book, many of the reproductions are of earlier paintings from his St Ives period: *Seagulls Nesting, Black-Backed Gulls, Flight of Wild Duck, Duck Shooting – the Punt Gunner* and *Flight of Curlew. Trink Hill,* exhibited at the Royal Academy in 1920, was painted entirely out of doors on the moor to the south-west of St Ives. It took two years to complete, waiting for the moment when the setting sun cast low rays over the undulating ground, giving solidity to a farmhouse, boulders and the grazing cows.

Leicestershire and Its Hunts was followed by *The Harboro' Country* in 1927. It describes the Fernie and Billesdon hunts in the part of the county around Market Harborough, Simpson having had too much material to put it all into one book as originally intended. It takes the same format as the earlier volume and includes two dramatic chapters on the Battle of Naseby during the Civil War. Among the colour plates there are fewer scenes of

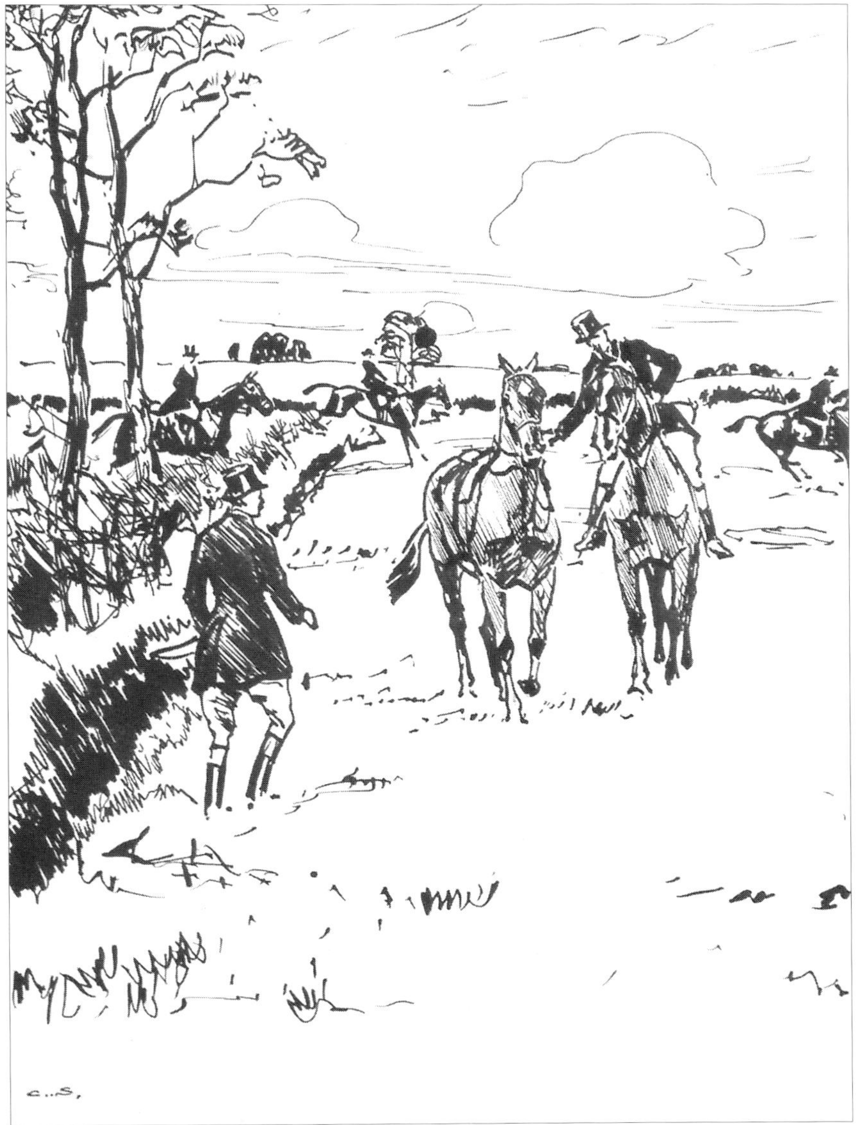

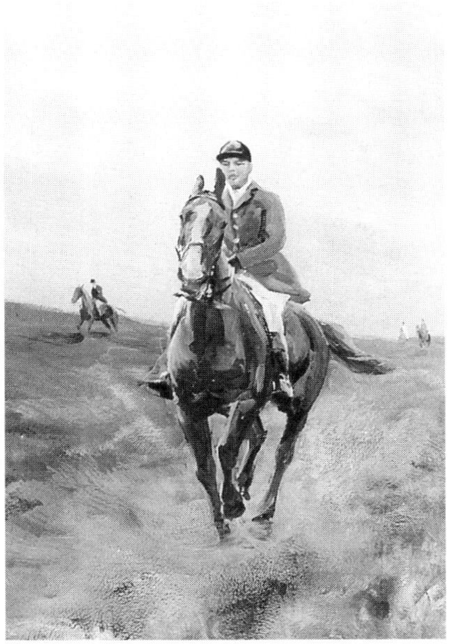

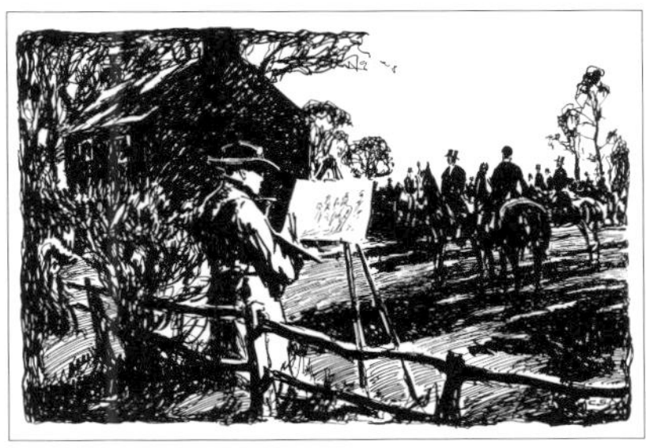

Detail from *Huntsmen on a Moor*
Oil on paper, 25 x 20 in
Courtesy of David Lay Auctions

Charles Simpson sketching at a meet of the
hunt, wearing an old Burberry to protect
himself from the weather and a turned-
down felt hat to shade his eyes. Self-portrait
for *The Bodleian*, the house journal of the
Bodley Head.

An example of good manners
Illustration from *Manners and Mannerisms*
Courtesy of Jordan and Chard Fine Art

the hunting field and two of hounds in kennels that are among his best
animal paintings. The frontispiece shows a fox in close-up, with the hunt
very small in the distance. Simpson had been waiting by a hedge when the
fox appeared alongside him and they looked at each other. He had a great
affection for foxes, and the ability to identify with them. 'One of the most
charming sights I have seen,' he wrote in later life, 'is a vixen with her cubs
in a wood, safe from harm, with no trap or poison waiting to exterminate
them.' He believed that hunting protected them and that otherwise they
might become extinct.[1] He continued to celebrate the chase in the third
book of the series, *Trencher and Kennel*, which dealt with the hunts in
Yorkshire: the Braham Moor, the York and Ainsty, Lord Middleton's Hunt,

75

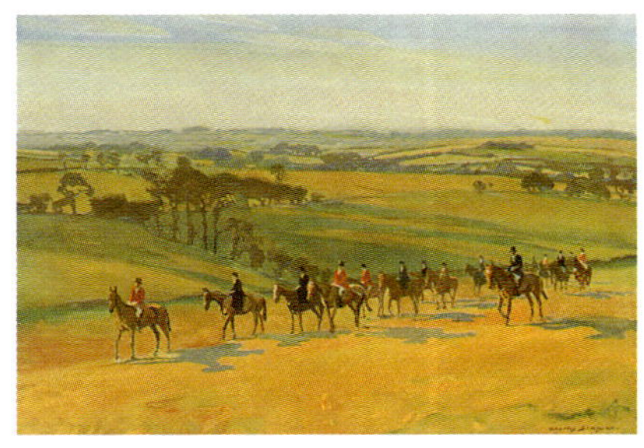

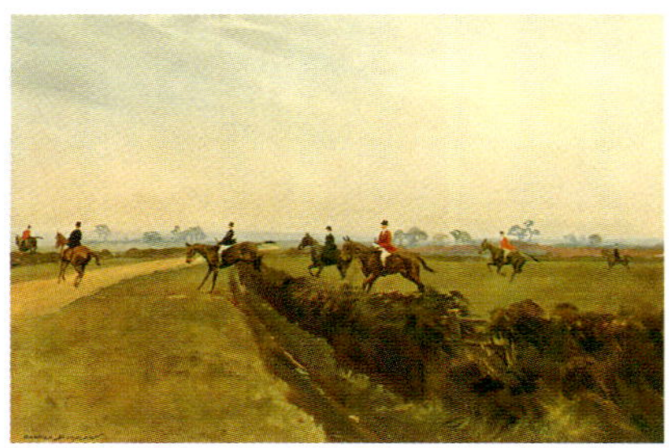

Looking towards Harrogate
and *The Sinnington Vale*
Illustrations from *Trencher and Kennel*

The Brontë Waterfall
Gouache, 21 x 15 in
Illustration from *Emily Brontë*
Photograph by Venture, Truro

On the Moors near Haworth
Gouache 15 x 21 in
Illustration from *Emily Brontë*
Photograph by Venture, Truro

the Sinnington and the Ferndale. It opens with a vivid description of a chase and contains possibly the best of the hunt drawings. Trencher-fed packs were not kept in large separate kennels but were looked after by the huntsman at the stables.

While working in Yorkshire he was able to gather material for his next book. It would be quite unlike the last three: a biography of Emily Brontë. He enjoyed literature as much as music and his interest in *Wuthering Heights* and its author was combined with his love for the open moors. He read all the background material dealing with the Brontë sisters and felt that the figure of Emily remained 'as elusive and mysterious as the moorland mist'. He made contact with the Brontë Society and visited Haworth on three occasions to make sketches in spring, summer and winter. His painting of the waterfall above the valley of the Sladen Beck was nearly washed out by a sudden thunderstorm. Staying at the Bull Inn, he met an old man of ninety-two who remembered seeing the sisters on their walks and who gave a description of them. At the Brontë Museum he read Emily's diary, which had recently returned from America and which provided new details of her life and work. In the incongruous setting of the RAF display at Hendon he discussed Emily Brontë with a Captain Sunderland whose family came from High Sunderland Hall. His description of the 'grotesque carving' above the gateway helped to establish it as the original for *Wuthering Heights*.

It was a successful book. He had new information, a clear story to tell and an enthusiasm for the person and the place. It has been superseded by other more literary and psychological biographies, but in its day it was

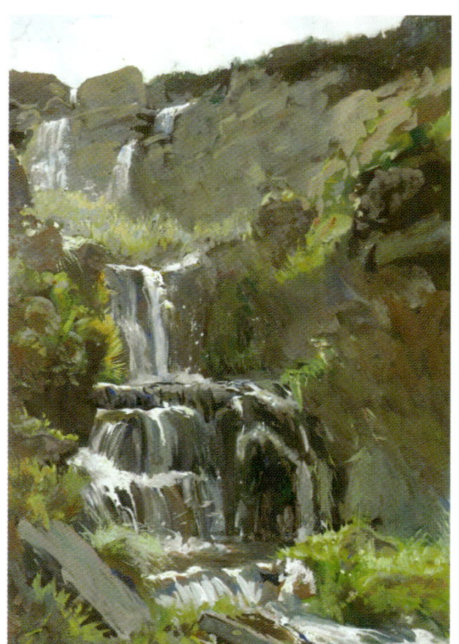

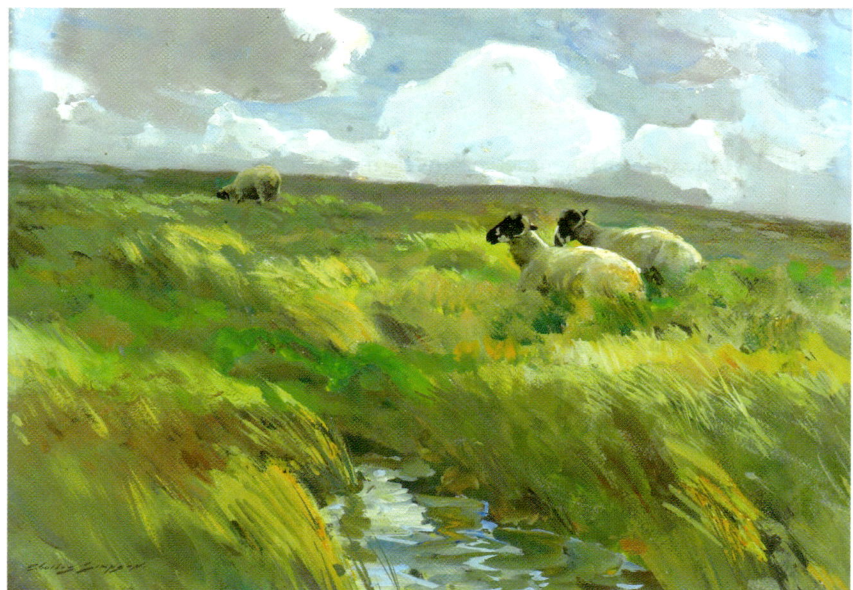

the best general life available. It was published in 1929 by *Country Life*. The *Daily Chronicle* thought it was 'probably the most accurate portrait that we can ever hope to have of the genius who wrote *Wuthering Heights*, the greatest novel ever written by a woman', though the *Times Literary Supplement* found the portrayal of Emily's character rather too suave. *The New Statesman* welcomed it as 'a contrast to the extravagancies too often raised by Emily Brontë. [Simpson] is very successful in setting her against the background, stern and beautiful, of her country, those wonderful moors for which, when she left them, she disconsolately pined… The book is very attractively illustrated by reproductions of paintings by the author.'

While writing the hunting books Simpson had met Major Guy Paget of Sulby Hall near Rugby. He was another wealthy landowner, at one time Member of Parliament for Bosworth and a Justice of the Peace. He had a reputation as a fearless rider with the Pytchley and Ferneley hunts. An old Etonian, he believed that foxhunting was 'an integral part of the Spirit of England, acting as a school which soon expels the coward or the sluggard, and brings out the finest in the British character'. [2] Simpson regarded him as one of his best friends and often stayed at the Hall. Paget collected sporting pictures – he showed eighty-five from his personal collection in an exhibition at the Alfred East Gallery in Kettering – and he bought from Simpson. 'Why is it that Charles Simpson can draw a pack of hounds running better than anyone else?' he asked. 'Because he hunts on an infernal motorbike and sees the pack from in front or from the flank, not from behind.' He bought *Dawn – the Cornish Marshes*, which had won a Gold Medal at Vienna, and he commissioned *Going to Covert: Major Guy Paget on Goliath, with the Pytchley Hounds outside Sulby Covert*.

Paget was always ready to put in a good word for him, make a speech or write an article. He thought Walter's equestrian portraits were worthy of Ferneley, the great early nineteenth-century sporting artist. [3] In his book *Sporting Pictures of England* he described him as 'the best bird painter living'. [4] He persuaded his rich friends to commission paintings: *Major Algy Burnaby and his Huntsman Walter Wilson, Arthur Thatcher outside Walton Holt, Mr Wright and the South Atherston*. In *Who's Who* Paget gave his hobby as writing and he had Simpson to illustrate his books. *The Flying Parson and Dick Christian* is the story of a Leicestershire huntsman. Simpson devised with the printer a process for reproducing chalk drawings in three colours.

Paget introduced him to Victor Emanuel, a rich American businessman with a passion for hunting. Every year he left New York to spend the season at Rockingham Castle near Market Harborough. Early in 1930 he listed

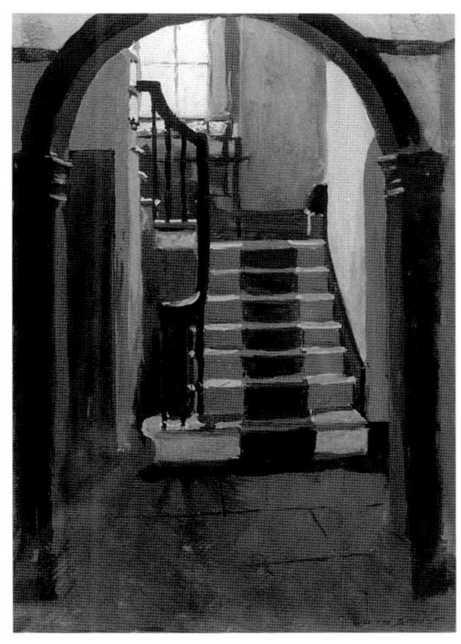

Parsonage Hall and Staircase
Gouache, 21 x 15 in
Illustration from *Emily Brontë*
Courtesy of David Lay Auctions

the pictures that he wanted Simpson to paint of his horses and family:

1. landscape with The Ghost, Francois and Ptarmigan
2. landscape with Top Hole, Rigaud and The Duke
3. family group in courtyard with Mr and Mrs Emanuel, Albert (aged 11) and Barton, with Roulette, The Duke, Little Boy and Blackie
   This picture to be 6' x 7'
4. a set of four horse portraits of Sandyman, Francois, Val and Silurian
   The whole to be executed for £1250

He would pay £500 down and the balance on completion of the work.

In his portraits of horses and figures on horseback Simpson satisfied his clients, showing the horse to advantage, the rider suitably elegant and the groom or huntsman appropriately servile. If they wanted him to include the fountain in the courtyard he would include it, even if it made the composition

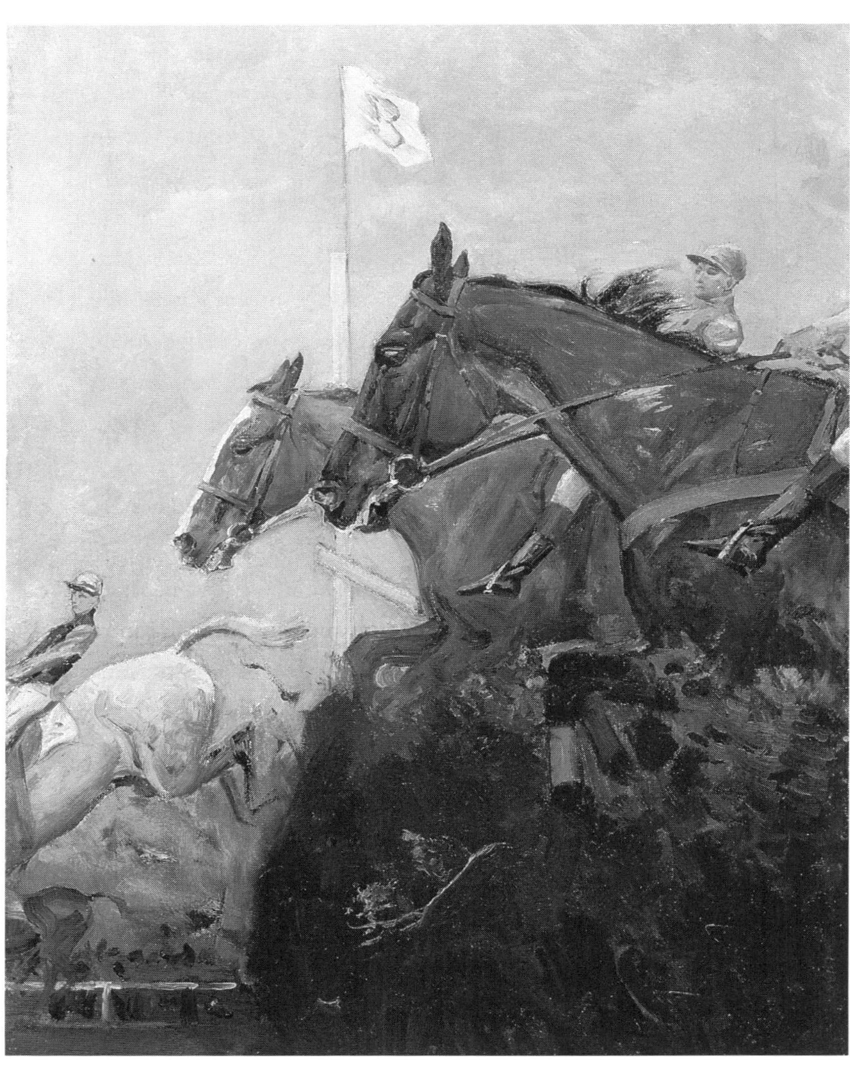

Over the Fence
Oil on canvas, 24 x 18 in
Courtesy of Sotheby's New York

difficult. He recognised that this was not likely to result in great art, but he produced a workman-like job. He was more inspired by the racecourse, attending the major events with Munnings or Paget. He was always at Epsom on Derby Day: 'the dark mass of the crowd behind the white rails, the coaches, each a miniature stand on which grey top hats and black coats contrast with flowery dresses, and far away the sweep of green round Tattenham Corner, all a kaleidoscope of colour in the sunlight.' He conveyed his enjoyment of the scene in gouache sketches done on the spot. He loved the tradition and stylishness of Ascot, the paddock with 'pools of shadow under the trees, the green of sunlit grass, and moving through the crowd a gay procession, gleams of light on jockeys' silks, scarlet, azure and gold, as impatient horses are led out onto the course.' At Aintree he regularly stationed himself at Becher's Brook in the Grand National to capture the moment when the horses rise over the fence, stumble on landing and start again. The angle of the jockeys in their colourful silks and caps as they lean back and then forward gives momentum to a picture. The curve of a rider's body as he falls from the saddle completes the circle of the composition. There is no stiffness, only colour and movement, thrill and excitement.

In the same period Simpson painted *The Prince of Wales with the Quorn* and *Lord and Lady Mountbatten with the Cottesmore*. For Major Jack Harrison he did a set of pictures showing his polo team *The Knaves* playing at Hurlingham. He also had exhibitions linked to the hunting books in the Midlands and at the Fine Art Society in London. *Stealing away from the Spinney* from the 1926 exhibition 'Famous Woods and Spinneys' shows a fox moving cautiously across an open field as the full moon rises over the trees. This is not just any fox but an individual, thin, sharp-nosed and hungry. There is tension in its arched back and lifted tail as it sets out on the prowl. At these exhibitions The Bodley Head displayed his hunting books and six other titles that he had illustrated. Whilst in Leicestershire and Yorkshire he contributed articles to *Country Life*, illustrating his work and reports on horse shows and race meetings.[5] He provided the illustrations for a contributor who wrote under the name of Crascredo, giving rise to speculation that this was Simpson himself.[6] He used the pseudonym The Wag for cartoons and children's books.[7] He designed a dinner service decorated with hunting scenes for Royal Doulton. His industry was prodigious: five long books, four of which required a huge amount of research, written and published within five years, as well as numerous drawings and paintings, though after 1926 he no longer submitted any work to the Royal Academy. To achieve all this he was frequently away from home. Ruth saw little of him and they led separate lives.

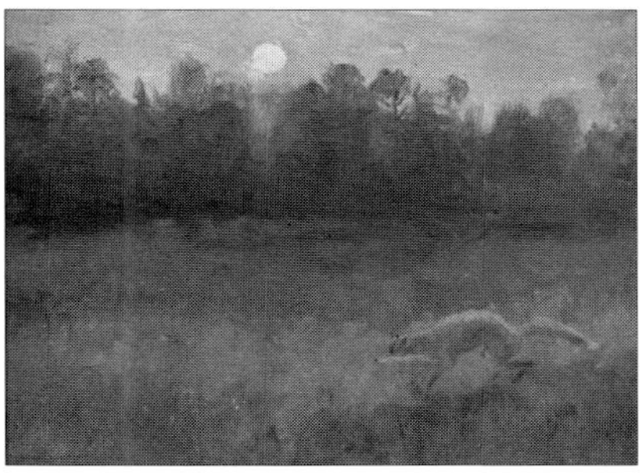

Stealing from the Spinney
1926, oil on canvas, 14 x 18 in
Photograph by Venture, Truro

RIGHT
Derby Day
Courtesy of The National
Horseracing Museum, Newmarket

BELOW RIGHT
Grand National, Aintree 1928
Gouache on board, 21.5 x 30 in
Dunedin Art Gallery, New Zealand

BOTTOM RIGHT
In the Paddock, Ascot
Oil on canvas, 20.5 x 29 in
Courtesy of Sotheby's New York

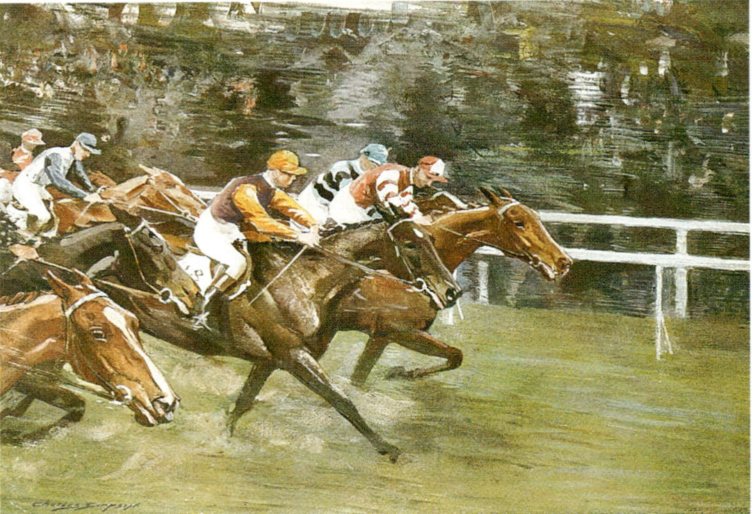

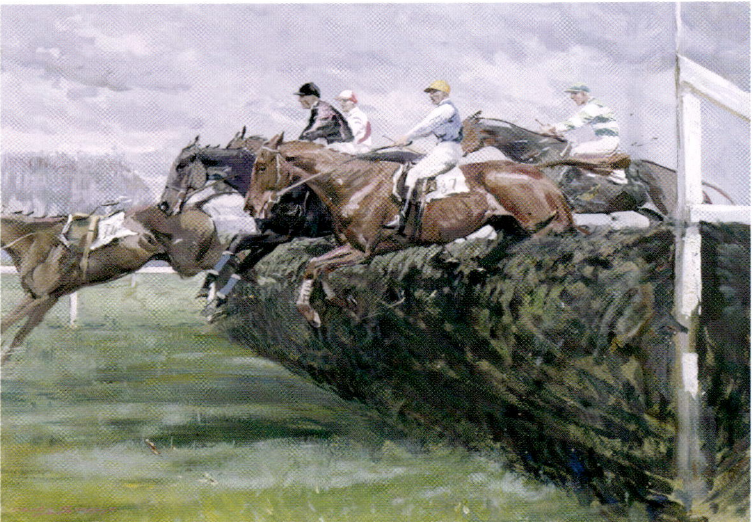

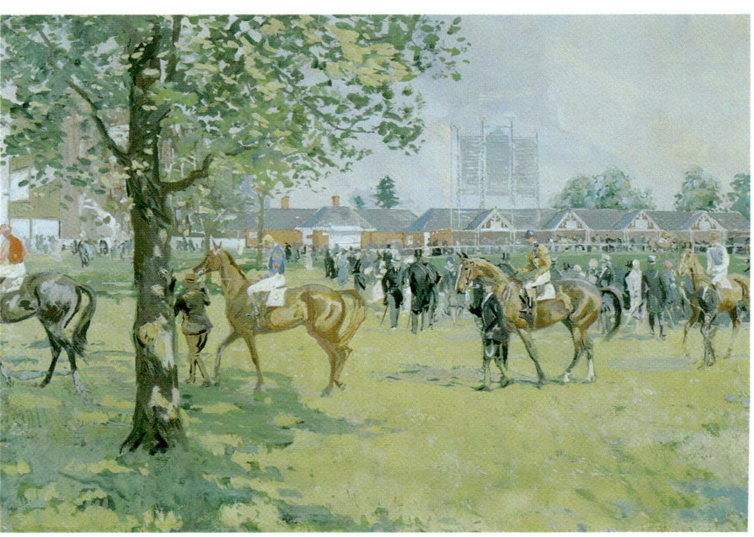

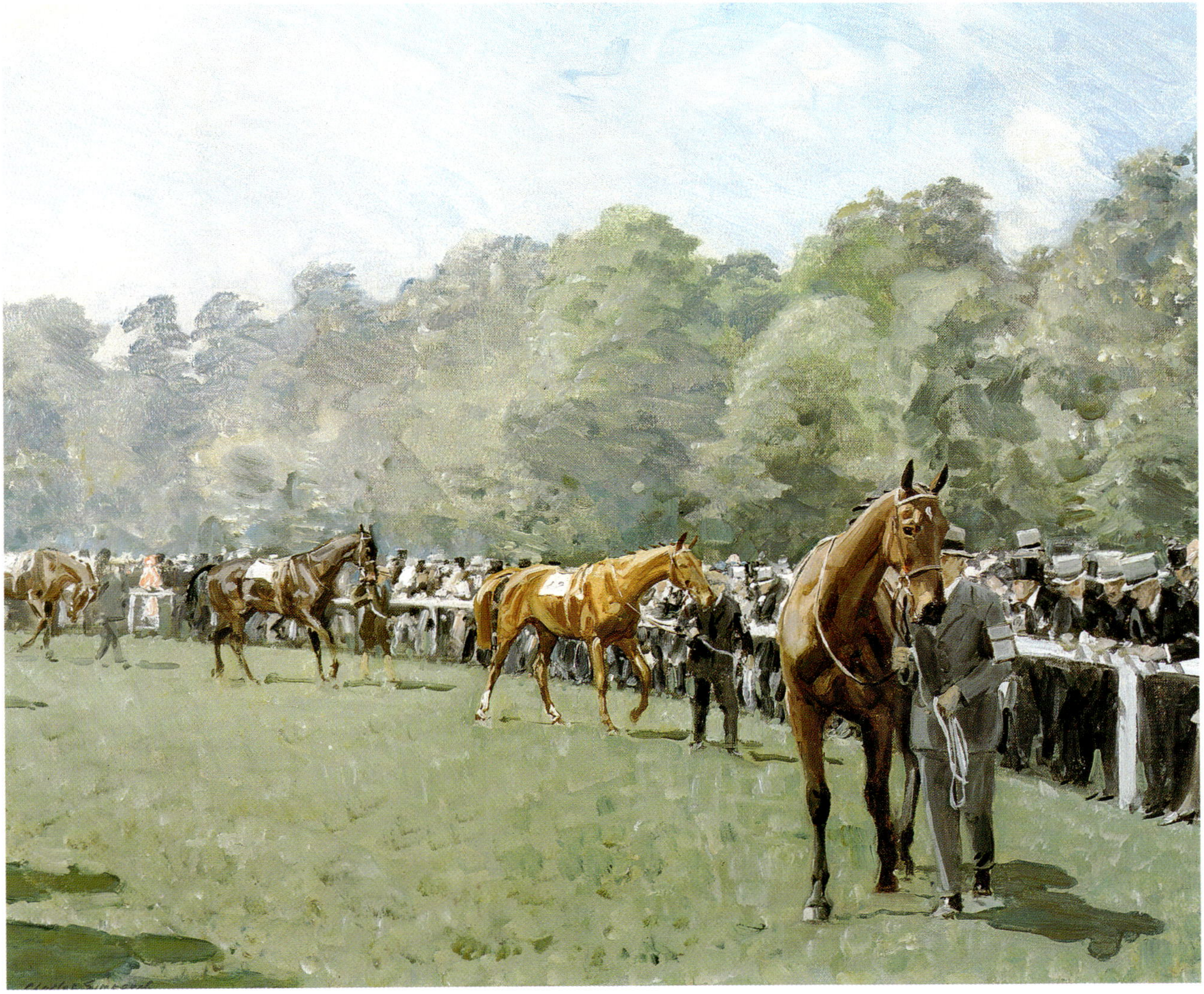

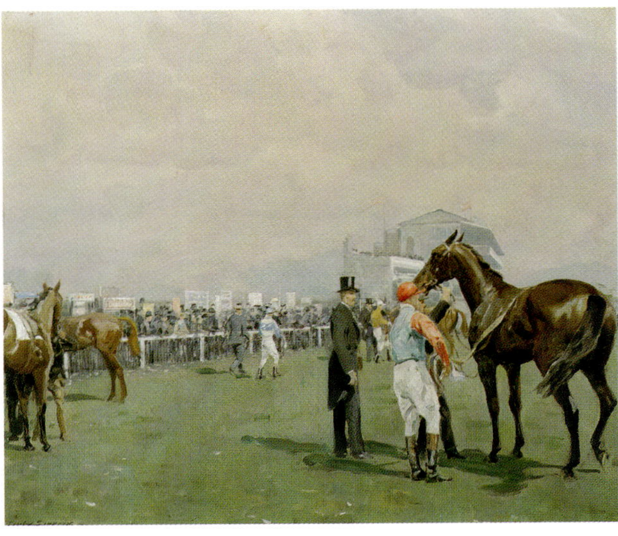

ABOVE
The Collecting Ring, Ascot
Oil on canvas, 20 x 24 in
Courtesy of Sotheby's New York

LEFT
Unsaddling after the Derby
Oil on canvas, 20 x 24 in
Courtesy of Sotheby's New York

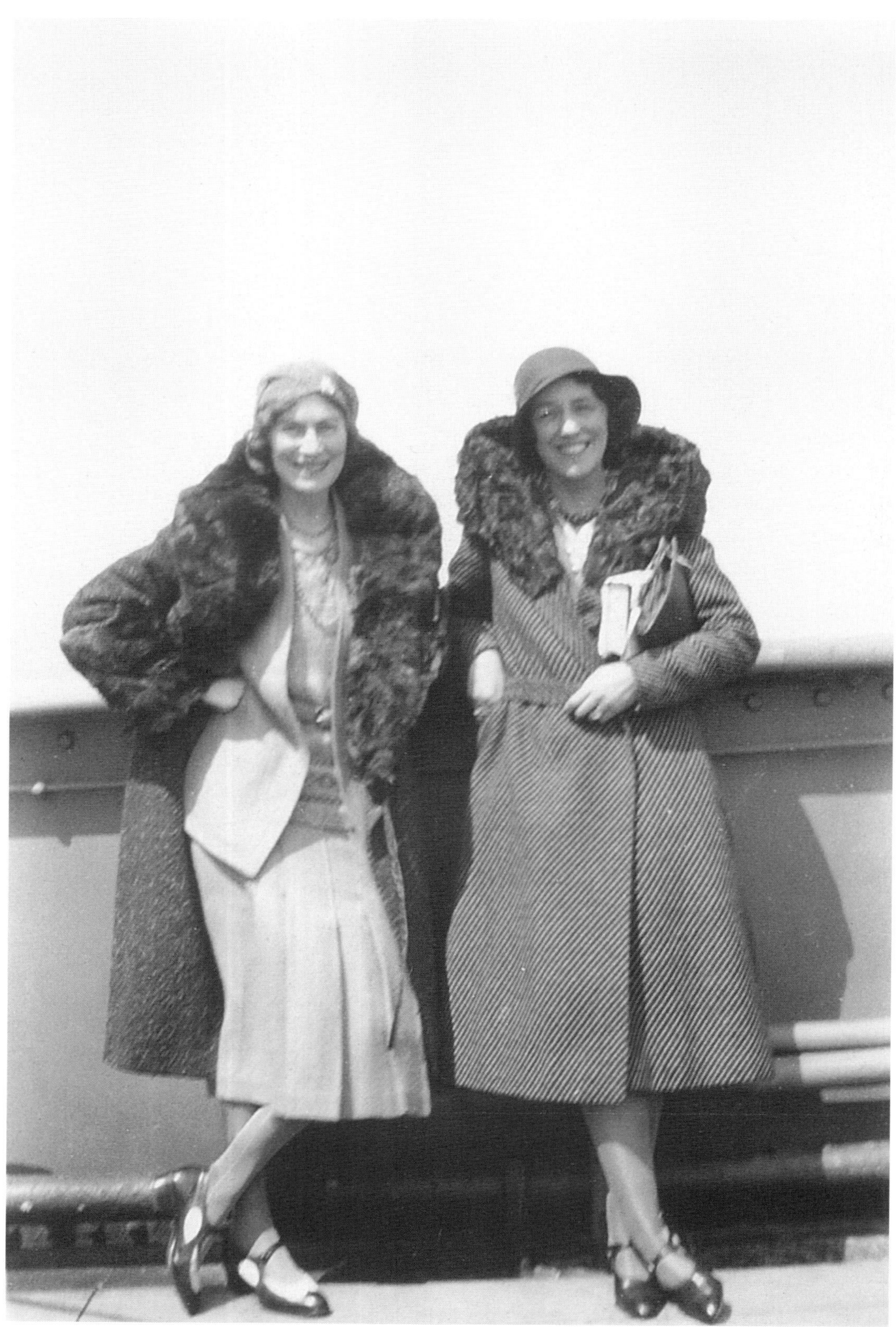

Colombo: The Voyage
of the SS Ranpura

For Ruth it had been a wrench to leave Cornwall. In St Ives she had been part of the artistic community, a continuation of her student days in Newlyn. She took an active role in the teaching and management of the school and was known as a portrait painter of promise. She had exhibited in London, Edinburgh and Plymouth, and had been praised for 'a freedom and freshness of technique that positively exhilarates'. 'Mrs Simpson shows how a portrait can be also made a real picture.'[1] Her subjects were her family and friends: her mother and father, Crosbie Garstin and Commander Bradshaw. Her best paintings were of other women of her own age, with whom she was able to empathise and whose dresses of contemporary materials brightened her palette, as in the portraits of Gertrude Harvey and Ella Naper. In *Maroon and Gold* colour becomes as important as capturing the character of the sitter, probably one of her students, who is posed in her dark purple dress against a simple background of glowing cadmium. Colour replaces names in the titles of her paintings – *A Study in Yellow, Orange and Green, The Yellow Jumper.* Her portraits of men, such as that of the American writer and illustrator of children's books Frank Verbeck, resident in St Ives, are darker in tone.

She had come a long way from her days as a student of Stanhope Forbes, and her sympathetic studies of modern twentieth-century women were developing towards still brighter colour and greater simplification. But she found life in London very different. She was more isolated, without students or artist friends to pose for her. She was neither well known nor forceful enough to gain commissions. She lacked a studio and the routine of going to work in it. She had never had much confidence in her ability and it didn't help that Walter was so prolific and successful. Within two or three weeks of meeting him she had confessed to her mother that encouraging as he was, she wished that he would leave her alone to get on at her own pace.

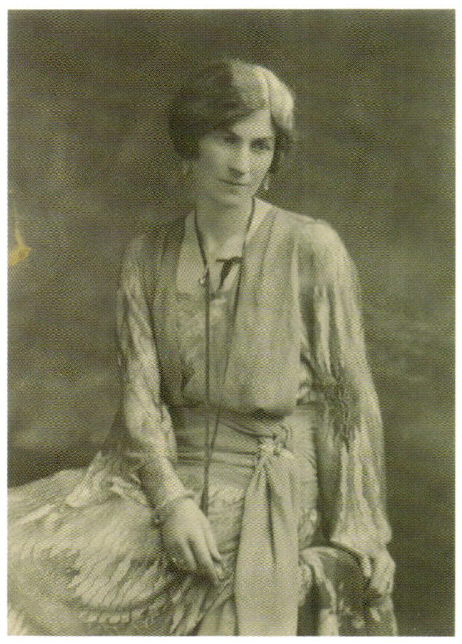

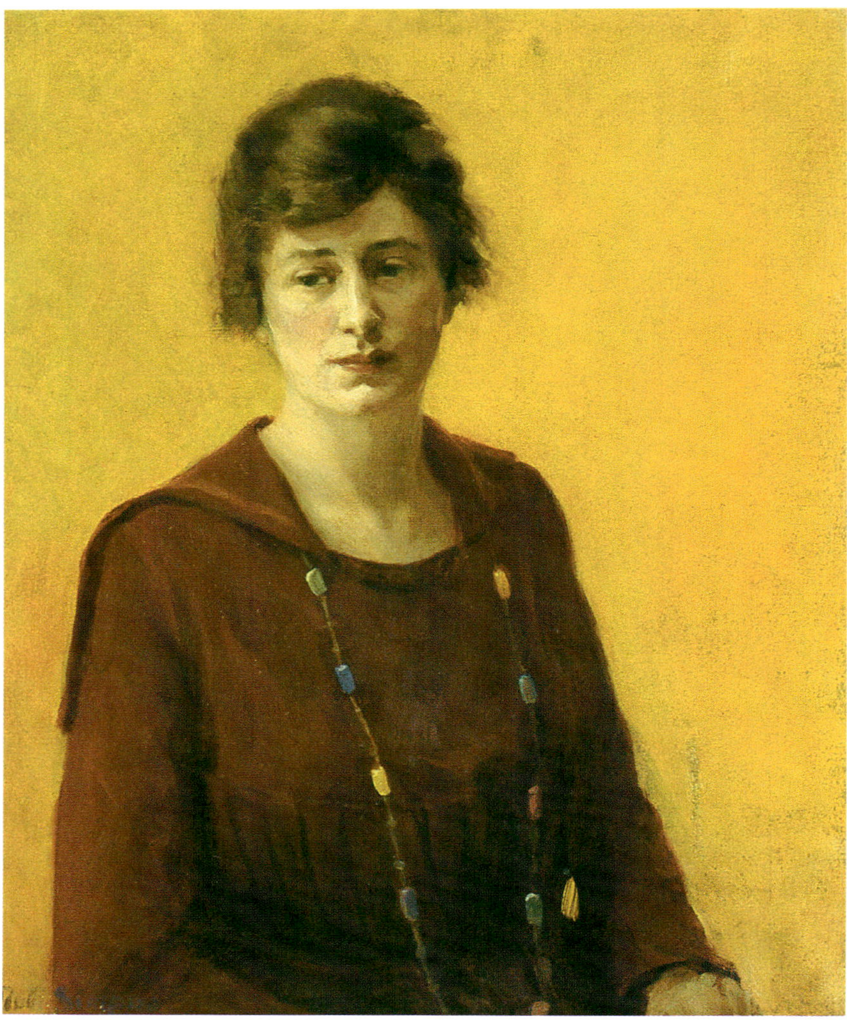

She had talent, but was discouraged by his greater talent and his appetite for work. She stopped painting.

Walter never took a holiday, finding his days in the hunting field or on the racecourse holiday enough. Ruth went without him, going abroad for the first time in the summer of 1924, almost as soon as they moved to London. Her passport gave her height as 5'5½"; her eyes were blue, her hair was brown and she looked very attractive in the photograph. She crossed from Dover to Calais and travelled on to Switzerland with friends. When she returned, their daughter Leonora was on the front cover of the *Woman's Pictorial*, reproduced in colour from Walter's Royal Academy picture of that year. *The Pergola* is a touching portrait; the wide-eyed child of about eight or nine stands with one hand holding the trellis and the other clutching her doll. She wears a round sunhat and a white dress that is tinted green by the light filtering through the foliage.

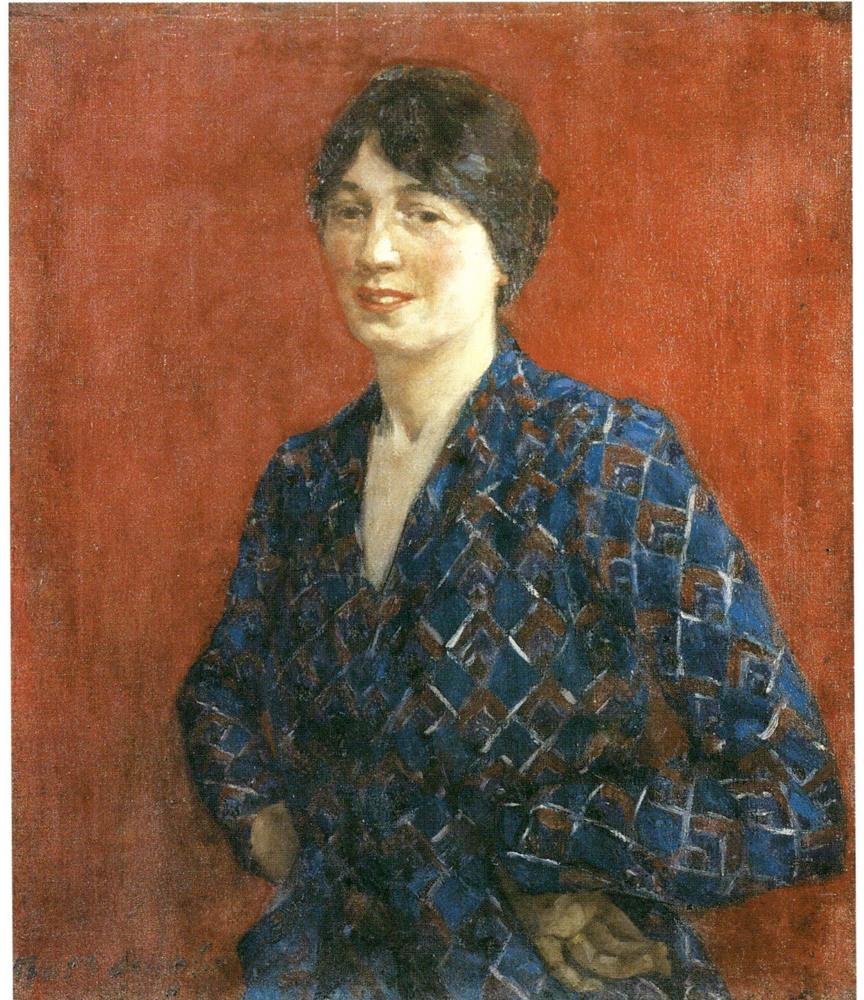

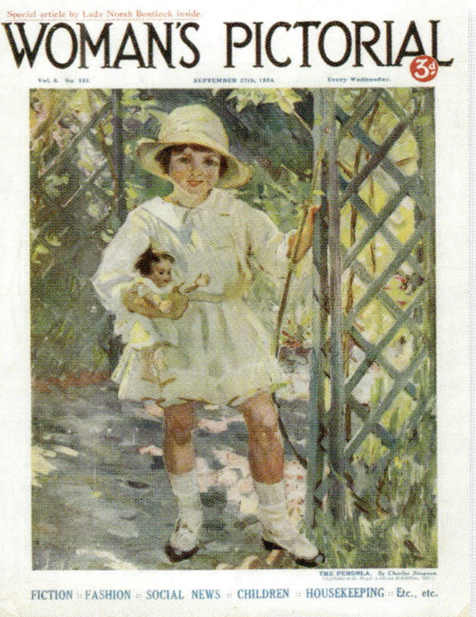

ABOVE
The Pergola
Charles Simpson
Illustration on cover of *Woman's Pictorial*
RA 1924, oil on canvas, 40 x 30 in
Royal Cornwall Museum, Truro

LEFT
Ella Naper
Ruth Simpson
Oil on canvas, 24 x 20 in

They lived in Brook Green, Hammersmith, and Ruth's London friends were better off than the artists they knew in Cornwall. Life was more expensive and Walter never stinted himself. He liked to stay in decent hotels; he enjoyed a good meal followed by port and a mild Havana cigar. His appetite was legendary and double portions were the norm. He belonged to the Arts Club and the Garrick, where the sporting artist Lionel Edwards remembered him and Munnings together as riotous company. He expected Ruth and Leonora to have whatever they wanted, but it was Ruth who worried about money. Walter had no aptitude for finance, and although *El Rodeo* was a success as a book and an exhibition, they were living beyond their means. Walter dedicated *Leicestershire and Its Hunts* to his father, sending him a de luxe edition, but then he had to ask him for help with his overdraft. The Major-General transferred £40 to his bank account to reduce the amount.

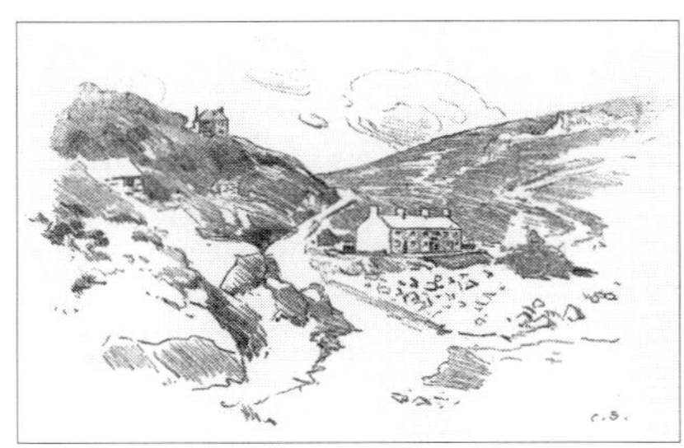

Lamorna: Flagstaff Cottage on the skyline and Morsylla in the terrace
Illustration from *Unknown Cornwall*

Ruth was not happy living in Hammersmith, where during the General Strike of 1926 Walter was attacked by gangs twice within a week as he walked home from his rented studio. They moved to Holland Park, where he had once lived as a child when his father was at the War Office. Here Ruth, who was always open to every infection, became unwell. The constant vomiting and diarrhoea, the high temperatures and headaches, left her weak and exhausted. Her illness was diagnosed as paratyphoid. The symptoms lasted for months and she thought that only in Cornwall could she recover. Walter wanted to move no further out of town than Richmond but in 1930 they rented Morsylla in Lamorna Cove. It was the third in a terrace of four cottages, built of local granite like the quay projecting from the side of the cove, and in the nineteenth century had housed harbour or quarry workers. It stood close to where the stream through the valley emerged from the trees and entered the sea, tumbling over rocks and spreading across the sand. On either side of the harbour the cliffs rose steeply. Ruth and Leonora moved in, Walter kept the flat in Holland Park.

Ruth's recovery was slow. She was always tired, the symptoms would recur and she spent days in bed. Leonora was an angel and they were both looked after by their housekeeper, Ribbie. When not feeling too unwell Ruth would have tea with John and Houghton Birch at Flagstaff Cottage, with Alfred and Cecily Sidgwick at Trewoofe Orchard or with Jessica Heath and her daughter Nancy at Menwinnion. Early in the year her life was brightened considerably by a proposal from a friend from Harrogate, Kathleen Whitehead, that she should join her in the spring on a cruise to Colombo. She made up her mind to get better by then. At the beginning of February Walter wrote: 'My own darling – it's come.' He drew a cartoon figure leaping for joy, a wide grin on its face. At last the cheque for £750 had arrived from Victor Emanuel, the balance owing on the group of pictures that Walter had painted for Rockingham Castle. It had been a strain waiting to be paid and Ruth now sent off to Dorothy's, the London clothes shop, for summer dresses on approval. Ella Naper came to help her choose but in the end they sent them back. Ella started to cut out and sew a dress for her.[2]

Ruth had her vaccinations and then on the first day of March she woke early with a very bad pain that got worse as the day went on. She remained in bed with hot-water bottles. Ella called the doctor, who diagnosed appendicitis. She could have no solid food but had to live on Bengers and Ovaltine. She thought it would be impossible now to accompany Kathleen Whitehead, but Kay had a suggestion. They had planned to join the boat at Marseilles, but if Ruth thought she could get to London they could board at Woolwich. It would save the long and difficult rail journey to the south of France. Ruth was determined not to let Kathleen down – or herself.

Walter returned on his motorcycle and went to see Ella Naper's pottery, the wood and corrugated-iron studio at the top of the valley. She had given it up after the death of her partner in the business, Kate Westrup. It stood empty and he planned to take it over. On Good Friday there were immense crowds in the cove and the St Buryan brass band played right outside the house. Ruth packed her trunks and wrote a letter to Walter, leaving it in her chest of drawers 'in case anything happened'. Friends came to say goodbye. With Leonora, she caught the train from Penzance to Paddington, where Walter, who had ridden back earlier, met them. The following day she spent in bed; she was sick, in pain and suffering from colitis. She hoped a sea voyage would cure her. Walter was working on pictures for *The Sketch* and *The Tatler* and Leonora went off to her grandparents in Yorkshire.

The special train left Liverpool Street station at 10.40 a.m. on Friday 17 April 1931. At the King George V Dock, Ruth had to be supported on both sides as she boarded the SS *Ranpura*, 16,600 tons with two tall funnels, of the P&O India Mail and Passenger Service. She went straight to bed in her cabin. She slept well and at Southampton the next day sent off thirteen postcards and two letters. The ship rolled a lot in the Bay of Biscay but at Gibraltar she went on deck for the first time, sat in the sun and drank a sherry before lunch. She went ashore at Marseilles and visited Aix with Kathleen. On the first day out into the Mediterranean she felt less pain and the following evening she danced with a tea-planter returning to Ceylon. W.A. McMichael and T.A. Slack, who worked for the British American Tobacco Company in Bangkok, attached themselves to the two ladies and escorted them ashore at Port Said, where they had dinner together. Through the Suez Canal Ruth wilted in the heat but stayed up dancing much longer. Her pain had gone.

She was becoming very fond of Tom Slack, dancing with him in the evenings and talking on deck in the moonlight. She wore her gold dress for the farewell dinner and ball and the four dined at a separate table. Mr Slack gave Ruth presents, a box of Indochina cigarettes and a blue silk handkerchief. They danced the foxtrot, waltz, polka, blues and Paul Jones to such tunes as *You're driving me crazy*, *He's my secret passion*, *Little white lies* and *Just a little closer*. Three weeks after leaving London they arrived in Colombo and transferred to the Galle Face Hotel, where the men too stayed the night. The next morning Ruth said goodbye to Tom, who was continuing on the *Ranpura* to Bangkok. 'It tore my heart out,' she wrote in her diary. 'I was happy with him.' She watched from the hotel as

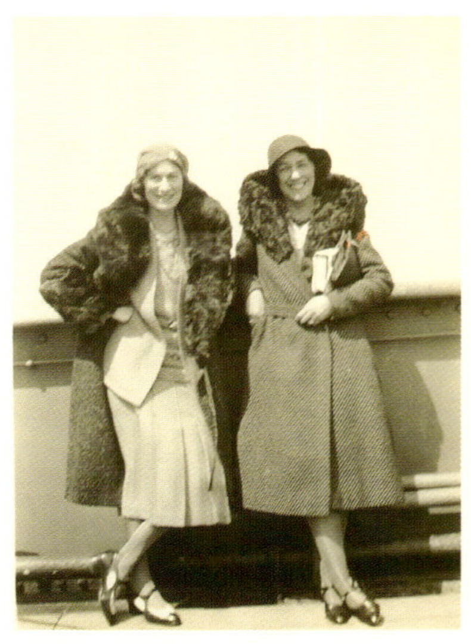

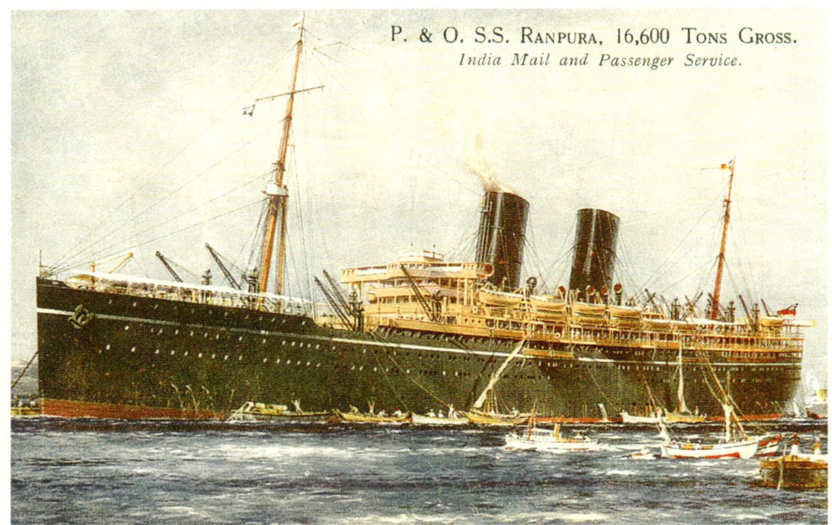

ABOVE
Ruth Simpson and Kay Whitehead on board
the SS *Ranpura*, 1931, photograph
WCAA

ABOVE RIGHT
Postcard of SS *Ranpura*, WCAA

Leonora as a bridesmaid c1930
Photograph

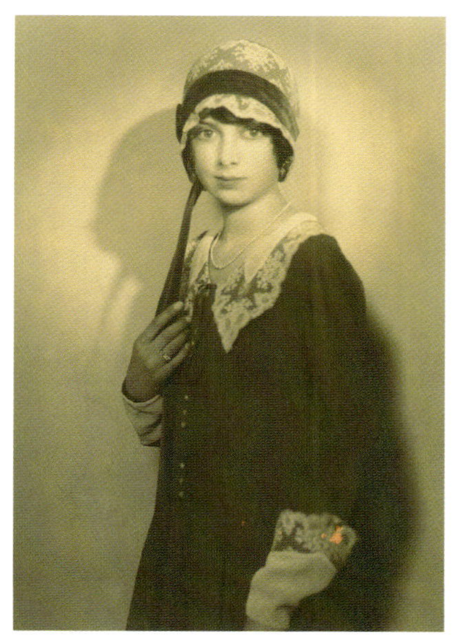

the boat left harbour, following it through binoculars until it was out of sight. Tom wrote to tell her that he too had gazed and gazed at the Galle Face, wondering if she was watching the boat sail away. He went below with an ache in his heart that 'I could not have believed possible and it remains'.

Ruth went to Kandy, shopped in the bazaars and rode in a rickshaw, but was miserable without Tom. With Kathleen, she boarded the *Otranto* for the return voyage, but the round of cocktail parties, dinners and dances had become boring, though she felt happier when Tom sent her a marconigram. They passed through the canal again and early one morning saw the plume of smoke coming from Vesuvius. At Naples she left the *Otranto* without regret. They spent five days in Rome and four in Paris, before the difficult return to London. Tom had sent a wiregram that Walter had opened. To make matters worse, the next day the post brought a whole pack of letters and cards that Tom had sent to Harrogate and Leonora had innocently forwarded. 'Awful day,' Ruth wrote in her diary. As quickly as she could she caught the Riviera Express from Paddington to Penzance. At Morsylla she was pleased to find that Colonel Paynter had had the larder turned into a bathroom.

Walter went as usual to Ascot and forgot Leonora's birthday. A week later he came down on his new motorcycle. As Ella's studio wasn't ready, he worked at Cappy, an empty cottage a little way up the valley. His father was writing a history of the Lincolnshire regiment and Walter was doing the illustrations. Ruth usually met the postman at the door but when three parcels arrived from Siam she could hardly conceal them. They contained pottery and twenty-six yards of cloth. She was very troubled about them and surprised when Walter didn't seem to mind. He even suggested that she might like a drawing to send to Tom Slack in return. She went to Cappy and chose one of the new war drawings and a rodeo sketch. With Walter in the studio she could write to Tom without interruption and walk up the road to post her letters. She had an arrangement with Kay; Tom would send his letters to her and she would enclose them in a letter to Ruth.

She felt she had to get away for a spell and went to stay with friends in St Ives, where she had her photograph taken to send to Bangkok. But the next day Walter telephoned and made her promise to come home as he said he was leaving before the weekend. She was annoyed when she found that he wasn't going until Monday. He finished all the illustrations except the frontispiece and delivered them to his father at Tavistock, on his way back to London; the Major General was delighted with them. At Morsylla, Ruth was miserable in the evenings and read poetry books lent her by Ella Naper. She wrote to Tom and waited for letters from him via Kay. But if she felt neglected by Walter, crushed by him as a person and an artist, her holiday romance with Tom Slack offered no permanent solution.

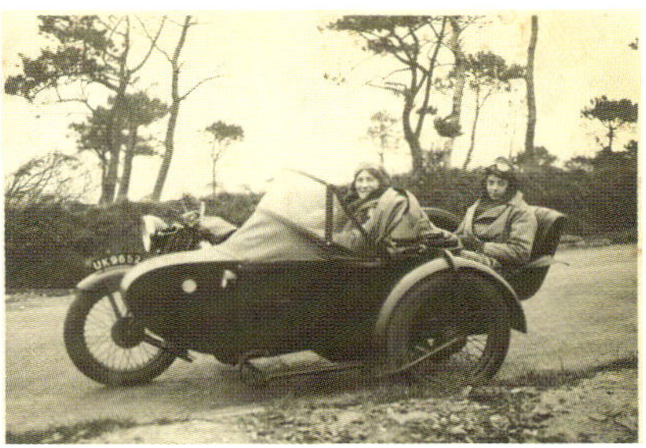

Ruth and Leonora in the sidecar of the motorcycle on Goss Moor, returning from Tavistock to Lamorna, 1931, photograph WCAA

Tavistock Goose Fair
Gouache, 20.5 x 28.5 in

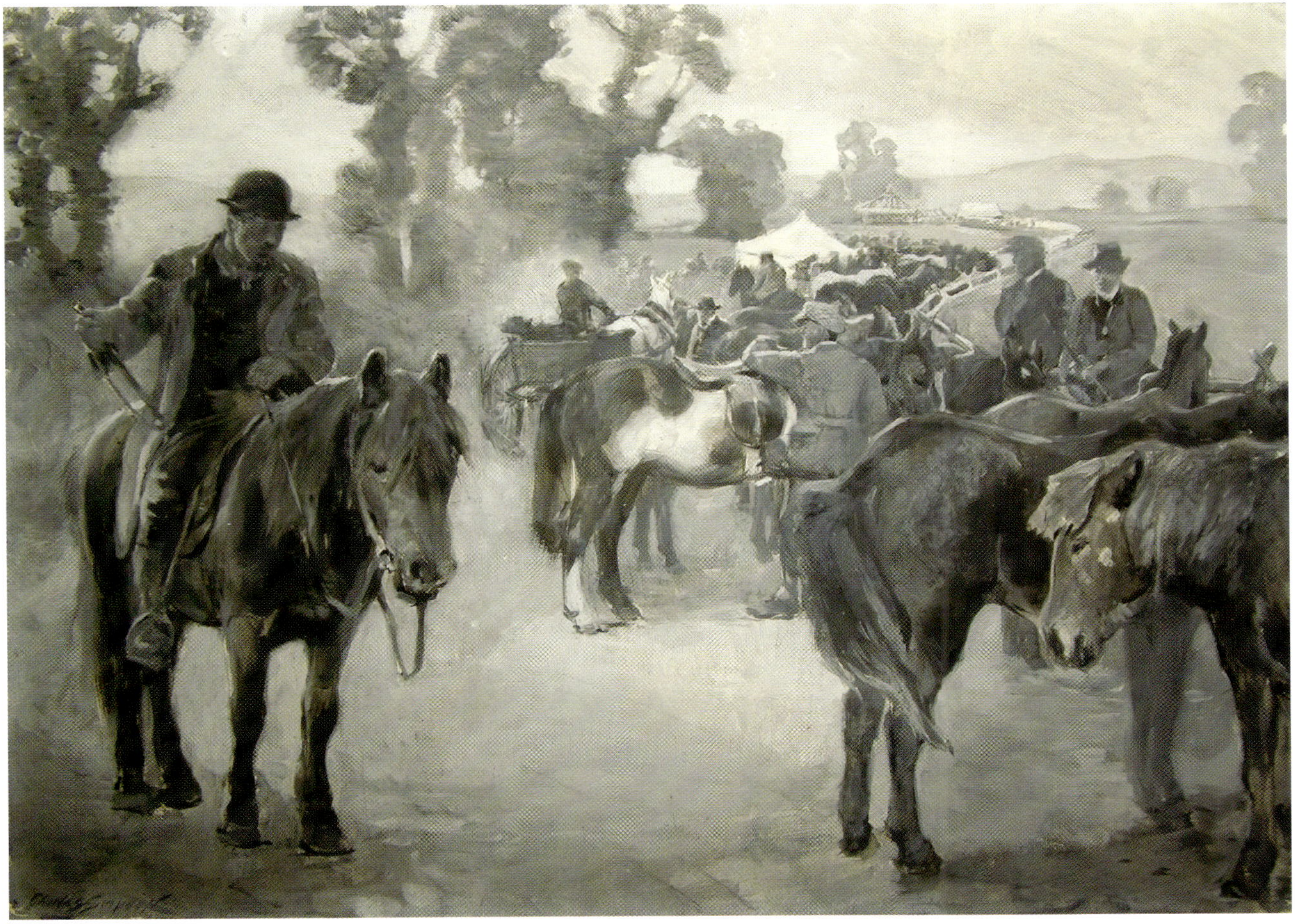

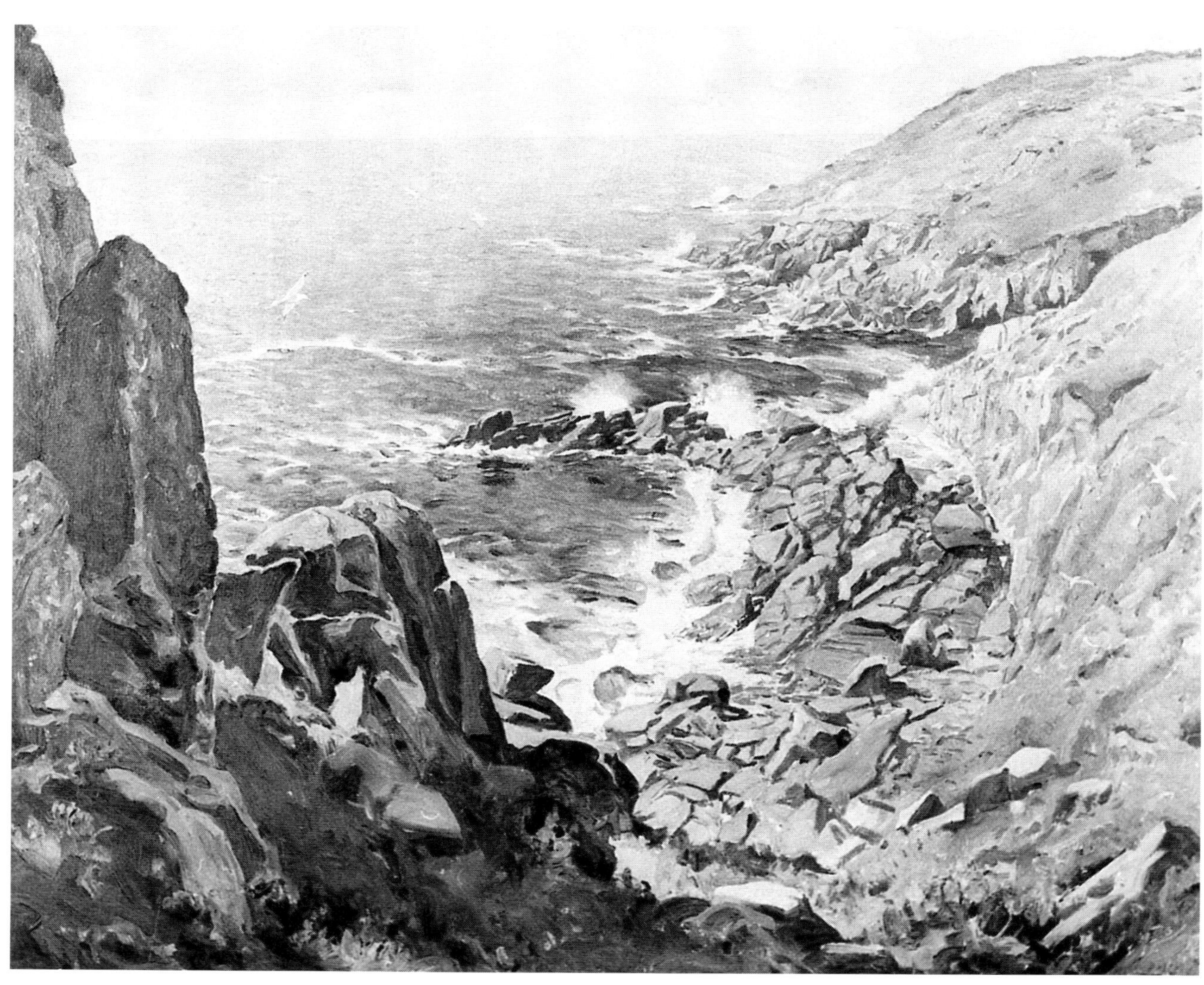

Carn Barges
Oil on canvas, 30 x 36 in
Courtesy of David Lay Auctions

CHAPTER TEN

Duncan's: Photography and Art

Ruth was distracted from her unhappiness that summer by the news
that William Duncan was selling his house and going to live in London.[1]
Duncan's, as the house was always called, stood high on the cliffs on the
western side of the cove, with magnificent views along the coast and over the
sea. It was approached by a lane that left the road further up the valley and
passed Cliff House. The main attraction was its situation; the house itself
was quite small and had been built from plans drawn up by Charles Naper.
With Leonora and Houghton Birch, Ruth went to view it and Leonora
approved. Ruth went to the estate agents in Penzance and made an offer of
£1500; Mr Duncan stuck to his asking price of £1600. She went to the Halifax
building society to discuss a mortgage and in Tavistock Walter broached
the subject with his father. His grandparents had left money in a trust for
Leonora. His father thought that since the Wall Street crash property was
a better investment than stocks, but the trustees wouldn't advance more
than two-thirds of the price. Ruth feared that the opportunity would
slip through their hands, but by September the house was theirs with a
mortgage for which Walter's father stood surety.

When Ruth's parents were staying at Bude in north Cornwall, she joined
them for two weeks' holiday. Her sister Rose with her daughter Deirdre
was with them and she also saw Belle Leader, who after her husband's
death in the war had moved there. She then spent a few days at Tavistock,
where Walter arrived from London with a beautiful turquoise handbag
for her and news that at such a difficult time for business he had secured
several commissions, a screen for Mrs Emanuel, more paintings for Guy
Paget and two pictures of the Fernie Hunt.

Back in Lamorna Ruth cut out curtains and chintz covers for the
settee and chairs, while Leonora went up to the house to distemper
the walls. Walter worked on his paintings at Lamorna Vean, Ella's old

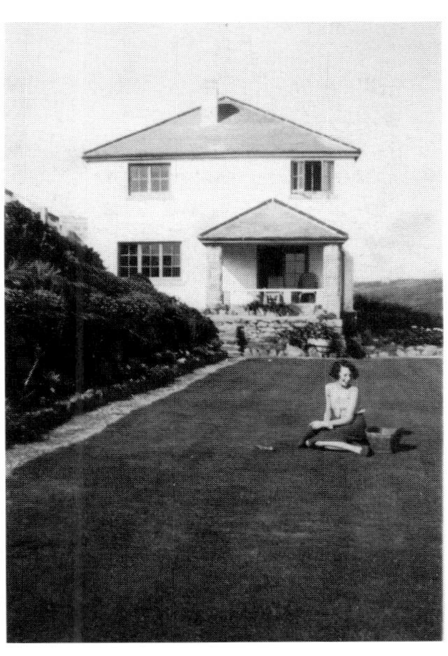

Leonora on the lawn at Duncan's
Photograph, WCAA

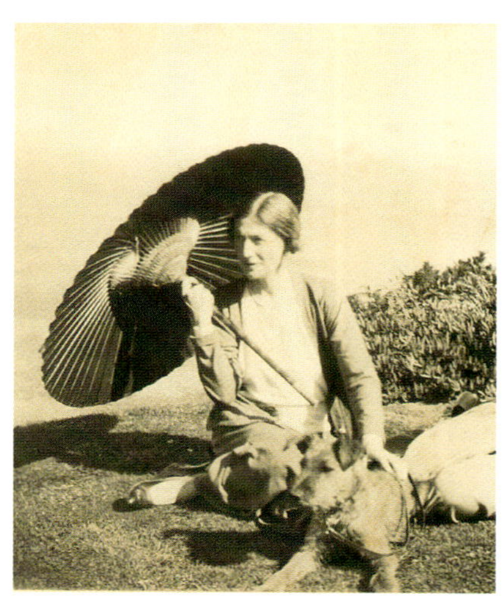

Ruth in the garden at Duncan's with
a Siamese parasol sent by Tom Slack
Photograph, WCAA

pottery. The bank was pressing them to reduce their overdraft and Ruth
went to Penzance to secure an extension. One glorious October morning
she and Leonora picked ten and a half pounds of blackberries and Ribbie
made jam in the afternoon. Before the end of the month Walter left for
his show at Doncaster Art Gallery, 'Racing and Sporting Pictures'. They
included paintings that he had done in September during St Leger Week,
when he set up an easel on the course and in Tattersall's sale ring. The
largest work was *The Finish of the St Leger*, painted from sketches, notes
and impressions and completed in the studio. It showed the winner,
Sandwich, followed by the rest of the field. It caught the movement of
the horses and the excitement of the crowd and was priced at £500. The
painting of the first day of the race meeting had been completed on the
spot and, like the yearling sale picture, was £200. There were paintings of
scenes at Epsom, Ascot and the water jump at the Grand National. The
exhibition was opened by Major Guy Paget, who suggested that buying a
painting was a better bet than putting money on a horse. The councillors
took him at his word and bought two paintings for the gallery, including
the St Leger finish.

While Walter was celebrating in Doncaster, Ruth fell ill again with
all the symptoms of paratyphoid. A gale was blowing into the cove and
huge seas broke over the quay. She stayed in bed, feeling depressed and
only bucking up when Ella called. She went into Penzance hospital for
examination under chloroform; the results showed no trace of paratyphoid
and no other irregularities. She needed more tests for the colitis, bouts of
which troubled her for the rest of her life.

In the new year they moved into Duncan's. Walter wanted to spend
more time in Lamorna now, painting the coastal scenery that he could
see from the house. He told Vulliamy that he wished to return to his
earlier style, and Vulliamy said he was very glad to hear it.[2] But it was
always necessary to leave Lamorna to find work. His most immediately
marketable paintings were scenes of hunting and horse racing. His 'Racing
and Sporting Pictures' continued its round of northern cities and Simpson
needed to be there for the openings, to meet possible clients and to make
contacts. Guy Paget was always ready to oblige with a well-polished speech.
It went to the Derby and Leicester municipal galleries, and at the Mappin
Art Gallery in Sheffield two paintings were bought for the permanent
collection, *Mallard Drake in Immature Plumage* for £20 and *Sunset on
Dartmoor* for £10, hardly spectacular prices but the number of people
visiting the exhibition was impressive – nearly forty-four thousand. Under

a different title, 'Paintings of Wildlife and Sport', the collection went to the Russell-Cotes Art Gallery and Museum in Bournemouth, where the gallery bought for £100 his major early painting *Duck Shooting – the Punt Gunner*, the Gold Medal winner in Paris in 1924. In impressive scale – it is eight feet wide – it shows a sunlit sheet of water and the sweeping movement of the ducks as they rise in alarm. The wildfowler in his boat is hidden in the distant rushes, revealed only by the barrel of a gun and a puff of smoke. The bird that has been hit falls head downwards in contrasting shape and motion. It is an impressionist painting, the golden sunlight made to glitter on the canvas by the use of touches of pure colour.

Simpson was in demand for child portraits, which also took him away from home. He had stayed with Lady Leconfield at Petworth House in Sussex to paint a portrait of her daughter, who afterwards sent him a thank-you letter with a child's picture of her pony. He got on well with children, writing letters to his young sitters and sending them drawings. One of his tricks – which amazed adults as well – was to draw with both hands simultaneously, the two hands joining up perfectly for the finished animal. He was naturally left-handed; as a child he had been given sixpence a week if he had managed his knife and fork properly at every meal. He became ambidextrous, but throughout his life always painted with his left hand.

A Mr Todhunter from Essex wanted him to paint his daughter on horseback with two dogs for a fee of one hundred guineas. The Comtesse de Pret Roose wanted a portrait of her two boys with her white Alsatian. 'Like all people who have their money in America,' wrote the agent, 'things are not so good for her at the moment, so you will have to be very reasonable.' *Michael and John* is a good example of his paintings in the thirties of the children of wealthy clients. They are riding in Rotten Row, Hyde Park, though without the Alsatian. The two boys in pale jumpers and jodhpurs sit confidently on their ponies and look out and down at the viewer. The sunlight coming through the gap between two tall trees falls on the boys and catches the necks and shoulders of the ponies, one with head raised, the other lowered. It is all sun and light; such a day it seems could last forever. This sense of permanence was just what his clients wanted and Simpson caught it perfectly in these last years before the Second World War.

He was a contributor to the monthly photographic review *The Gallery*, writing articles on composition and a regular column in which he commented on photographs sent in by readers. These were not holiday snaps but serious work from photographers of all nationalities. The by-line

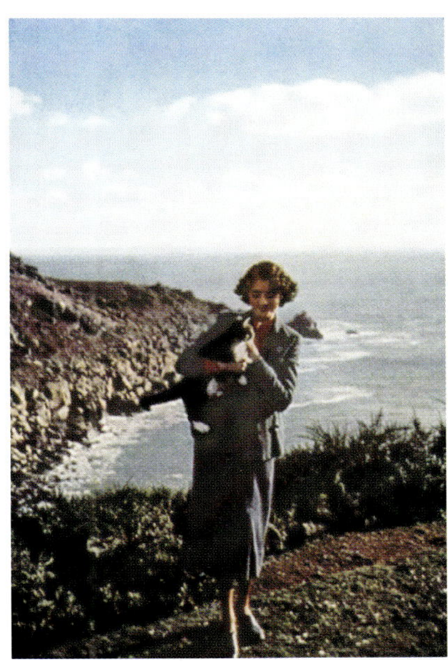

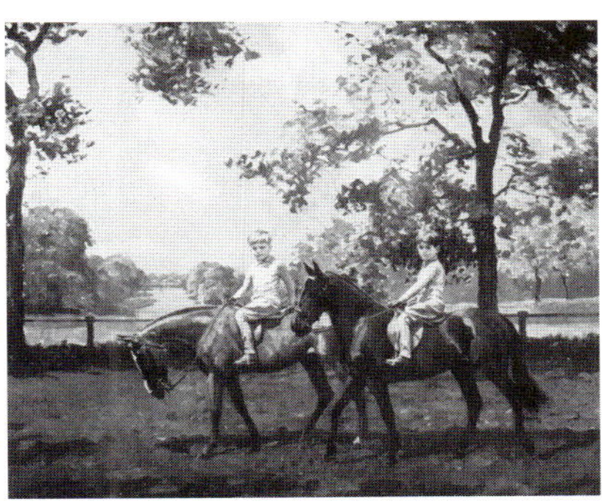

Leonora in the cliff-top garden at Duncan's
From *Photography of the Figure*

Michael and John
Oil on canvas, 40 x 50 in

for the analyses was Charles Simpson R.I. The articles showed every sign
of being written by him and were illustrated with views of the Cornish
coast but were signed E. Gordon Barker, a pen name derived perhaps from
the 'sharp notes' in music. His work in *The Gallery* led to a commission
for *Composition for Photographers: an Artist's Guide*. Its aim was to show
what sort of knowledge an artist must acquire and how it could be adapted
to photography. Simpson does not suggest that a photograph should imitate
art, but it needs to obey the same rules of composition.

The book sheds light on Simpson's own practices and values. The artists
who influenced him most, he says, were John Constable, the first painter to
treat the sky with a vigour equal to his treatment of the earth, and Claude
Monet. The big subjects of landscape – mountains, sunsets and picturesque
ruins – were no longer the only themes. Monet showed in the paintings of
his garden with the lily ponds that other and smaller subjects were enough
if the artist could endow them with feeling. Photography can do this by
taking a familiar scene from an unusual angle, some corner of the field
of vision: shallow water over sand, seaweed along the tide line, heather
like a miniature forest, the face of a quarry in the sun. Design comes first,
recognition second.

In his teaching, writing and practice, Simpson always placed great emphasis
on composition, by whatever name it was called: arrangement, design, pattern
or organisation of space (which E. Gordon Barker thought sounded more
like town planning). A photograph or painting works not through the objects
it portrays but in the way they are arranged. He illustrates this with two
sketches, one of a meadow, stream, cattle, trees and a bridge where nothing
relates. A shift of viewpoint groups the cattle together, the stream connects
the foreground to the bridge in the distance and the whole has pictorial unity.
He had a horror of 'spotty' pictures, where the contents are dotted around in
a naturalistic way without any cohesion. On the other hand, a picture
should not seem too 'hammered out'; however much care is taken with
the composition it should still seem spontaneous.

He considered the introduction of figures the greatest test of an artist's
ability. An indifferent painter will introduce them where they are not
wanted – a river must have a fisherman, a cottage porch an old woman,
a country lane some children picking blackberries. 'So trite! So obvious!'
He advises the study of Gainsborough, Corot and Watteau, who combined
figures and landscape perfectly. An amusing pair of sketches illustrating
some of the basic mistakes of composition shows figures on a quayside.
In the first a man is beheaded by the line of the horizon passing through

his neck, another appears to have been hanged by a rope and a third
has a mast growing out of his head. The second sketch shows how these
misfortunes could have been avoided. In portraits artificiality and absence
of surface quality are the chief faults. The placing of a head should not
make it look like the head on a postage stamp or a railway booking clerk
seen through his pigeonhole. The last chapter deals with nude photography,
most of which he finds dull and lacking the colour that gives life.

In his own photographs of the nude he used light and shadow
– chiaroscuro – to give a sculptural quality to the model, highlights
rounding the form against a plain background. He did not favour posing
the model in the landscape, which was too distracting and too reminiscent
of 'sun-bathing magazines', and he thought that most studio settings only
suggested 'the more tawdry trappings of grand opera'. He preferred a more
formal treatment of the human figure that in its simplicity moved towards
abstraction and he recognised – to his own surprise – similarities with
modern sculpture.

Photography of the Figure, published the following year, continues
from the earlier book. Colour film has become more widely available
and he considers its implications. A picture that may be a satisfying
arrangement of mass and line in black and white can be thrown off
balance by the introduction of colour, drawing the eye away by its strong
accents. The photographer has to use colour to create movement, give
contrast and arrest attention. At twice the price of the earlier book, it
contained over a hundred photographs in colour and monochrome of
children, draped and nude figures, (with examples of his own work),
character studies and portraits. Simpson's writing on photography was
influential in establishing the medium as an art form and for some this is
his most lasting legacy.[3]

For three years he published one book a year and in 1939 Batsford
brought out *Animal and Bird Painting*. Simpson recognises in the
introduction that there is something old-fashioned about the idea of animal
painting. Pictures in gilt frames of cattle and sheep looked down from the
walls of manor houses that have long gone or given way to the sparseness
of modern décor. They were part of a country life that has disappeared,
the horse replaced by the tractor and grazing lands lost beneath bricks and
mortar. His touchstone for an animal painting is *Oxen Going to Work* by
Constant Troyan. It is early morning, the mist hangs about the trees and
the cattle cast long shadows before them. The tall pole of the drover makes
an angle to the flat horizon. Every inch of the canvas conveys the hour of

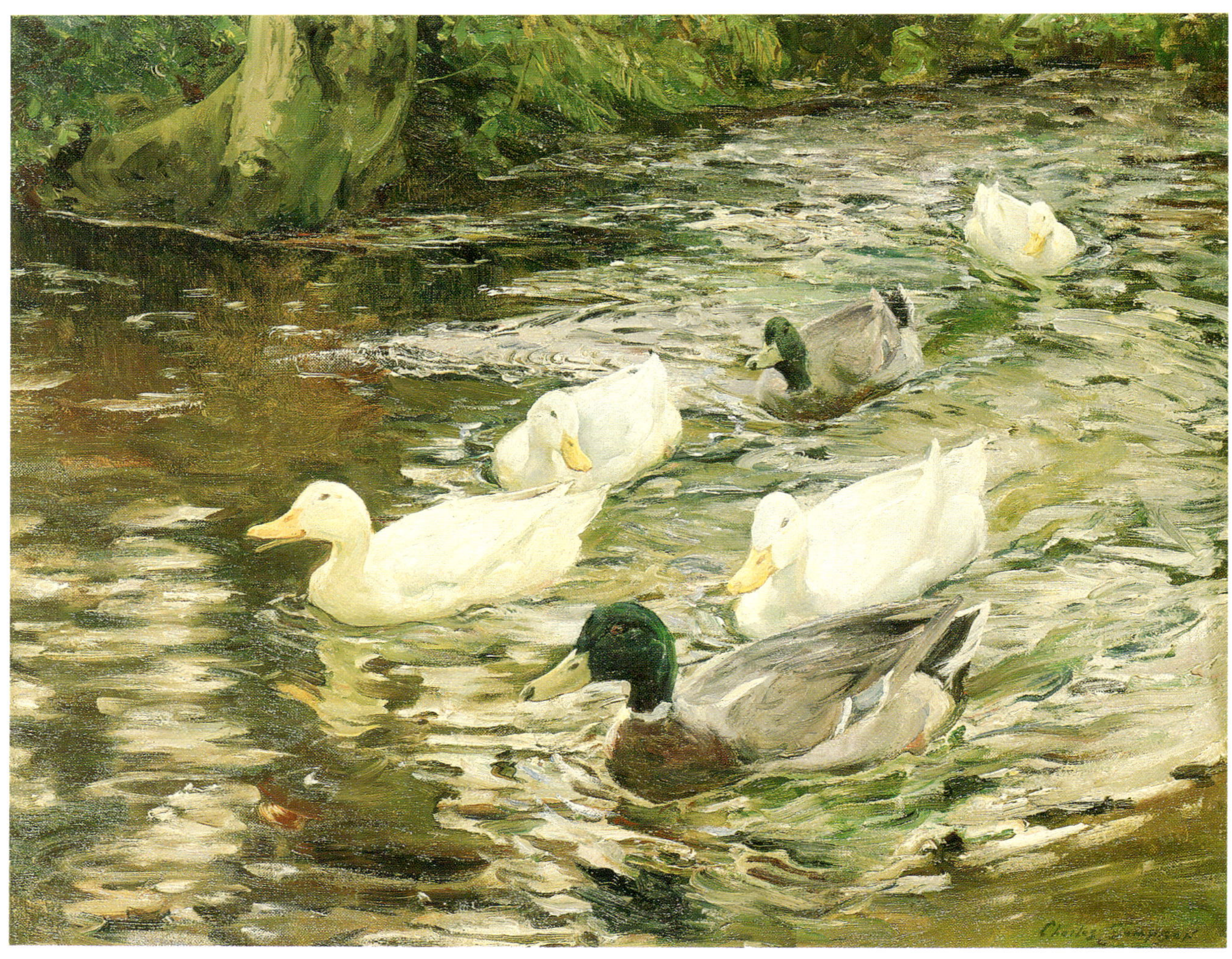

ABOVE
Mallard Drakes and Aylesbury Ducks
Oil on canvas, 24 x 30 in
Courtesy of Burlington Art

PAGE 97 TOP
In the Shade of the Sycamores
Oil on canvas, 32 x 36 in
Courtesy of Burlington Art

PAGE 97 BOTTOM RIGHT
Blue Tits on a Coconut
Oil on canvas, 14 x 10 in

the day. It has grandeur, dignity and simplicity of construction; man and beast are in their oldest relation to the earth.

He admires the Swedish artist Bruno Liljefors – with whom Simpson was often compared – as a painter whose creatures are part of the landscape, blending with it rather than standing out 'like film stars'. Animal painting is mediocre when the artist is so preoccupied with the animal itself that he paints not what he sees but what he knows of its anatomy, the details of bone, muscles and skin. The true artist responds to the weather and time of day, the form of the animal modified by light. It will be different in the brilliance of dawn, the intensity of noon, the glow of the afternoon and the deepening tones of the evening. Beneath cloudy skies the shape is moulded by subtler variations. The animal he paints changes every hour; the light never reveals every surface detail.

In a schematic approach, Simpson devotes a chapter to each animal or

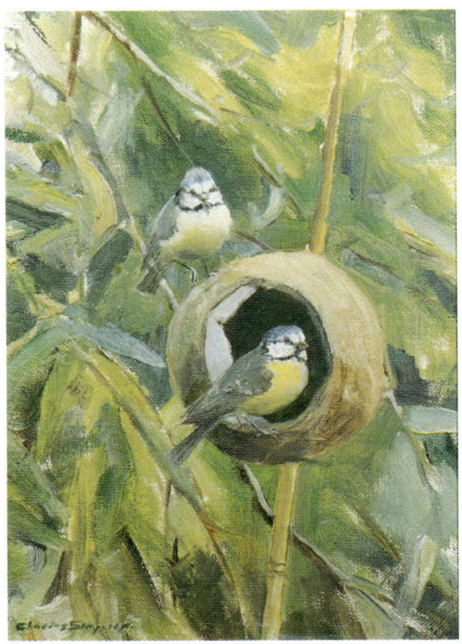

group of animals, beginning with the horse. A.J. Munnings has a sculptor's grasp of form and is the only horse painter who comes near to Stubbs, achieving the sinuosity of his *Hambletonian*. He picks out George Clausen and Arnesby Brown for their paintings of farm animals. Some artists show little understanding of how horses are harnessed. He explains the different methods of yoking, the collars, traces and reins, and gives details of the construction of ploughs. He describes the various breeds of cattle. The most difficult to paint are the reds of Devon and Sussex, as red cows in green pastures create too uniform a harmony of complementary colours. Sheep are irritating to paint because they are restless feeders and when one changes direction the others follow. Arnesby Brown catches the way a flock moves, just as one sheep is about to break away. There is mellow sunlight in Algernon Talmage's *The Young Shepherd* and the figure of the shepherd boy breaks with convention. Only the artist who does not have to earn

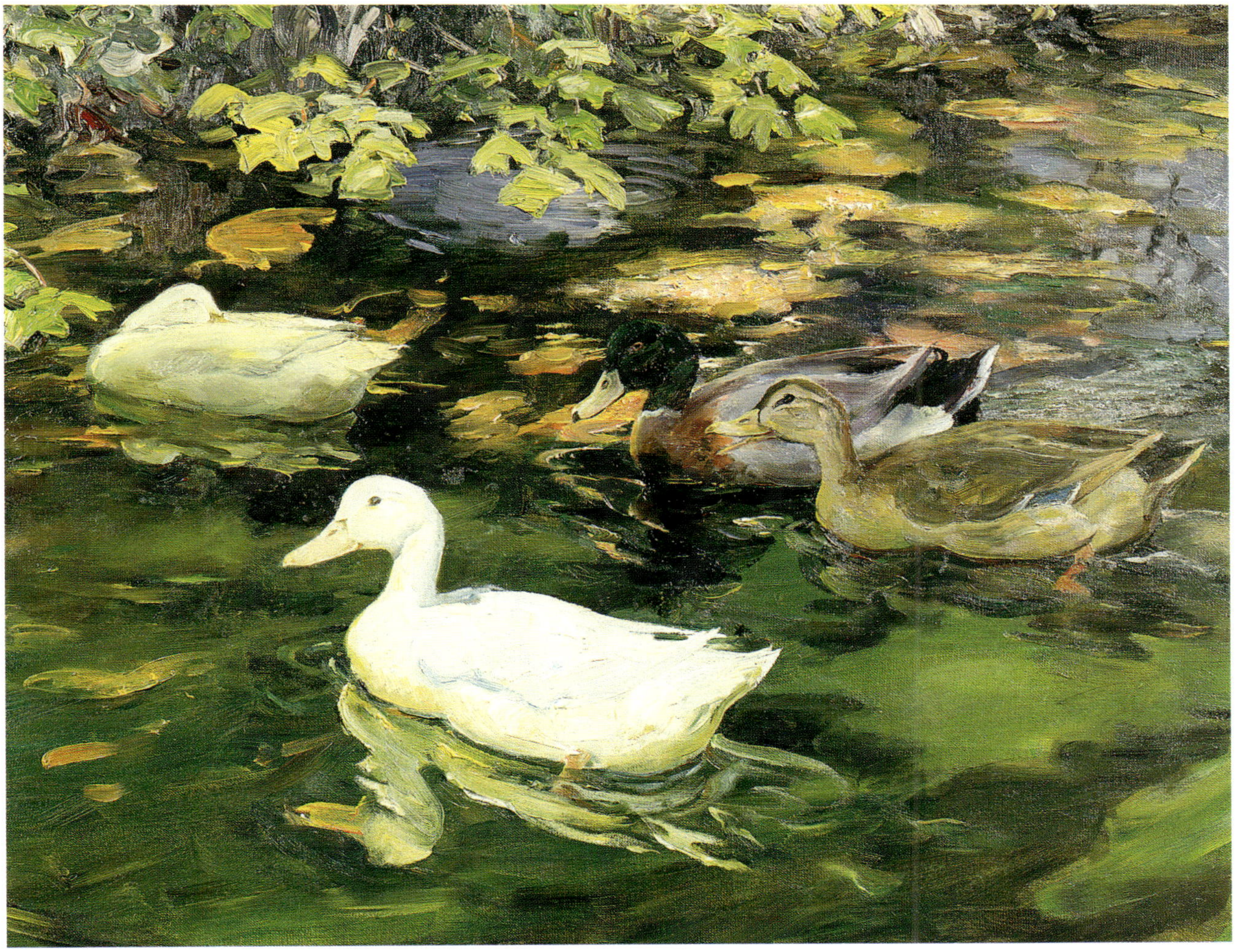

97

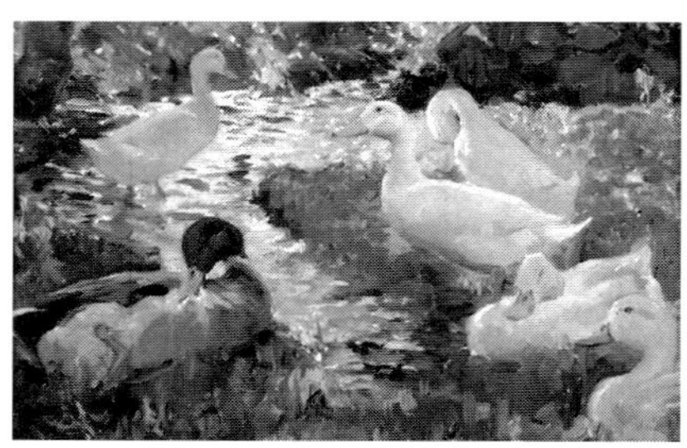

Mallard and Aylesbury Ducks
Oil on canvas, 16 x 24 in
Courtesy of Canterbury Auction Galleries

a living is free to paint as he likes. The huntsman wants a record of the scene that led to the fox's brush mounted on the wall; the breeder requires a picture that shows all the finer points of the animal he has bred. For the true artist, subject is a matter of minor importance. He may treat the same familiar theme time and time again, always finding some new problem of colour or design.

Charles Simpson on animal painting seems a perfect match of author and subject. It should be a fascinating book but in the end it disappoints. It has passages that give the reader an insight into the painting of animals and the problems they present to the artist. His commentaries on particular paintings are interesting and he can describe a scene in a way that brings it vividly alive. He has a vast knowledge of country life, the big game of Africa and European art. But the writing is overloaded with information. The chapter on dogs begins with six pages on their descent from wolves and the different breeds, before looking at Landseer's *The Old Shepherd's Chief Mourner* and Lucy Kemp-Welch's *Trust* as successful examples of a genre that on the whole 'has sunk to the level of the Christmas calendar'. His enjoyably acerbic comments are in the tradition of Stanhope Forbes's 'crits'. The cocks and hens of a certain type of landscape painter are 'feather mops with blobs of sealing wax on their heads'; on the other hand too much detail means 'a descent to the level of some children's annual with pictures of "our feathered friends"'. In their publicity Batsford referred to the book as a labour of love, but for all its passages of insight it seems more laboured than loved.

But at Duncan's Simpson did manage to return to the paintings that gave him most personal satisfaction. Carn Barges is a headland a short walk from the house along the coastal path and here he painted two contrasting pictures from the same spot, *Dying Light, Carn Barges* and *September on the Cornish Coast*. The first was painted on an August evening, when the promontory on the right is dark against the evening light and the lichen-covered granite boulders on the left catch the last rays of the sun. In the second the lighting is reversed and the promontory is luminous while the boulders become a dark mass against the sky, all detail lost. They were exhibited together at the Royal Academy in 1936, his first submission for ten years. Carn Dhu is the headland on the eastern side of the cove and his painting from there of Tregurnow Cliff was shown the following year. He also painted in the valley, returning to his favourite subject of ducks on the Lamorna stream or at Clapper Mill. 'No one can paint ducks like Charles Simpson,' was the received opinion in Newlyn and Penzance, and

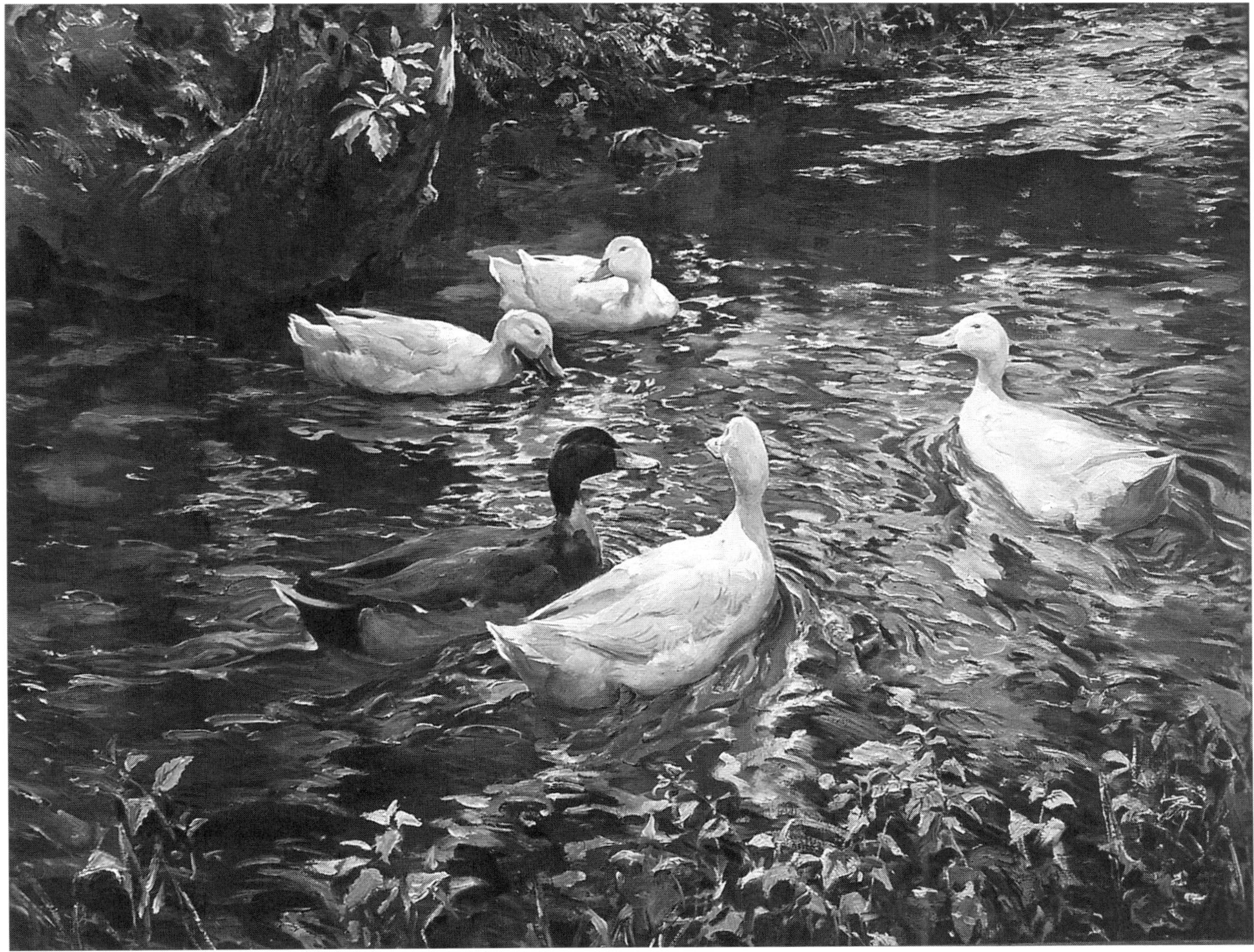

no one has ever observed them better. 'To make a duck swim – that is a test of accurate observation,' he wrote. He thought that they were often painted too high in the water, as though they lacked ballast. His ducks sail out over a pond, their breasts cleaving the water and sending ripples around their sides that die away across the surface until they reach the far bank. They express all the tranquillity and permanence of rural life.

Sun and Shadow on the Water
RA 1946

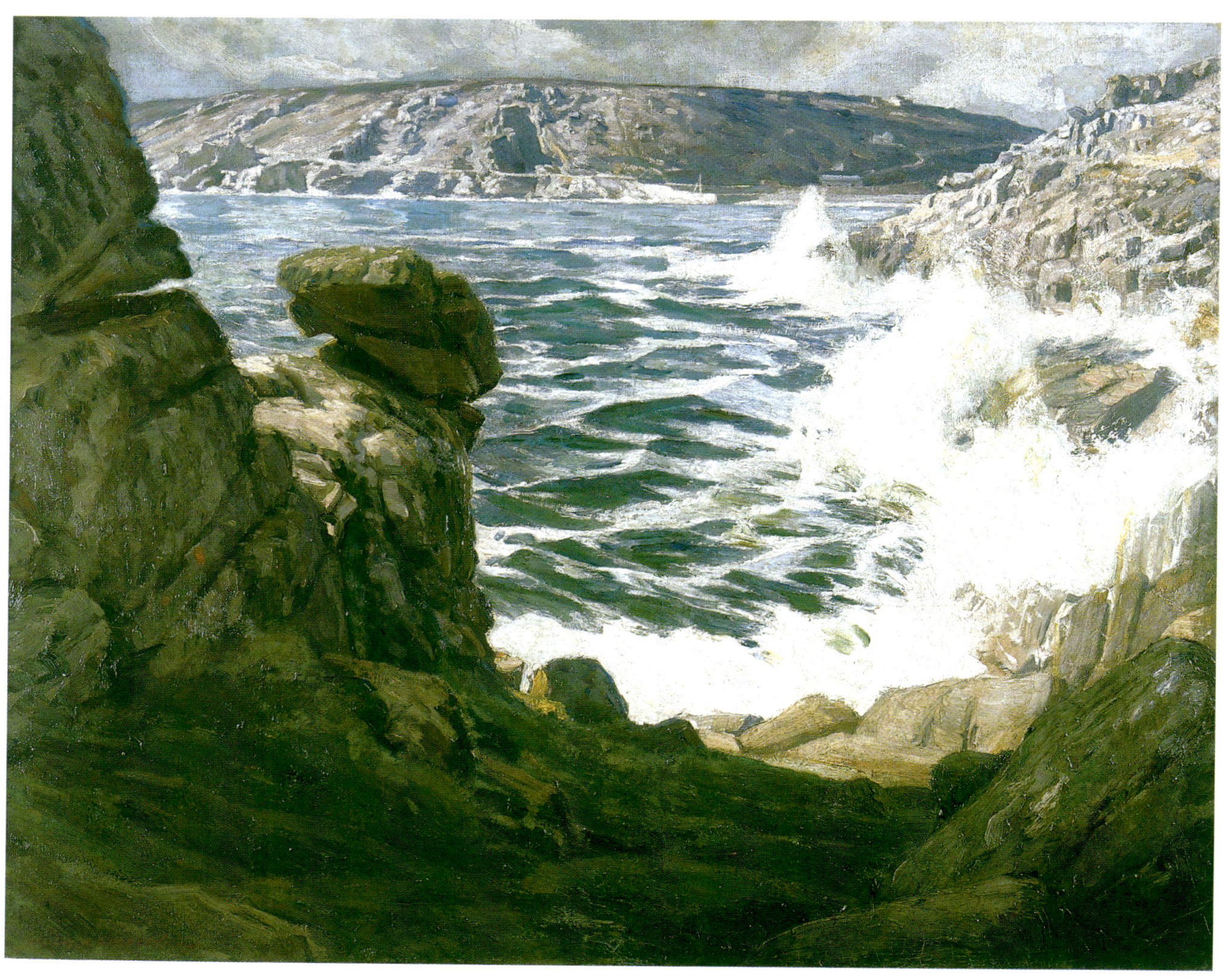

View from Carn Dhu
Oil on canvas, 48 x 60 in

Dorset: The Country
of The Woodlanders

Just before the outbreak of the Second World War Simpson had a commission
from the Royal Artillery Institution, Woolwich. They had been left money for a
painting commemorating the heroic action of a gun crew in the South African
War. With his usual thoroughness he sent for photographs of uniforms, asked
to borrow a helmet and water bottle and made sketches for their approval. But
once war was declared there were no more commissions for paintings and his
detailed proposal for a book entitled *A Painter Among Birds* was not taken up.
It was a release that brought material worries of its own. They had no income
and he considered applying for jobs. He typed out his curriculum vitae, playing
down all the Royal Academy exhibits and published books, and emphasising
his experience as a motorcyclist and his ability as a mechanic. He became a
deputy chief warden in the ARP, the defence against air attack, and an auxiliary
coastguard. They were hardly able to survive on his pay.

It was monotonous keeping watch on the Cornish coast through the long
hours of the night, his only company a rat running across the stones of Lamorna
quay. German bombers flew overhead on their way to South Wales, sometimes on
their return unloading any remaining bombs before heading out to sea. One night
during a raid on Falmouth Docks a plane was hit and with an engine missing
badly limped down the coast. A British fighter plane was on its tail, so it dropped
its bombs into the sea, the first off Carn Dhu and two more off Carn Barges. The
next morning a lot of dead fish came in on the tide and when the news spread
several villagers went down to collect them. Joe Ladner, one of the characters in
Harold Knight's painting *The Council*, reported that he 'got a nice fry'.

But mostly there were few excitements and the long hours of night duty took
their toll. Walter's health broke down. He was depressed about the war; all that
seemed permanent had gone and he saw little hope of ever rebuilding the old life.
Then a letter came that offered a job and a chance to get away. Frank Heath had
died in 1936 and his widow Jessica had left Menwinnion. She had bought a house

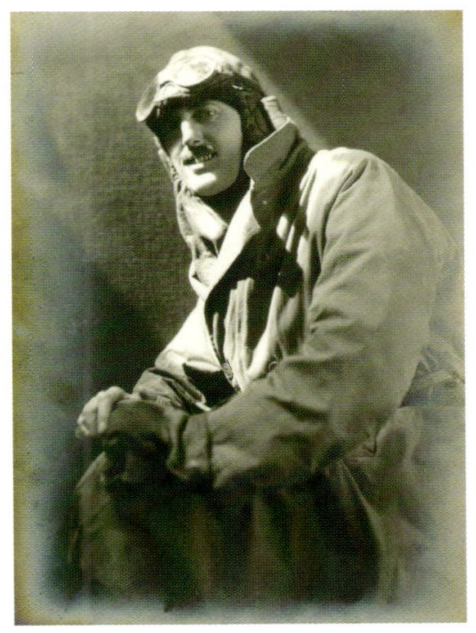

Simpson in motorcycling gear
Photograph, WCAA

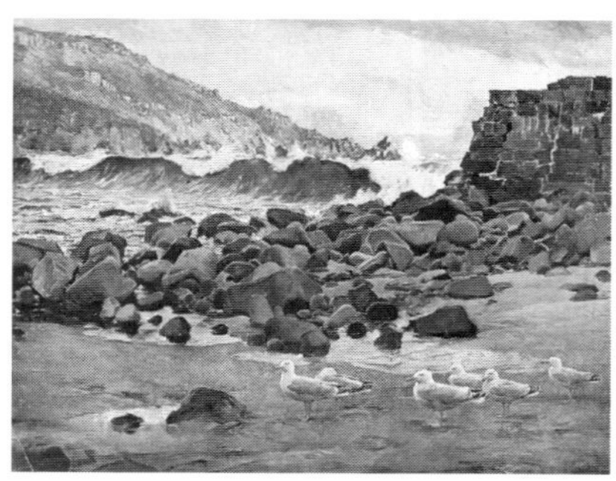

Evening Light at Carn Dhu, Cornwall
R A 1945

at Frampton in Dorset, intending to return to her native Ireland as soon as the war ended. It was a place for her three married daughters to return to in wartime, though only one daughter, Nancy, was then at home. Nancy's husband was in the army and it was she who wrote to Ruth and Walter. The nearby Frampton Court had been the estate of Richard Brinsley Sheridan, grandson of the playwright. The mansion had fallen into ruins but the land was farmed by Commander Sutton and his wife Kitty, who lived in the former dairy beside the original coach-house and stables. Jessica spent part of each day looking after their baby daughter. The commander was away at sea, they had lost all their help on the farm and Kitty ran it on her own. Would Walter like to be a farmhand in Thomas Hardy's Dorset?

They let Duncan's and moved to Frampton. Leonora was in the Land Army, managing a dairy herd at Boskenna, and at weekends went to the Napers at Trewoofe. Walter and Ruth arrived at Jessica's long low white house in the early summer of 1942 and he was engaged as cowman and labourer at the farm. Kitty treated him as a hired man during the day, ordering him about and making sure he worked hard. Out of working hours he was her social equal again. He found the situation not without its humour.

His first job of the day, at seven in the morning, was to catch and milk Gertrude, a Guernsey who reminded him of the cows of his childhood at Pickhurst Manor. He cleaned out the horseboxes in the stables, fed the puppies in the kennel and looked after the goat, tethering it on fresh grass. When he found it lying dead one morning, he went to tell Kitty.

'You!' she said sharply.

He expected a telling-off and disclaimed responsibility.

'Y.E.W.,' she spelt out. 'Bury it!'

A branch from the yew hedge had blown across the grass within reach of the goat and it had eaten the poisonous leaves.

Walter and Ruth soon found a place to rent. Marl Cottage had an overgrown garden that ran down to the river Frome and a view across the valley to the earthworks of Maiden Castle on the distant skyline. The next-door neighbour was a thatcher and a wheelwright lived down the road. It was like living through the pages of a Thomas Hardy novel and Walter read *The Woodlanders* again; it gave him the sense of unchanging times that he longed for.

The commander came home on leave and they worked together, making fences that the bullocks could not break down and building a silo. After a morning's work they went along to the little redbrick inn in Frampton for a glass of ale. All the young men had gone to the war and there were only old men left in the bar. With their talk of sheep and the market it seemed more than ever the world of the past. Walter was sorry when the commander's leave was over, as there were no more visits to the pub and Kitty set him to dig a large plot for root vegetables. He weeded and cleared the ground, removing the waste in a two-wheeled cart. He took the place of the pony between the shafts and found it quite calming, trundling the cart down to the rubbish heap and dragging it back up the slope. As the last load approached he looked forward to lunch that Ruth was preparing at the cottage.

On a sunny June afternoon a gymkhana was held in a large field by the river. All Frampton was there, farmers from neighbouring villages and townsfolk from Dorchester. Wagons and cars were drawn up around the field, a white marquee gleamed in the sun and riders competed in the ring. Simpson was asked to judge the jumping competition; he awarded first prize to Kitty. Just before the tea interval the atmosphere became ominously still. A bright afternoon turned dark and the rain poured down. People rushed for shelter but were soaked before they could reach their cars or crouch under farm carts. The roof of the marquee sagged. It was like the ruin of Michael Henchard's fête in *The Mayor of Casterbridge*.

Earlier in the year Walter had scattered fertiliser over the fields from a bag slung before him, casting handfuls in the manner of Millet's sower, just as men had sown seeds from remotest times. When the grass was ready to mow he drove the hay rake, sitting high on the iron seat, with Kitty's brown hunter between the shafts. The men borrowed from neighbouring farms raked and piled the grass into haycocks and Kitty brought jugs of cider from the house. They built the ricks and thatched them before the weather broke.

On Sundays, when he finished work at eleven o'clock, he cleared the garden with billhook and saw, felling a large tree and stacking the wood for winter. He made a bird-table outside the window at which they sat for their evening meal and watched the birds that came to it, mostly marsh tits. When they started to have a fire in the evenings he made a milking stool from the bole of a tree, boring holes for the legs with a red-hot poker. He brought home a stray cat to be company for Ruth, though in their simple life at Marl Cottage they spent more time together than they had for years. At night they fell asleep to the sound of the river and the occasional hoot of an owl.

The days on the farm were much the same as they had been for centuries, rolling on through springs and summers, autumns and the sleep of winters. It was easy to forget the war, even though there were the vapour trails of aircraft in the sky, the twisted wreckage of a crashed plane in the wood, a tremor in the earth when bombs fell on Portland. It all seemed as remote as the relics of ancient battles among the earthworks of Maiden Castle. With this simple life of hard work and fresh air in a countryside where time seemed to stand still, Walter recovered his mental and physical health.

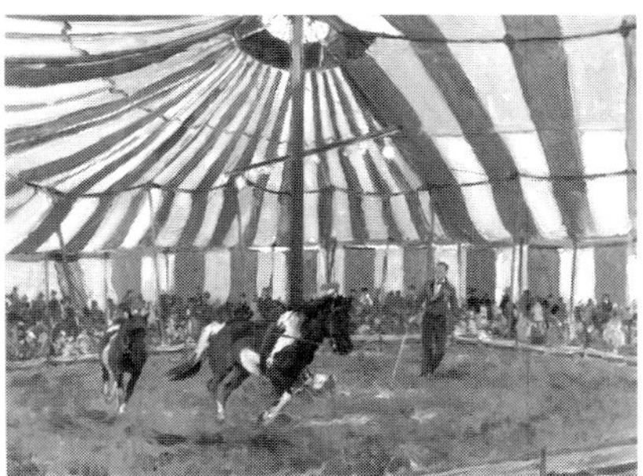

The Big Top
Oil on canvas

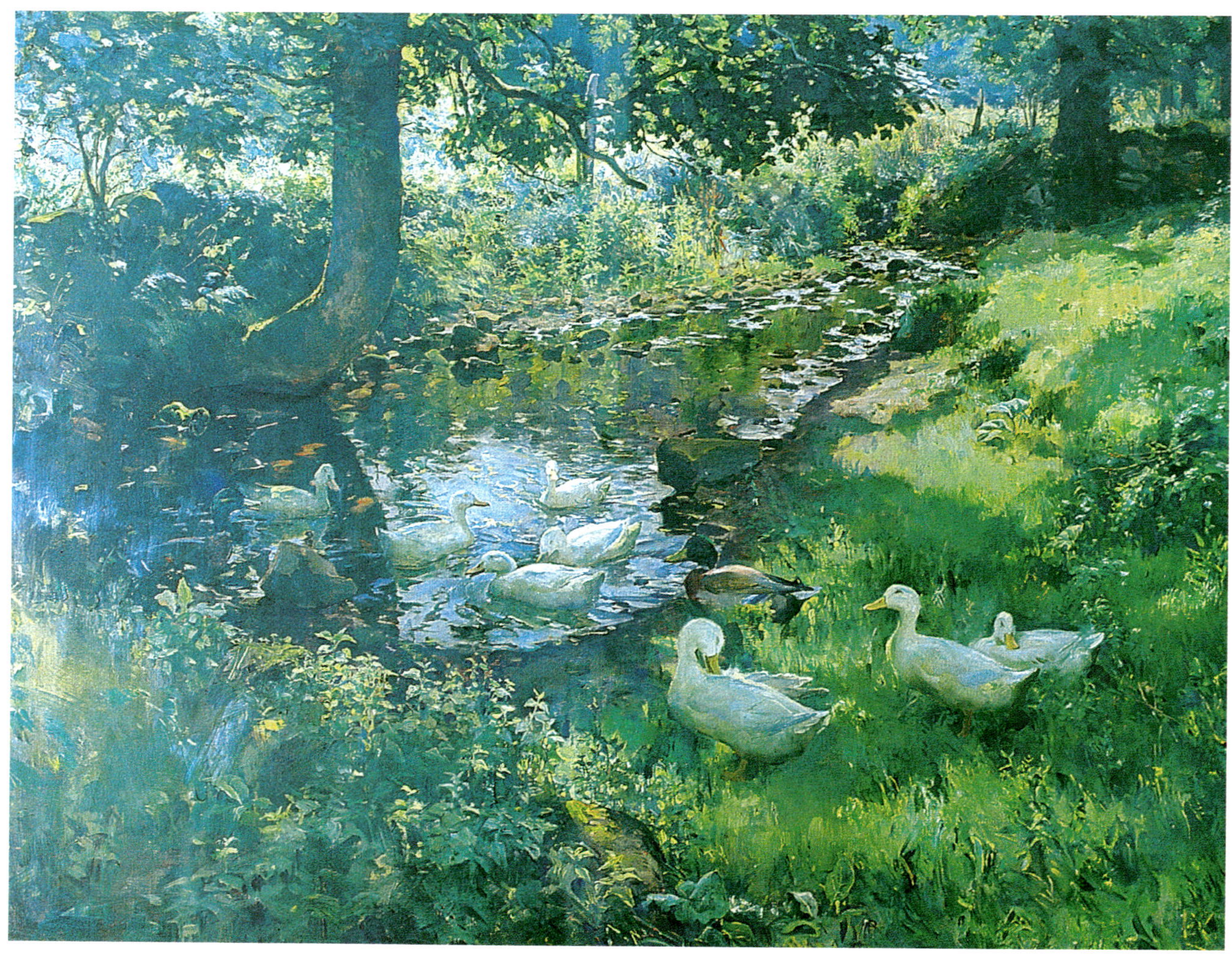

The Stream at Clapper Mill
RA 1945, oil on canvas, 48 x 58.25 in
Newport Museum and Art Gallery

To Youth the Heritage
Oil on canvas
'*This title was given to the picture as
typical of the bombed house and the
heritage of war's aftermath for the
younger generation.*' Charles Simpson

The painting shows Cathryn Robins
seated in the window of Stanley House
overlooking war damage

CHAPTER TWELVE

They returned to Cornwall before the war ended and as there were tenants
in Duncan's they rented a house in Raginnis and then in Green Lane at
Paul, both close to the small fishing village of Mousehole. Simpson began
to pick up his life again as an artist and writer. At the 1944 Royal Academy
he exhibited *Wheeling Gulls and Glittering Water*, painted on the harbour
side at Newlyn. The dazzling sunshine is reflected from the sea and from
the wings of the circling gulls. Two fishing boats are moored near the quay
in the rippling water. The gulls fill the picture, with two or three large
birds in the foreground and others receding into the distance, their wings
forming a pattern against the sky. *The Stream at Clapper Mill*, shown
the following year, is another painting of light. It shines through leaves
on to the gently flowing Lamorna stream where Aylesbury ducks stand
on the bank or float on the water in dappled shade. It was bought from
the exhibition by Newport Art Gallery and Raphael Tuck acquired the
reproduction rights, beginning an association that lasted many years.

When they repossessed the house that had been their home for fourteen
years it now seemed too isolated. Ruth had to ride in the sidecar to go shopping
in Penzance and petrol was rationed. Walter had his sixtieth birthday and they
decided to move into the centre of town. They sold Duncan's and in 1945 bought
Stanley House on the main street in Alverton at the west end of Penzance. It is
an elegant Regency building of dressed granite, three storeys high with wide bow
windows on the first and second floors. It stands right on the pavement at the
end of a terrace. Before moving in they had alterations made, which took a year
because of the shortage of electricians and masons. Ruth wrote to Leonora, who
had left the Land Army and joined the ATS, the women's military service, asking
her what colour she wanted her room painted. Ruth did the decorating herself.

The front rooms had high ceilings, high enough to hang one of Walter's
large pictures of seagulls swooping over the waves. His studio was on the top

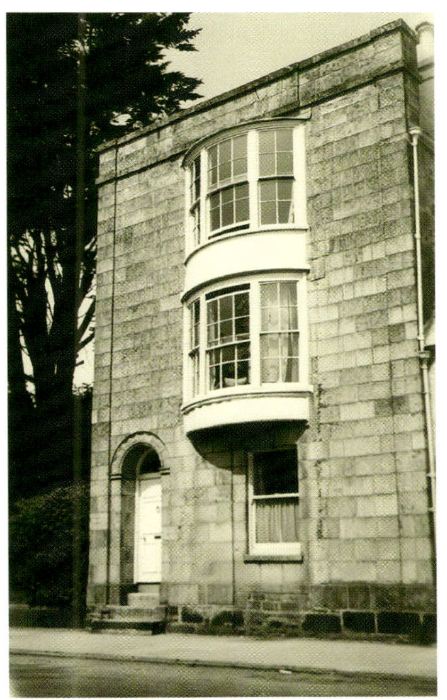

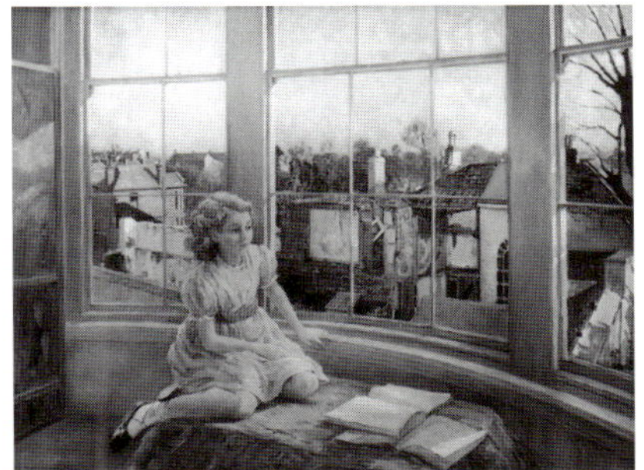

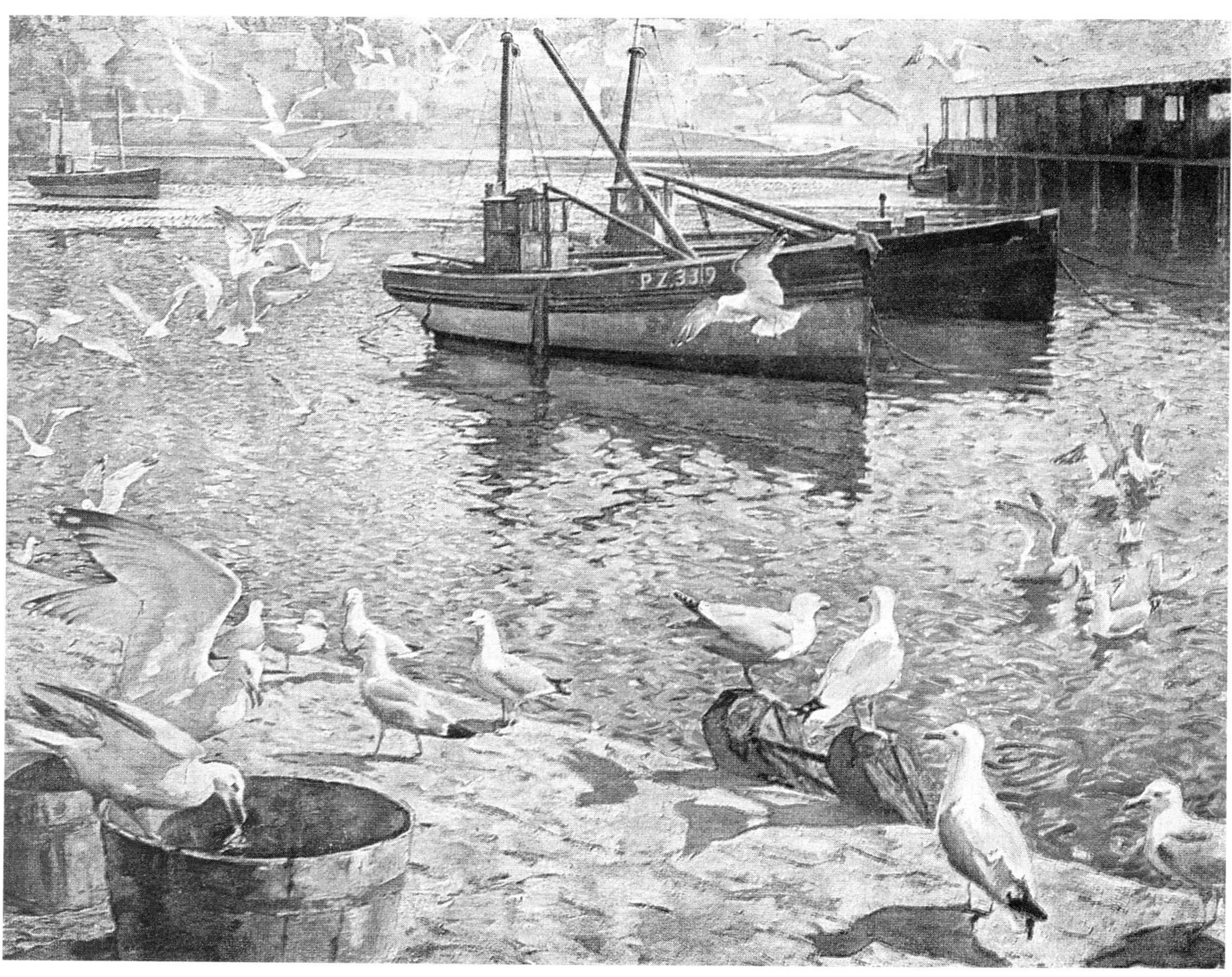

Wheeling Gulls and Glittering Water
RA 1944

floor looking out over the town to the sea. He had rejoined the St Ives Society of Artists during the war and took part in their touring exhibitions, the 1945–1946 tour visiting northern cities. An exhibition was sent to South Africa in 1947 to coincide with the visit of King George VI. The Cape Town Gallery offered to retain for sale *Wheeling Gulls and Glittering Water* if he would reduce the price from £200 to £175 and *Swimming with the Current* at £40. The Society had another major show at the National Museum of Wales in Cardiff, combining the work of traditional and modern artists, where he exhibited alongside Barbara Hepworth and Ben Nicholson. *On Newlyn Pier* was accepted by the Royal Academy, followed the next year by *Midsummer Mosaic*, another scene of ducks on a stream in dappled light with luxuriant summer growth along the banks. Lionel Edwards thought it the best painting in the show. During the London Olympics Simpson was represented at the Sport in Art exhibition at the Victoria and Albert Museum. At the same time he was quite prepared to take on humbler work, farmyard scenes for children commissioned by Raphael Tuck and inn signs at £15 each for the brewers Ind Coope and Allsop of Burton on Trent: The Ship, The Poundfold Inn and The Leopard and Fox.

In 1948 he published his last and most interesting book. *The Fields of Home* contains an evocation of a happy late-Victorian childhood. Simpson conveys the young Walter's excitement at 'going to Pickhurst'. Everything is sharp and clear, all the boy's senses alert: the sound of the click of the gate swinging back after their arrival and the horses' hooves on the gravel, the scent of lavender and roses as they approach the house; in the fields the scent of buttercups and the keener tang of daisies, the earthy smell of horse mushrooms beneath a tree. He sees every detail and absorbs the atmosphere of house, garden and farm. Inside the cowshed at milking time 'the quiet was broken by a steady rhythm on the polished sides of the pail. We did not talk for a while. The drowsy murmur of the sighs of the cattle passed from stall to stall. The robin came back, cocked its head on one side, picked at chaff-dust on the floor, and flew to the closed half-door that shut off the straw yard. There it broke into a trill of song, silhouetted against a beam of light in which dust motes floated.'

The boy observes with a child's freshness of vision and the adult remembers with nostalgia. For Simpson, Pickhurst Manor was 'a land of lost content'. When he returned in later life he found a network of roads and small houses, with only a bank of wild strawberries to remind him of what it had once been and the joy he had known there. He conveys the boy's almost Wordsworthian rapture in the countryside and these sections of the book merit comparison with the writings of Richard Jefferies and W.H. Hudson. But when he leaves his childhood and devotes the last third of a short book to the Cornish landscape the prose becomes dense. Once the story of his life is discontinued there is no longer any narrative drive, only pure description. This is always beautifully observed: 'The northern cliffs frown upon the sea, an unbroken barrier of rock, grey as the jackdaw's mantle, sombre as the raven's wing.' The sentence has the rhythm of a line of verse and when this continues for page after page it becomes the sort of 'poetical' prose for which there is little taste today. To the modern reader all of Charles Simpson's writing is overburdened, either with facts in the critical books or with description in his more personal works. He is a better painter than writer but those who admire his paintings will always hold *The Fields of Home* in affection.

When the Western Union Fleet visited Mount's Bay, he climbed on to the roof of the Pavilion Theatre to paint the warships from the fleets of Britain, France and the Netherlands at anchor in the bay, the promenade in the foreground decorated with flags forming the strong diagonal

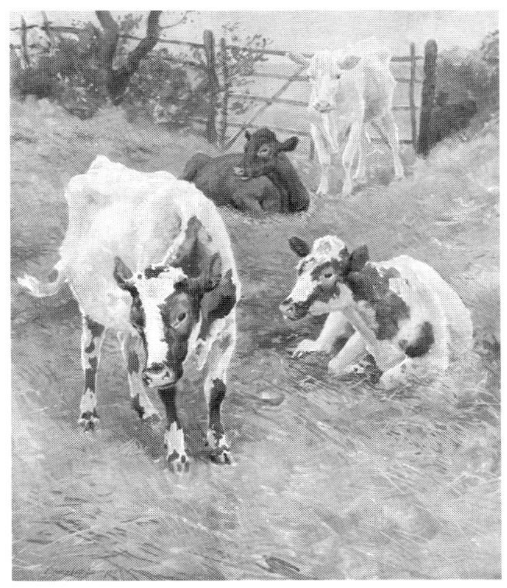

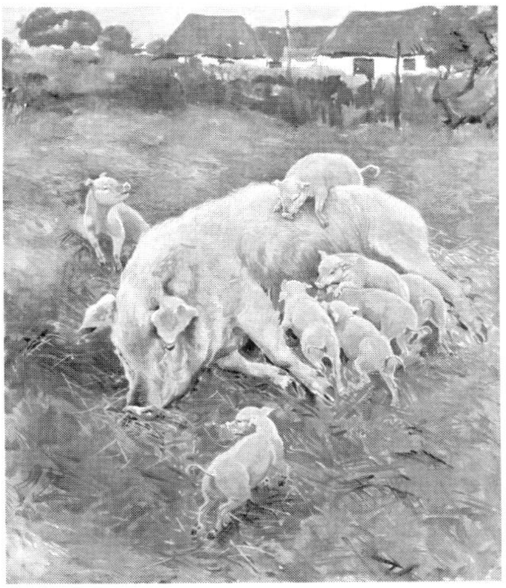

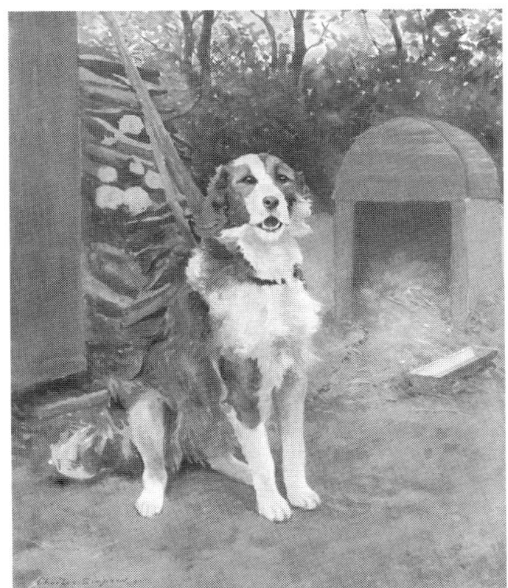

Three illustrations for a children's book of farm animals

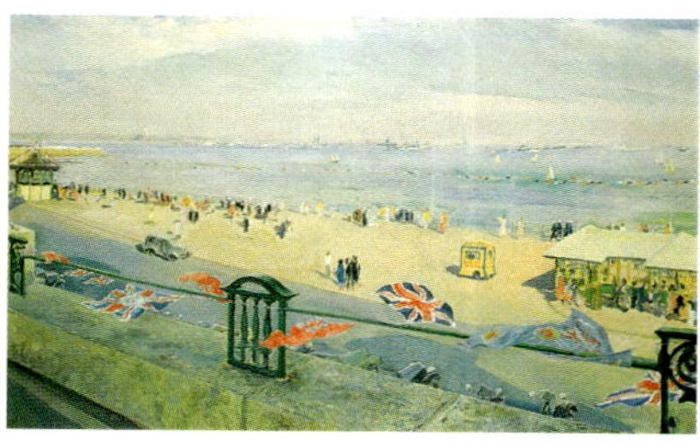

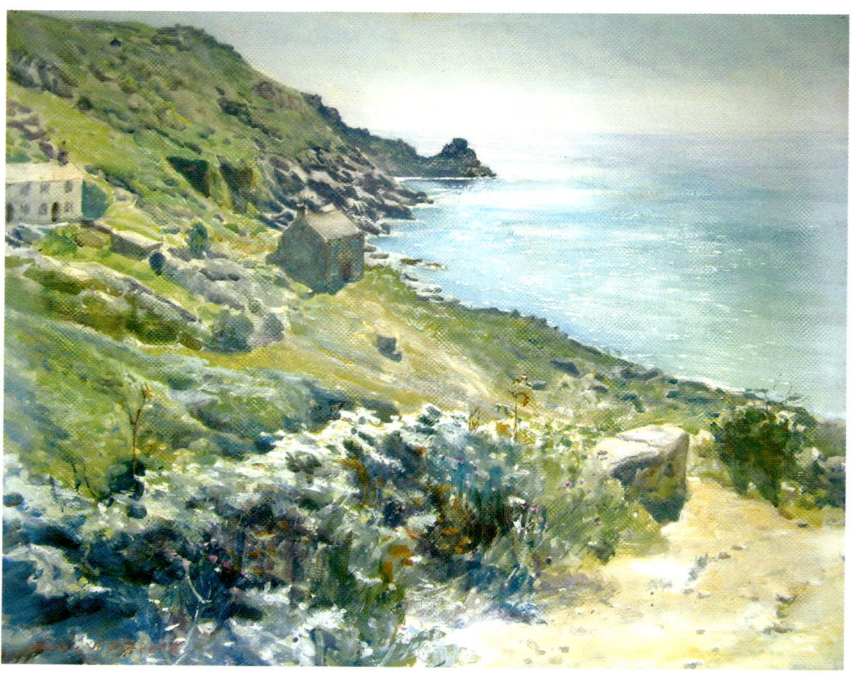

composition that he always favoured. He renewed his association with the Newlyn Society of Artists, which had closed its gallery again during the war, and served on the committee until 1954, when he retired for health reasons. His place was taken by Peter Lanyon, a succession that was symbolic of the changing art world. The younger generation coming to the fore were abstract artists like Peter Lanyon, John Wells and Bryan Wynter, and in the St Ives Society tension rose between the traditionalists and the moderns. With a great deal of ill feeling on both sides, the society split and the moderns, led by Barbara Hepworth and Ben Nicholson, formed their own group, the Penwith Society. Away from St Ives, Simpson was not directly involved in all the bitterness and resentment, though his sympathies were with the traditionalists. He showed with them in the Festival of Britain exhibition of 1951, entering *Lamorna Stream in Early Spring* (£50) and *Herring Gull, Lamorna Cove* (£40). Although not a member of the Penwith Society, he contributed by special invitation to their Festival show as well, one of the few artists with pictures in both exhibitions. He was not as openly hostile to innovation as Alfred Munnings, whose half-drunken outburst against 'so-called modern art' in his retirement speech as president of the Royal Academy he would have listened to on the wireless. Simpson once wrote that at the end of the day the artist, laying aside his palette, glances at the mosaic of colours and thinks 'By Jove! They have a quality that has been lost in the same colours so carefully applied to the canvas. The picture looks tame, the palette animated. Why not treat the canvas like the palette, simply making a pattern?' But Monet was as modern as he went.

His last Royal Academy exhibit was in 1953; *The Tide Line* had first been shown there nearly thirty years earlier. The Academy was no longer as important as it had been; painters now advanced their careers through dealers and galleries. Although the moderns were getting all the notice, public taste remained largely conservative and there was more of a market for familiar rather than avant-garde work. Simpson still had steady sales and there were loyal collectors of his paintings. The headmistress of a school that had been evacuated to Penzance during the war bought the large *Sunset over the Cornish Moors* for £200, to hang in Westwing School at Langford Court, Bristol. Jennifer Rowe, whom he had once sketched on Porthminster Beach, rang his doorbell one day. She was now married and on holiday in Cornwall with her husband. It was their twentieth wedding anniversary and they wanted a special present. That very day he was packing the painting of her sitting on the edge of the sandpit to send to an exhibition in Bolton. 'How extraordinary!' he kept saying. 'How extraordinary!' They bought the picture that she had last seen forty years earlier.

George Lane manufactured health products in Gloucestershire and collected Simpson paintings, starting a correspondence with him. He began in 1952 by buying *Evening Light at Carn Barges* for £60. He then asked Simpson to send him one of his screens decorated with wild teal and a watercolour of mallards at the agreed price of £41. Later he bought *Ploughing in the Wolds*, painted when Simpson was researching the Yorkshire hunts. Touring Cornwall

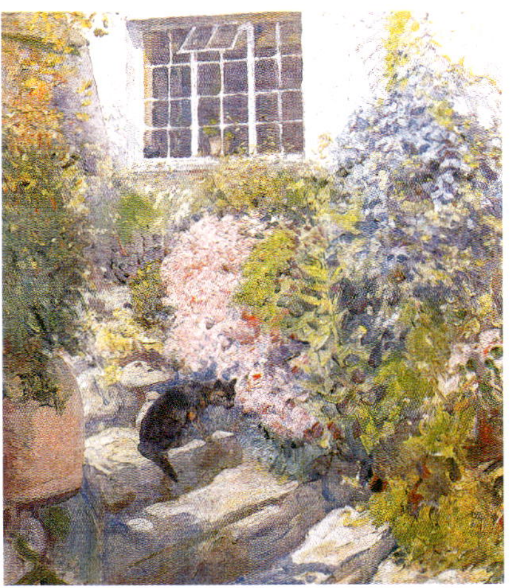

ABOVE
Cat on a Sunny Path
Oil on canvas

BELOW LEFT
Lamorna Cove from the Sea
Gouache, 25 x 30 in

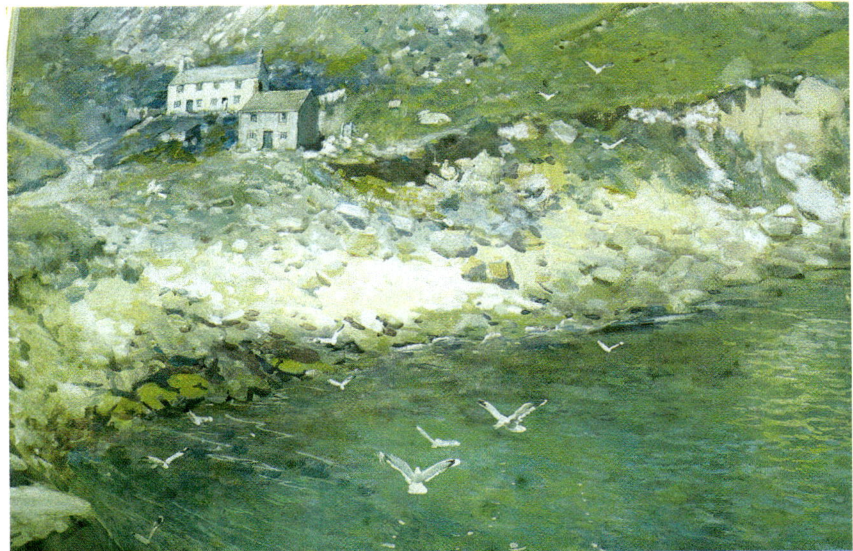

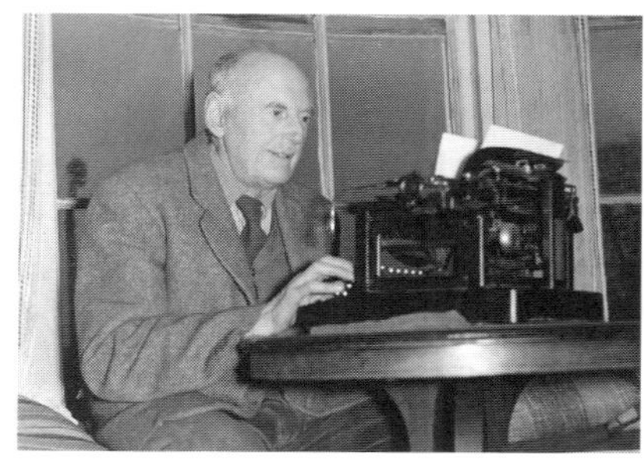

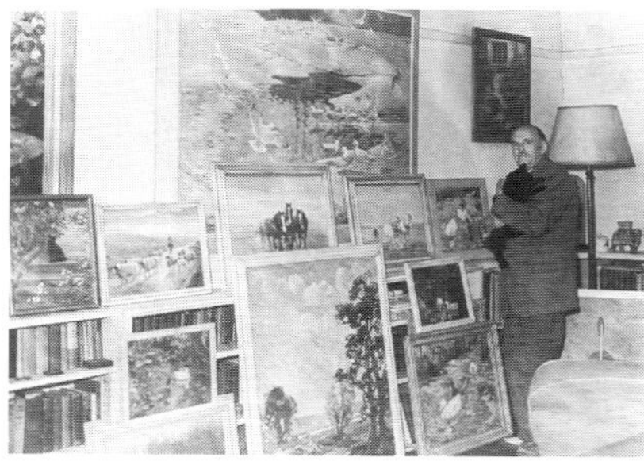

Charles Simpson at his typewriter in the bow window of Stanley House during the 1960s

Charles Simpson in Stanley House with some of his paintings

with a caravan, the Lanes were delighted to see *Clodgy Moor* for sale in the window of Alfred Smith's furniture store in Penzance and bought it for £30. A rather miffed Simpson pointed out that the sale brought him no benefit at all. He had no idea who had put it into Smith's but the Lanes had got an incredible bargain. It had been painted about 1908 and was one of the best from that period. He sold a similar one at Cheltenham for £400 and another painted from the edge of the moor won a Gold Medal at San Francisco in 1915. If he hadn't been out when they called he would have taken them to the exact spot. He heard from the Broadway Gallery that they had considered a picture of white horses ploughing. If they were interested he could let them have it for much less. In other letters he told them that if they ever got a sale for him, perhaps from people coming to admire their collection, he would offer them a picture as commission. He would take £40 or £50 for his large painting of the north Cornish coast that was 'just like looking through a window'. At Christmas and Easter he had small exhibitions at John Peak's framing shop in Causewayhead in Penzance.

He continued to write photography criticisms, now for *Camera World*, and he became involved with the English Ring Actors, a company based in Eastbourne that brought plays by Somerset Maugham, Terence Rattigan, Bernard Shaw and others to the Pavilion Theatre in Penzance. The association began when he helped them with their production of *The Brontës of Haworth Parsonage* and he became one of the directors. He made sketches of their pantomime *Aladdin*, exhibiting one at the Royal Institute of Painters in Watercolours (R.I.), of which he had been a member since 1923 and where he showed every year.

In the mid-fifties he was disturbed by a threat to Lamorna that seemed to confirm his worst fears about a changing world. Colonel Paynter had died and his daughter Betty inherited the estate. It was impossible to keep it going and with death duties of £33,000 to pay she sold the cove and three farms. It still didn't solve her financial problems and she applied for planning permission to build one hundred and twenty-six houses, a permanent site for a hundred caravans and a petrol station. Those who loved the valley were appalled. The plan was rejected but the anxiety continued when a revised scheme for twenty-three houses was submitted. Leading artists signed a letter to *The Times* appealing for support to save 'this unique and lovely valley'. A large crowd attended the public enquiry in Penzance in February 1955 and there were frequent interruptions from the hall, cheers and ironic laughter, long bursts of applause. After the views of the planning authority and local residents had been heard, Charles Simpson and John Tunnard, realist and surrealist, spoke for the artists. Simpson said that his paintings of Lamorna had been shown all over the world. Even the modified plans would have altered the character of the valley forever. To his great relief – and that of many others – the inspector found against the proposal. His generation had seen more changes than any other, before or since, but at least his beloved Lamorna had been saved.[1]

Television ownership was expanding rapidly and show jumping had become a popular sport as a result of television coverage. The most successful riders and their mounts became household names and Simpson's painting of Colonel Llewellyn on Foxhunter, a commission that Munnings had turned down because of gout in his fingers, led to a run of requests for portraits of horses and riders. He stayed with Colonel W.E. Lyon, editor of *The Horseman's Year*, at his house near Stow on the Wold and painted his wife on a favourite horse. Always keen for a sale, he wrote to George Lane: 'Should you hear of anyone who wants a horse painted do let me know. I have painted so many that I can always do them from photographs and description of colour if it is not possible to see the horse.' He offered a sketch as commission. His most famous horse and rider portraits were painted for Pat Smythe, whose competition riding made her an early television celebrity. The two paintings show her on Tosca and Prince Hal, and were done not from photographs but when he stayed with her at Miserden House near Stroud in Gloucestershire. In November 1956 she opened an exhibition of eighty-one of his paintings in Cheltenham, including the two in which she featured and preparatory sketches. Her presence ensured maximum publicity.

A paragraph in *The Cornishman* in May 1957 reported that Mr Charles Simpson had switched from painting horses to kittens. He replied to their 'little joke', saying that for the past week wherever he'd gone he'd been greeted with amusement. 'I hear you are painting kittens now, Mr Simpson.' To put the record straight he said that for some years he had written and illustrated children's books and was then at work on one about a cat and her kittens. Simpson was always very fond of cats. At Lamorna they had a farm cat, George, whose portrait was reproduced in a Medici calendar. Their cat at Stanley House was called Hamlet because he could never make up his mind whether to jump off the wall. Most of his work for children was unsigned. It included a delightful *Farm Panorama* with animals that could be cut out and arranged, like the one he had made for his sister Mary many years before.

When *The Stackyard* came up at auction he sent Ruth to buy it back. It had been painted at Chywoone Farm in about 1914 and shows a cockerel with

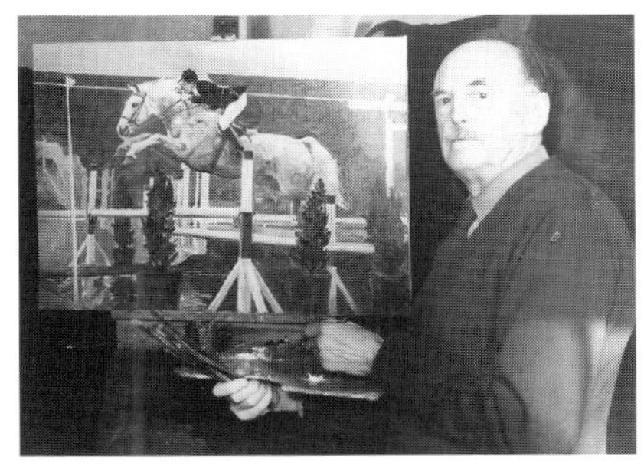

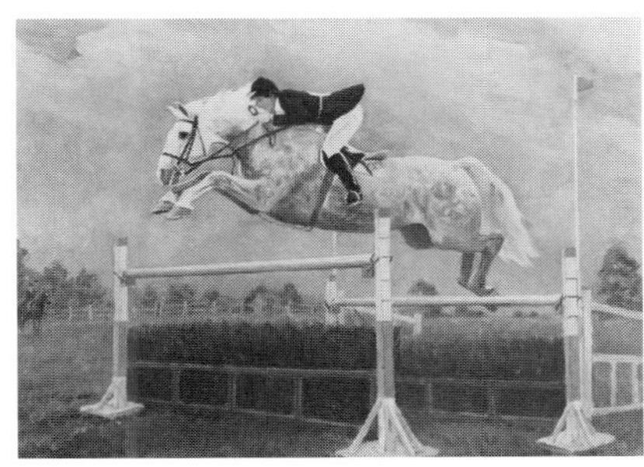

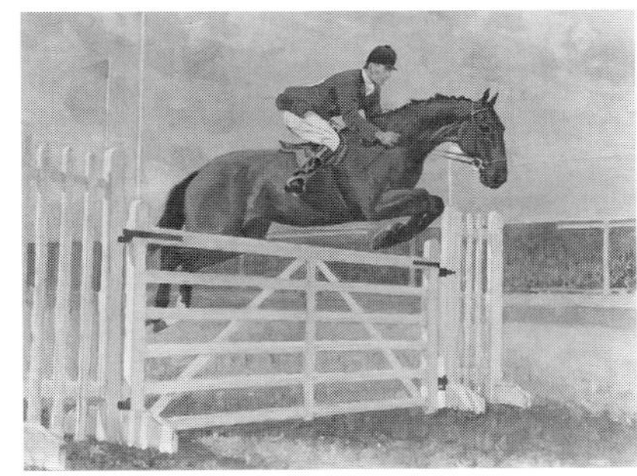

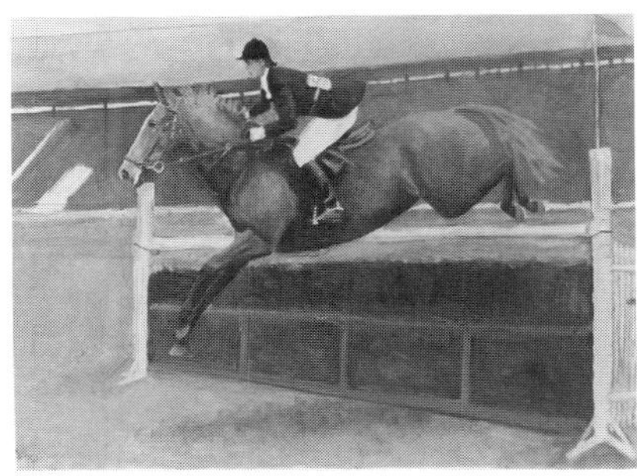

Charles Simpson with *Pat Smythe on Tosca* 1956; *Pat Smythe on Tosca*; *Harry Llewellyn on Foxhunter*; *Pat Smythe on Flanagan*

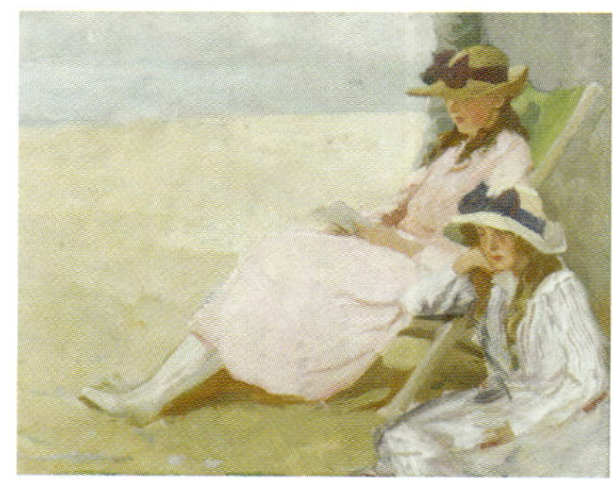

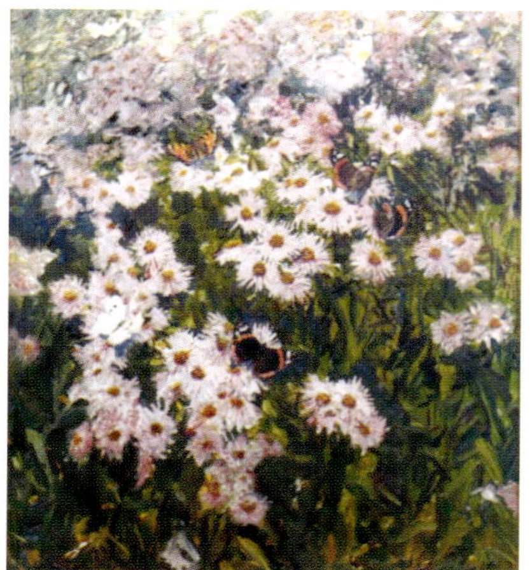

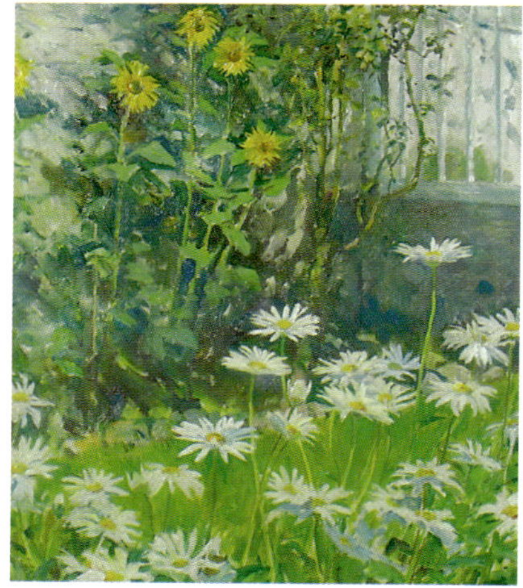

six or seven hens scratching at a pile of straw, and two ducks foraging at its base. The paint is thickly applied, building up ridges that give the texture of the golden-brown straw. The birds are no more than streaks of white paint moulding their shape, with a dab of red – stand back and they become farmyard fowls. The Khaki Campbell duck almost disappears against the straw, defined mostly by its shadow. The glow of the straw contrasts with the wintry trees against a cold sky and the dark mass of a hayrick. It was his favourite painting and he kept it by him for the rest of his life.

For three years his solo touring exhibition visited major municipal galleries, ending in Bournemouth in 1958. The Russell-Cotes Gallery again bought a painting, adding *The Bird Table* to its earlier *Duck Shooting – the Punt Gunner*. The next year he was seventy-five but he had no thoughts of retiring, still exhibiting at the Newlyn Gallery and delivering his pictures in the sidecar of his motorcycle, adapted to take a six-foot canvas. He painted another portrait of Pat Smythe, this time on Flanagan and done from photographs. In February 1963 he reports that he has 'just finished a picture of a friend's two daughters on their horse and pony returning from a ride and also painting a large picture of Lamorna Cove and two smaller ones for the summer exhibition'.[2] He kept up a correspondence with his collectors, suggesting paintings they might like to buy.

To celebrate their golden wedding in May the Simpsons were joined by Leonora and by his sister Gaynor, Lady O'Dowda. It had been fifty years of an essentially loving marriage, but Walter was very autocratic and had never given Ruth a chance to fulfil herself. She now became seriously ill and he expected Leonora to give up her own life to look after them. When their daily maid gave in her notice and went off strawberry picking, Leonora left her job at Harrods in London and returned home permanently. Ruth died in Barncoose Hospital, Redruth, on 25 November 1964. Walter was lost without her and after her death never took up a paintbrush again.

Resting – on Porthminster beach
(Vera and Phyllis Cuningham)
1919, oil on canvas, 24 x 30 in
Photograph by Venture, Truro

Butterflies and Michaelmas Daisies
Oil on canvas, 14 x 11 in

Sunflowers and Daisies
Oil on canvas, 24 x 20 in

Charles Walter Simpson died at the age of eighty-six on 3 October 1971. There was no obituary in *The Times*; the world had lost interest in painters of his generation. Yet before the end of the decade their rediscovery began. David Messum has described how travelling through the West Country in search of pictures he was struck by the quality and freshness of the Newlyn School. He put on his exhibition *A Breath of Fresh Air* at Beaconsfield in Buckinghamshire in 1974, containing mostly work by Stanhope Forbes and Walter Langley. In 1978 the County Museum in Truro in conjunction with the National Trust brought together works by Newlyn and St Ives artists in *Painting in Cornwall 1880–1930*. There were five pictures by Charles Simpson, amongst them the painting of Leonora as a child standing beneath the pergola, given by her to the museum in memory of her father. Ruth's portrait of Frank Verbeck was also included. For many visitors who had grown up without ever seeing any of the work of these artists but who had gathered that they were old-fashioned and academic, the show was a revelation. The reappraisal continued in the first major survey of the school, *Painting in Newlyn 1880–1900*, shown in Newlyn, Plymouth, Bristol and Birmingham in 1979, and *Painting in Newlyn 1900–1930*, shown in Newlyn and Plymouth in 1985. A combined exhibition went to the Barbican in London later the same year. They included six paintings by Charles Simpson; apart from *Penzance from Newlyn*, five of the six were actually painted in St Ives: *Resting – on the beach at St Ives, The Sandpit – on Porthminster Beach, The Sandcastle, Nannie and Billie* and *The Herring Season: from my Studio Window*. There was a single work by Ruth, the portrait of Minnie Triggs as *The Milkmaid*.

The interest created by these exhibitions and the catalogues by Caroline Fox and Francis Greenacre contributed to the increasing value of Newlyn School paintings, though Simpson's work did not rise as spectacularly as some of his contemporaries such as Harold Harvey. He has not been easy to classify, having links to the Newlyn, Lamorna and St Ives artists without being entirely one of them. His work too is so various; to some he is primarily a bird painter, to others a sporting or equestrian artist. He was a landscape and seascape painter, but there are also his pictures of figures on a beach. He devoted much of his considerable energy to writing about sport and the countryside, literature, art and photography. His versatility has affected his reputation.

Even so, in a repeat exhibition of *A Breath of Fresh Air* in the spring of 1990, *Skinning Fish, St Ives* was priced at £6,850 and *Gulls on the Quayside*, a 1912 oil on canvas of white wings against tan sails in Newlyn harbour, at £28,500. His sketch of Phyllis and Vera Cuningham leaning against the side of a boat at low tide in St Ives harbour, painted in 1919, sold at Sotheby's in April 2000 for £32,000 or £37,300 if the commission is added. As Simpson might have said, there was no benefit for him in the sale. He had struggled all his life to make a living and had sometimes compromised. But when he painted the things he loved, the countryside and its creatures, he endowed them with the sense of beauty and timelessness that he always sought.

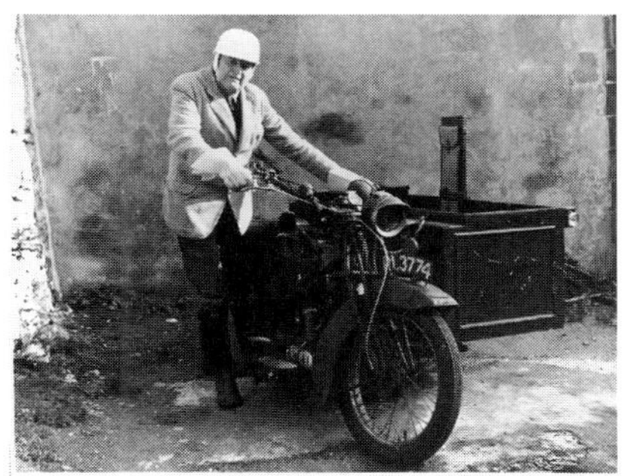

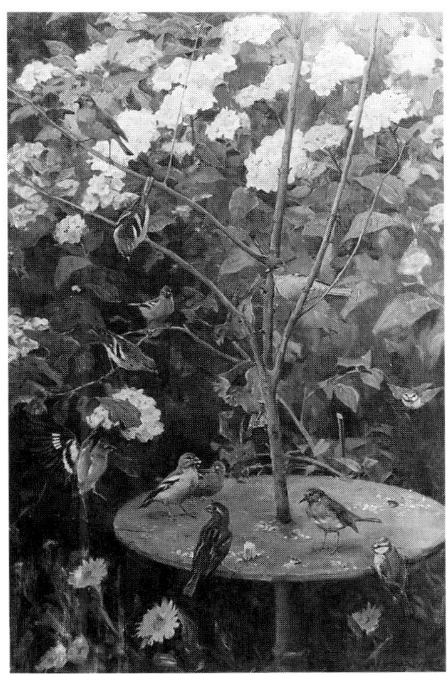

TOP
In his seventies, Simpson still delivered pictures in the sidecar of his motorcycle, adapted to take six-foot canvases

ABOVE
The Bird Table
Oil on canvas, 36 x 24 in
Russell-Cotes Art Gallery, Bournemouth

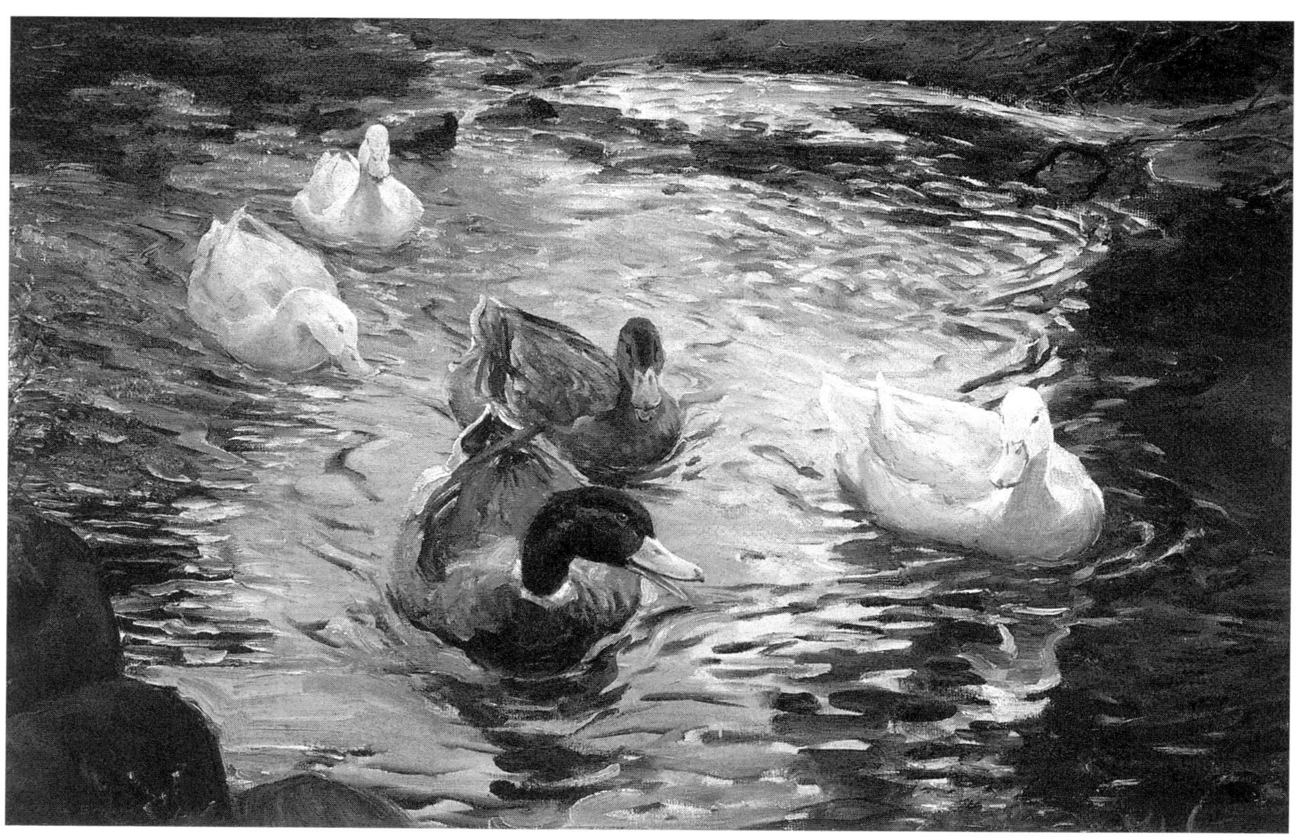

A Breeze on the Water
RA 1917, oil on canvas, 24 x 36 in
Courtesy of Leon Suddaby

1. **Pickhurst Manor: Boyhood**

   The Fields of Home, Charles Simpson, F.Lewis, Leigh-on-Sea 1948

   1   This folder is now in the West Cornwall Art Archive (WCAA).

   2   The need for the open air led him later in life to travel everywhere
       by motorcycle.

2. **Bushey, Newlyn and Norfolk: Apprenticeship**

   Lucy Kemp-Welch, Laura Wortley, Antique Collectors' Club 1997

   An Artist's Life, A.J. Munnings, Museum Press 1951

   Calico Pie, C.E.Vulliamy, Michael Joseph 1940

   Animal and Bird Painting and unpublished autobiographical note
   by C.W.S.

   Information from Garnet and Vivienne Hocking

   1   Laura Knight in her autobiography *Oil Paint and Grease Paint,*
       Nicholson and Watson, 1936, refers to Charles Simpson as one
       of the best students at the school and Simpson himself wrote
       that he married 'a fellow student'. But he was never a pupil of
       Stanhope Forbes.

   2   Fox and Greenacre suggest that Simpson brought Munnings to
       Newlyn, having already stayed with him in Norfolk. Simpson
       stayed with him at Church Farm, which Munnings did not occupy
       until after 1905 or 1906, though he was always vague about dates.
       'There is no one now to say precisely when he forsook Norfolk for
       Cornwall,' wrote Reginald Pound in 1962. He thought that a young
       woman student at Calderon's School of Animal Painting in Essex
       recommended Newlyn and Munnings made two or three short stays
       before settling there in 1911. It seems likely that he met Simpson in
       Cornwall on one of his early visits.

3   Garnet Wolesley (1884–1967) studied at the Slade School of Art and
    moved to Newlyn in 1908. His favourite subjects were young people.
    After the First World War, during which he served in the navy, he
    became a fashionable society portraitist. He married Joan Trevelyan
    in 1937 and gave up painting to manage her large Somerset estate.

4   *The Paper Chase* was printed at The Newlyn Press, run by R.T.
    Dick and J.D. Mackenzie at the Gwavas Studio. In 1912 they
    printed *The Merry Maidens*, the magazine of Penzance High School
    edited by Phyllis Gotch and again illustrated with woodblocks by
    Charles Simpson.

3. **Paris, Aldershot and Sussex: 'An accomplished artist'**
    Unpublished article by C.W.S.
    A Pastorale, Charles Simpson, St Ives 1922
    100 Years in Newlyn, ed Melissa Hardie, Patten Press 1995
    Autobiographical note by C.W.S. and letters

1   Mary married her young man and they went to farm in Canada.
    Their son Charlie Hoey died in Burma in 1944 and was awarded the
    VC. Another son Trevor was killed in France.

2   19 April 1911. The other witness was Gertrude's sister, Sophie.

3   Simpson wrote poetry throughout his life. It tended to be elegiac in
    tone, as in the lament for the tree in Alverton that had survived the
    bombing of the war but was felled to make way for new building.
    Other titles were *On Beethoven, On Handel's Largo, After the
    Storm, Cliff, December* and *Swans.* They are conventionally poetic,
    though *The Tramp* begins promisingly in a Wordsworthian manner:
    A tramp lay down upon some littered straw
    Beneath a few split beams by way of roof
    And where the moonlight filtered to the floor
    Between the rafters' trellis work he saw
    The stars above, strange, silent and aloof.

4. **Ruth Alison: 'A great and wonderful love'**
    Letters from Ruth to her mother and father, WCAA

1   Alec Walker and Kathleen Earle married after the war and
    established the Cryséde silk factory in Newlyn, where Kay designed
    the dresses that were sold in their shops throughout the country.

2   The model, Minnie Triggs from Tredavoe Farm, later became nanny
    to the Simpsons' daughter, Leonora.

3   Their father John Bodinnar was a cooper. When Kay and Alec
    Walker set up the Cryséde factory, Sophie worked on the dyeing
    process and later managed their shop in Newlyn. She joined the
    Land Army during the Second World War. She never married and
    looked after her mother Ann, who lived until she was ninety-six.

5. St Mary Abbots: The Wedding

Letters from Ruth and Walter to each other, WCAA

6. Leonora: Little Gonwin and Lamorna

What A Go! Jean Goodman, Collins 1988
The Englishman, Reginald Pound, Heinemann 1962
Lamorna Birch, A Painter Laureate, Austin Wormleighton, Sansom &
Company 1995
Oil Paint and Grease Paint, Laura Knight, Nicholson and Watson 1936
Letters from Ruth Simpson to her mother, WCAA

1   It had been one of two tea gardens in Carbis Bay. Later it became a
    caravan park; the farmhouse was demolished and it is now a housing
    estate.
2   W.H. Hudson in *The Land's End* gives a chapter to 'the native
    naturalist', the ferryman at Lelant and his stories of birds and seals.

7. St Ives: The School of Painting

George Fagan Bradshaw, David Tovey, Wilson Books 2000
Artists and Bohemians, Tom Cross, Quiller Press 1992
Matthew Smith, Malcolm Yorke, Faber and Faber 1997
St Ives 1883–1993, Marion Whybrow, Antique Collectors' Club 1994
Prospectus and letters in Simpson Archive, WCAA

1   Charles Pearce, quoted in Whybrow
2   When Vera Cuningham (1897–1955) went back to London she took
    lessons from Bernard Meninsky (1891–1950) and became his model
    and mistress before having a passionate affair with Matthew Smith
    (1879–1959). She posed for the highly coloured nudes that made
    his reputation. She developed a very individual style in her own
    dark paintings of distorted female figures, promoted post-war by
    the Creuze Gallery in Paris. *A Wet Day*, renamed *The Tent*, sold at
    Bonhams in June 2004 for £16,000 or £19,666 with commission.
3   *Western Daily Mercury*, August 1920
4   The fishing boats unloaded the herring into gurries, wooden boxes

with shafts nailed to the sides, providing handles for two men to carry them to the packers.

5   It clearly took place much earlier than 1922 though it is not dated. I have placed the two visits in 1910 and 1911 because they fill gaps at those times in his known whereabouts and would explain why he did not meet Ruth on her first visit for the summer term of 1911.

6   David Tovey in *Creating A Splash,* Wilson Books 2003, argues that Simpson was the dominating force in the colony and that the formation of the St Ives Society of Arts was an attempt to overcome the feeling of stagnation after his departure.

8.   London, Leicestershire and Yorkshire: Horses and Hunts

1   *The Cornishman,* 16 April 1964

2   The memorial service for Guy Paget (1886–1952)

3   *The Studio,* August 1945

4   Published by Collins 1945

5   Simpson published at least eighteen articles in *Country Life.* 1926: 'The Ascot Procession', 'Some Famous Woods and Spinneys', 'The Art of Lionel Edwards' (a book review) and 'The Sportsman's Bag' (a review of a book by Crascredo). 1927: 'Dartmoor Hunting', 'The Oakley Country', 'The Bramham Moor', 'The Roses of Towton' and 'The Passing Seasons' (another review of a Crascredo book). 1928: articles on racing, the Royal Tournament and Olympia; 'The Colour of Scotland', illustrated with two colour reproductions of *Evening in a Scottish Deer Forest* and *On the Pool below the Rapids.* 1929: articles on racing at Cheltenham, Aintree, Sandown, Epsom and Ascot; the International Horse Show and the Royal Tournament.

6   It has been suggested that Crascredo was a pen name for Simpson. *Manners and Mannerisms* contains fifteen essays that appeared originally in *Country Life.* The title piece deals with good manners in the hunting field and irritating mannerisms, such as taking a fence too fiercely and making encouraging noises to the horse. Crascredo appears to ride himself and in one article calculates the exact cost of keeping a horse down to the last penny. In *No Joke* he seems to have personal experience of the First World War. Other books such as *Horse Sense and Sensibility* were illustrated by Lionel Edwards, hardly likely if he were Simpson. And if he were, he would have reviewed his own book, *The Sportsman's Bag.* In Crascredo's *Hunting Lore* he contributed to the text. 'I wrote the verses and many

other parts of the book, we had great fun with it, but I remember that Lionel Edwards…was rather pained at this humorous treatment.' (Letter to Richard Mather, 31 May 1962). Crascredo was obviously not Simpson but a close friend; Guy Paget fits all the evidence.

7 The seven books illustrated by The Wag were published by *Country Life* between 1928 and 1930. They had commissioned a practical guide to horse-ownership from Lt-Col M.F. McTaggart in the form of letters from an experienced colonel to a novice subaltern and asked Simpson to provide illustrations. They were horrified when he produced cartoon-style drawings that made fun of the subject and said so in a preface, explaining that they included them only at the author's insistence. Simpson called himself The Wag of the Regiment and used the name for subsequent cartoons. They were admired by Paget, who wrote that with a few blobs and lines Simpson could conjure up a pack of hounds emerging from a wood. However, they are very variable; some convey a simple idea with economy, others are mediocre. The best are probably those that illustrate the children's book, *Hildebrand* by John Thorburn. See Appendix Two.

9. Colombo: The voyage of the SS *Ranpura*

Ruth Simpson's 1931 diary, a Christmas gift from Houghton Birch and her only diary in WCAA apart from a journal for the month of August 1934 when she went with friends on a yachting cruise to the Scottish Islands.

1 *Western Daily Mercury* and *Western Morning News*, reprinted in *The St Ives Times*, 20 and 27 August 1920

2 The jeweller Ella Naper (1886–1972) lived at Trewoofe. See *Ella and Charles Naper, Art and Life in Lamorna*, John Branfield, Sansom & Company, 2003

10. Duncan's: Photography and Art

Ruth's diary; catalogues and letters, WCAA

1 William Matthews Duncan was a Scottish businessman who loved art and fishing, a lifelong friend of and adviser to Lamorna Birch. He had retired to Lamorna in 1922 to be close to Birch.

2 Simpson and Vulliamy lost touch with each other for many years. In 1935 Vulliamy wrote again, after 'five years of misery' that he had not wished to inflict on anyone else. He reviewed his life: 'On the whole I suppose I have been successful.' His *Life of Wesley* went into three editions, his *Life of Boswell* into two. He had described

his experiences in the Near East anonymously in *Fusilier Bluff* and had written several 'spoof' crime stories under the name of Anthony Rolls: *The Vicar's Experiments, Lobelia Grove, Family Matters* – 'the tangible profits are not very considerable'.

3   Simpson also wrote on nude photography in a long introduction to *Artist's Model*, John Everard, The Bodley Head, London, 1951.

11. Dorset: The Country of *The Woodlanders*

Unpublished typescript by Charles Simpson, WCAA

12. Penzance: Stanley House

Letters in WCAA

Creating A Splash, David Tovey, Wilson Books 2003

Boskenna and the Paynters, Jim Hosking, published privately 1999

Daily Telegraph, 10 February 1955

Artists of the Newlyn School 1880–1900, Caroline Fox and Francis Greenacre, Newlyn Orion Galleries 1979

Painting in Newlyn 1900–1930, Caroline Fox, Newlyn Orion 1985

Painting in Newlyn 1880–1930, Caroline Fox and Francis Greenacre, The Barbican Gallery 1985

1   John Tunnard lived at Trethinnick where Laura Knight's studio had once been. He came from the same English establishment background as Charles Simpson, but rejected it completely. He was passionately anti-hunting, a keen naturalist and painted dream-like landscapes inspired by ancient Cornwall and modern technology.

2   Letter to Richard Mather, 20 February 1963.

A P P E N D I X   O N E

A Pastorale: published privately at St Ives 1922, 51pp in a hand-bound
  numbered and signed edition of 75 with 16 woodcuts

El Rodeo: John Lane at The Bodley Head 1924. Demy 4to, 15s net

Leicestershire and Its Hunts: John Lane at The Bodley Head 1926. Demy
  4to, 256pp, 31/6 net, 28 illustrations in colour and 55 in black and white
  De luxe edition of 75 numbered and signed copies, £5.5.0

The Harboro' Country: John Lane at The Bodley Head 1927. Demy 4to
  240pp. 24 illustrations in colour and 52 in black and white.
  De luxe edition of 75 numbered and signed copies

Trencher and Kennel: John Lane at The Bodley Head 1927
  24 illustrations in colour and 52 in black and white
  De luxe edition of 75 numbered and signed copies

Emily Brontë: Country Life 1929. 205pp, 15s net, 20 illustrations in colour

Composition for Photographers, An Artist's Guide: H.F. and G. Witherby
  1937. 38 reproductions from paintings and photographs 32 sketches and
  diagrams by the author

Photography of the Figure: H.F. and G. Witherby 1938 100 illustrations, 21/-

Animal and Bird Painting: B.T. Batsford 1939. 136pp. Illustrated by the
  author and with reproductions of famous paintings

*The Fields of Home, A Book of English Field and Hedgerow, Coastline
  and Moorland*: F. Lewis, Leigh-on-Sea 1948. Crown 4to, 114pp, £1.5.0;
  19 illustrations in monochrome and 3 in colour. De luxe edition of 100
  signed copies £3.3.0

Books illustrated by Charles Simpson

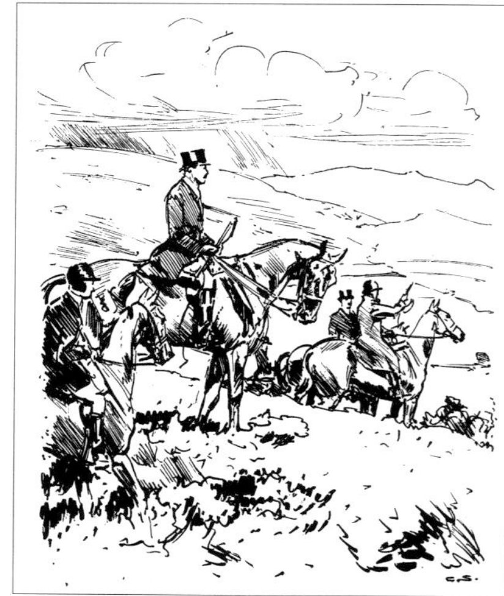

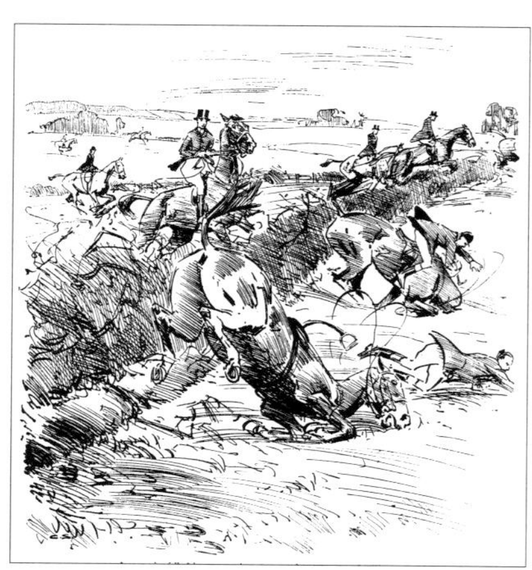

Compiled by David Tovey

Unknown Cornwall, C.E. Vulliamy, John Lane at the Bodley Head 1925; 30 illustrations in colour, 15 in monochrome and 67 in b/w

Manners and Mannerisms, 'Crascredo', Country Life 1929; 11 full-page and 2 half-page b/w illustrations and vignettes in the margin in green ink

Son of a Gun, Major Kenneth Dawson, Country Life 1929; 155 pages, nearly all with green ink illustrations in the margins or as chapter headings, plus a frontispiece. Letters of advice on shooting

The Gone Away – A Romance of the Dales in Three Acts, Dorothy Una Ratcliffe, John Lane at the Bodley Head 1930; colour frontispiece *The Ford* and eight full-page illustrations plus many smaller vignettes

The Fellowship of the Horse, Lt-Col S.G. Goldschmit, Country Life 1930; b/w frontispiece and 30 full-page b/w illustrations plus 6 illustrations for each section of the book

Practical Jumping, Major J.L.M. Barrett, Country Life 1930

Wit and Wisdom of the Shires, 'Coronet' (Colonel Walter Faber MFH, DL, MP), Edgar Backus, Leicester 1932, with a foreword by Guy Paget; an account of the hunting seasons of 1921–1927, with 50 illustrations

The Flying Parson and Dick Christian, written and edited by Guy Paget and Lionel Irvine, Edgar Backus, Leicester 1934; 40 full-page illustrations, 25 in colour and many vignettes in b/w

The Autobiography of 'Sir' Bernard Montgomery, Guy Paget, British Technical and General Press 1952; the story of Paget's hunt terrier, 'translated from the doggerel', with b/w ink drawings

Charles Simpson has sometimes been confused with the Canadian artist and illustrator Charles W. Simpson R.C.A. (1878–1942). The subject matter is usually sufficient to distinguish them.

Books illustrated in cartoon style by The Wag (Charles Simpson)

From Colonel to Subaltern – Some Keys for Horse Owners, Lt-Col M.F.
McTaggart, Country Life 1928. The first book illustrated by The Wag,
who called himself 'The Wag of the Regiment', it is a series of letters
from an experienced countryman to a novice

From Major to Minor – Some Keys for Anglers; Major Kenneth Dawson,
Country Life 1928; letters of advice on angling

Hunting Lore, 'Crascredo', Country Life 1928; 244 pages, alternate pages
having Wag illustrations plus others in the margins

The Olympian Alphabet, The Wag, Country Life 1928; a children's rhyming
alphabet about show jumping, written and illustrated by The Wag

Hildebrand – Literary horseplay for boys and girls, John Thornburn,
Country Life 1930; 28 full-page coloured drawings and others in b/w

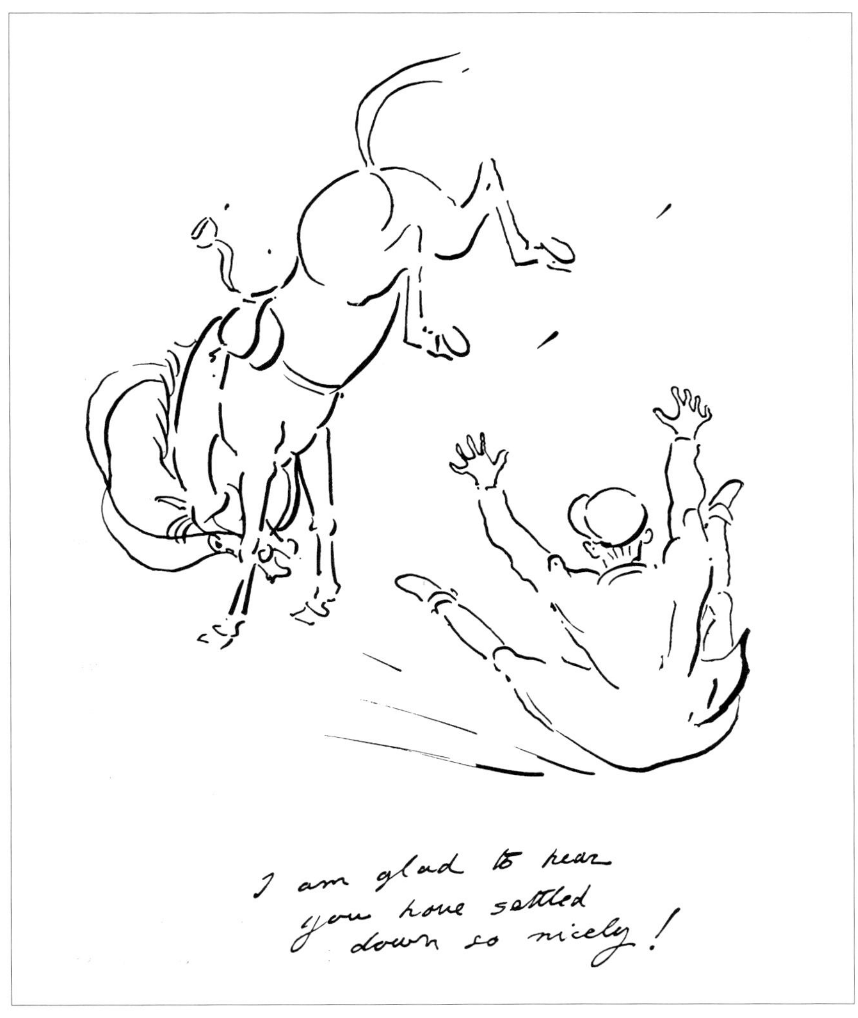

**I'm glad to hear you have
settled down so nicely!**
Illustration from *From Colonel to
Subaltern*, 1928, under the pseudonym
The Wag

APPENDIX THREE

1910	The Graphic Gallery, The Strand, London: The Great Flood of Paris
1913	The Baillie Gallery, Bond Street, London: Ducks and other Farm Studies
1919	St Ives Art Gallery (Lanham's): with Ruth Simpson
1920	The Shore Studio, St Ives: Cornish Bird Life
	Plymouth Municipal Art Gallery: the Wild Bird Series
	Devon and Cornwall Galleries, Plymouth: The Freedom of Dartmoor – with portraits by Ruth Simpson
	The Laing Art Gallery, Newcastle upon Tyne: Exhibition of Works by Charles Simpson R.I., including the Wild Bird Series
c1920	The Modern Gallery, Newcastle upon Tyne: Pictures in Oil, Watercolour and Tempera
1921	The Saville Gallery, Newcastle upon Tyne: Wild Bird Paintings
1922	Leicester Galleries
	St Ives Art Gallery (Lanham's): preview of the London exhibition
	The Grieves Art Gallery, Old Bond Street, London: Paintings and Screens by Charles Simpson R.I., R.B.A. – with portraits by Ruth Simpson
1924	The Arlington Gallery, Old Bond Street, London: El Rodeo
	Plymouth Municipal Art Gallery: El Rodeo, with paintings of Devon and Cornwall
	The Laing Art Gallery, Newcastle upon Tyne: The Herring Fishing Season
1925	The Fine Art Society, London: Exhibition of Hunting Field Sketches, Leicestershire 1924–25 and of the Grand National 1925
1926	The Fine Art Society, London: Famous Woods and Spinneys
1927	The Fine Art Society, London: Famous Yorkshire Hunts

1929   The Fine Art Society, London: Racing and Hunting, Pictures
of the Brontë Country

1930   Paston House Gallery, Norwich: Hunting and Steeplechasing
Pictures, Usher Art Gallery, Lincoln

1931   Doncaster Art Gallery and Museum: Racing and Sporting Works
(transferred to Derby, Leicester and Sheffield)

1932   Leicester Museum and Art Gallery: An Exhibition of
Leicestershire Hunting Scenes, Sporting and Other Paintings

1933   Russell-Cotes Art Gallery, Bournemouth: Paintings of Wildlife
and Sport

1934   The Fine Art Society, London: Rodeo and Grand National

1935   The Sporting Gallery, Bond Street, London: Grand National and
Hunting Pictures

c1950   McClure's Galleries, Glasgow: Pictures by Charles Simpson R.I.

1956   Grundy Art Gallery, Blackpool: Paintings of Sporting and
Country Subjects (transferred to Sunderland, Rotherham,
Northampton and Cheltenham)

1958   Russell-Cotes Art Gallery, Bournemouth: Sporting and
Country Subjects

2005   Penlee House Gallery and Museum, Penzance

1908-1914	Passmore Edwards Gallery, Newlyn
1914-1928	Walker Art Gallery, Liverpool: Autumn Exhibitions (12 works in 10 years)
1915	Panama Pacific International Exposition, San Francisco (awarded Gold Medal)
1917-1924	St Ives Art Gallery (Lanham's)
1922	Plymouth Municipal Art Gallery: Newlyn and St Ives Schools Royal West of England Academy, Bristol: Autumn Exhibition Walker Art Gallery, Liverpool: Jubilee Exhibition: *The Flight of Wild Duck*
1923	Paris Salon (awarded Silver Medal)
1924	Paris, VIII Olympiad Exhibition of Sporting Pictures (awarded Gold Medal) Edinburgh Royal Academy
1930	Foyle Art Gallery, Charing Cross Road, London: Drawings made to illustrate books published by The Bodley Head
1936	Towner Art Gallery, Eastbourne: This England
1937	Russell-Cotes Gallery, Bournemouth: Coronation Exhibition (visitors voted *Dying Light, Cornwall* second most popular picture in the show)
1940	Royal Academy, London: United Artists Exhibition in aid of the Red Cross
1943-1955	St Ives Society of Artists
1945-1946	STISA touring exhibition to Sunderland, Gateshead, Middlesborough, Carlisle, Darlington and Swindon
1946	Alfred East Gallery, Kettering: Sporting Pictures from the collection of Major Guy Paget

	The Royal Glasgow Institute of Fine Arts
	(and in 1947, 1948 and 1951)
1947-1956	Passmore Edwards Gallery, Newlyn
1947	Cape Town Gallery, South Africa: STISA exhibition
	National Museum of Wales, Cardiff: STISA exhibition
	City of Liverpool Art Gallery
1948	Victoria and Albert Museum, London: XIVth Olympiad Sport
	in Art Exhibition
	Sunderland Art Gallery: Society of Marine Artists
1950	Penwith Society, St Ives
1951	The Cooling Galleries, New Bond Street, London: Society
	of Animal Painters, Sculptors and Engravers
	STISA: Festival of Britain Exhibition
	Penwith Society, St Ives: Festival of Britain Exhibition
1956	Passmore Edwards Gallery, Newlyn: Summer Exhibition
	(At 150 guineas *Clouds over Godrevy* was the most expensive
	picture in the show)

APPENDIX FIVE

Compiled by David Tovey

Blackpool: The Grundy Art Gallery

Leonora and the Pet Goat, oil on canvas

Bournemouth: The Russell-Cotes Art Gallery

Duck Shooting – the Punt Gunner, oil on canvas

The Bird Table, oil on canvas

Steer Roping – Leaving the Chute, oil on canvas

Derby Museum and Art Gallery

Otter Hunting – the Kill, oil on canvas

Doncaster Art Gallery and Museum

Finish of the 1931 St Leger 1931, oil on canvas

Tattersall's Sale Ring 1931, oil on canvas

Bolton Wood, w/c

Bolton Abbey, Wharfedale, w/c

Gateshead: The Shipley Art Gallery

The Duck Pond, tempera

Otter Hunting, tempera

Herring Gulls, oil on paper

Harrogate Art Gallery

The Herring Season – Packers on the Quay, gouache

Newcastle: The Laing Art Gallery

The Afterglow, oil on canvas

Marshland, oil on canvas

Herring Gulls and a Black Back, R.A. 1913, oil on canvas

The Herring Season, R.A. 1924, oil on canvas

Newport Art Gallery

The Stream at Clapper Mill, Lamorna, R.A. 1945, oil on canvas

Study for Ducks at Clapper Mill, oil on canvas

Nuneaton Art Gallery

At Covert Side, w/c

Bogwood – York and Ainsty, w/c

Paisley Art Gallery

On Dark Water, oil on canvas

Penzance: Penlee House Gallery and Museum

The Western Union Fleet, Mount's Bay, 1949, oil on canvas

On loan from the Newlyn Gallery

Penzance from Newlyn, oil on canvas

Hunting Drawings (2)

Maroon and Gold (by Ruth Simpson), oil on canvas

Plymouth: City Museum and Art Gallery

The Line Fishing Season, 1919, oil on canvas

Sheffield: The Mappin Art Gallery

Mallard Drake in Immature Plumage

Sunset on Dartmoor, oil on canvas

South Shields Museum and Art Gallery

Silver Morning, w/c

Otter Hunt, w/c

The Curlew, Twilight, w/c

Sunderland Museum and Winter Gardens

Sailing through the Sunshine of Early Spring, oil on canvas

Truro: The Royal Cornwall Museum

The Pergola, oil on canvas

The Injured Seagull 1915, w/c

Frank Verbeck (by Ruth Simpson), oil on canvas

Windsor: The Royal Collection

Queen Mary's Dolls' House, 4 miniatures

Overseas Collections

Perth: The Art Gallery of Western Australia

Broken Ice, oil on canvas

Christchurch Art Gallery, New Zealand

On the Beach 1919, tempera

Landing Herrings, oil on canvas

Dunedin Art Gallery, New Zealand

On the Quay, the Herring Season, St Ives, gouache

The Grand National, Aintree, 1928, gouache

1907 *Autumn Ploughing*

1908 *The Hayfield*

1910 *Milking Time*

1911 *Winter on a Cornish Moor*
The Pond

1912 *Ducks on the Water*

1913 *Herring Gulls and*
a Black Back
Autumn Sunset
Seagulls

1914 *The Duck Pond*
The Mackerel Season
The Aylesbury Duck

1915 *Low Tide*
Ducks

1916 *The Serbian Retreat*
into Albania
Silver Wings

1917 *A Breeze on the Water*

1918 *The Tent*
On the Beach, St Ives
Wind-blown Water

1919 *The Line Fishing Season*
Low Tide

1920 *Trink Hill*
Leonora and the Pet Goat

1921 *The Breakwater*
The Rock

1922 *Black-backed Gulls*
The Flight of Wild Duck
On the Fringe of
a North-Easter

1923 *Seagulls Nesting*
The Five Points, Cornwall

1924 *The Tide Line*
The Herring Season:
from My Studio Window
The Pergola

1925 *Duck Shooting –*
the Punt Gunner

1926 *Sunrise on the Estuary*

1936 *September on the*
Cornish Coast
Dying Light, Carn Barges,
Cornwall

1937 *Tregurnow Cliff from*
Carn Dhu, Cornwall
Sunrise on the Estuary

1940 *The End of the Pier*
at Low Tide

1944 *Wheeling Gulls and*
Glittering Water

1945 *Evening Light on Carn*
Dhu, Cornwall
The Stream at Clapper Mill,
Lamorna

1946 *Sun and Shadow on*
the Water

1947 *The Stream in Spate*

1948 *Midsummer Mosaic*

1953 *The Tide Line*

APPENDIX SEVEN

The Studio no 65, 1915. C. Wood, pp 128, 212; no 81, 1921.
C. Wood, pp 91-95

The Connoisseur no 52, 1918, p232; no 74, 1926, p 60; no 76, 1926, p 63

Apollo Magazine no 7, 1928, p 43

Bulletin of the Russell-Cotes Art Gallery and Museum, 12 Dec 1933.
'Paintings by Charles Simpson R.I.', pp 49-51

Apollo Magazine, Oct 1944. 'Charles Walter Simpson R.I.' by Guy Paget,
pp 86–88.
4 b/w reproductions

The Artist, Nov 1949. 'Artist of Note' by Cecil Wade, pp 65–66.
2 b/w reproductions

The Horseman's Year, 1955

Horse and Hound, 10 Oct 1996. 'Engine Oil Saves the Artist' by Charles
Lane, 5 colour reproductions

The British Sporting Art Trust, Spring 1998, Essay no 34: 'Charles Simpson
R.I.' by Charles Lane